THE RAPTURE
WHAT THE BIBLE REALLY SAYS

THE RAPTURE

WHAT THE BIBLE REALLY SAYS

W. MICHAEL HARLEY

TATE PUBLISHING & *Enterprises*

Published by Tate Publishing & Enterprises, LLC
127 E. Trade Center Terrace | Mustang, Oklahoma 73064 USA
1.888.361.9473 | www.tatepublishing.com

Tate Publishing is committed to excellence in the publishing industry. The company reflects the philosophy established by the founders, based on Psalm 68:11,
"The Lord gave the word and great was the company of those who published it."

Book design copyright © 2009 by Tate Publishing, LLC. All rights reserved.
Cover design by Joey Garrett
Interior design by Stefanie Rooney

Published in the United States of America

ISBN: 978-1-60696-051-6
1. Religion, Christian Theology, Eschatology
09.02.25

DEDICATION

This book is dedicated to my dear mother, Hallene, who went home to be with her Lord about the time I began this book four years ago. During her long lifetime, she was always unafraid of truth and of tomorrow, always understood and practiced love. Along the path she trod, she left no breadcrumbs since she did not intend to return this way.

ACKNOWLEDGMENTS

This book would never have seen the light of day had several primary influences not guided its birth. First, I want to thank my confessed, longtime best friend, confidant, and very special lady, Dorothy Clayton, who made me feel competent enough for the task. She encouraged me in each stage of the project and gave unrelenting hands-on assistance as we neared production. My spiritual inspiration came, of course, from the Holy Bible but was guided and developed in my association with the Reformed Presbyterian Church, U.S.A. and Pastor Jack Davidson of Cascade Presbyterian Church, at Eugene, Oregon, who introduced me to Reformed theology. I drew a lot of knowledge and understanding from Mr. Harold Camping of Family Stations Inc., who is the finest teacher of the Bible I ever encountered. His books inspired me to want to tell more of the story most people have never heard. Literary agent Priscilla Palmer appreciated the first draft sufficiently to insist I expand it from the original six chapters. That added nearly three years of effort to the task. To Bill Randolph, high school classmate; retired executive at Mercedes Benz; my chief, long-distance encourager and reviewer, who was the first to read the entire finished first draft; thanks for believing in me and for being so certain I had a story to tell. I owe a hug to Chuck Grove, whose *nom de plume* is Howard Bond. Howard was a fellow newspaper columnist, poet, and good old sidekick, whose humor and command of the language cemented our friendship. A practicing Roman Catholic, he stepped up at my suggestion, and ruthlessly (he thought) proofed the original manuscript. I can't thank him enough. Although our theologies differed somewhat, his review was inestimably valuable to me and was, as always, humorous. Finally, I want to acknowledge the support and opportunity to publish, afforded by Dr. Richard Tate and his hardworking staff at Tate Publishing, especially my editor, Matt Halstead, and graphic designer, Joey Garrett. God bless them all. WMH

CONTENTS

Preface 11

Why This Book? 23

The Need to Coordinate Doctrines 35

It's Best to Start at the Beginning 43

The Dispensationalists 55

Pitfalls of Dispensationalism 79

Which Kingdom of What? 103

Fundamentalism, Briefly 115

The Schofield Charade 125

The Millennium 145

The Father of Evangelicalism 151

Paul and the Judaizers 169

Judaizing Congregations Today 181

Shall We Believe the New Testament? 189

Light from Galatia 203

Power and the Cornerstone 217

A Promise of Moses 229

The Promise for Jacob 241

Introduction to Part II 255

Noah's Ark, the Rapture: Is There a Connection? 259

Night Time, When Thieves Lurk 277

Feasts of Leviticus Whisper, "Rapture" 289

Times of Sodom and Gomorrah 295

Resurrection Day and the Rapture 303

Times of the Prophet Daniel 307

Author's Notes Concerning Part Two 327

A Critique of Part Two by Howard Bond 331

A Christian Zionist Author 347

The Immortals 361

Notes 367

Bibliography 369

PREFACE

It was the darkest of times in America. Religious dogmas and superstition everywhere ruled in the Protestant churches. It was exactly as the Bible warned it would be - a time of great apostasy. It was the twenty-first century!

Had Martin Luther or John Calvin presented the teachings popular in the twenty-first century denominations, popular heresies that pass for the gospel, not even a thin veneer of original Christianity would remain today. Had that giant among men, John Wycliffe, versed in the law, in theology, philosophy, logic, and languages, mirrored the eschatology of Protestant denominations today, there might never have been a dedication to future generations in his English translation of the Bible!

William Tyndale abhorred the conduct of the church in his day—its corrupt bishops, begging friars, indulgences, and self aggrandizing Popes. Today he would be afraid for the survival of even the tiniest remnant who still manage to know the real Jesus. The measure of all this, of course, is the conduct of not only the large, wealthy religious corporations of our day, but also of the biggest names in what is known loosely as Christianity. Such people will not allow the doctrines of the Apostle Paul in their congregations. They deny the truth of the New Testament as it pertains to the end of time. They are denying the truths of the Bible but go unquestioned by the faceless drones in their congregations.

After the death of Constantine in the fourth century, the Roman Church achieved a powerful foothold into what then remained of the true Christianity. The misnamed "Holy" Roman Empire governed the western world of that day, exercising an unholy monopoly over education, spiritual life, and safety of the populace. Outbreaks of religious freedom did occur over the centuries, but most were ruthlessly repressed by Romish Popes. That shortly brought what we know as the "Dark Ages." Then, because a handful of priests from that Roman government that was called a church were able for the first time to actually read portions of the Bible for themselves, the Reformation resulted. A few Catholic priests who valued Bible truth became Protestants. The truth set these men, and eventually a continent, and later the world, free for the first time to read the actual teachings of Jesus Christ. Today, largely as a result of modern communications, especially the TV tube, Protestant worshippers are in the Dark Ages again when it comes to actual knowledge of what the Bible contains, especially regarding study of the end times. Yet here we are actually living in those times!

Any man or woman who has actually studied the Bible in a diligent attempt to learn what is contained there concerning the last days of our world, knows full well that the books, movies, videos, DVDs, and teaching of the fundamentalists bear little resemblance to the teaching of God found in the Bible. But such people are rare. Most churchgoers today actually seem to prefer not to know what truths exist outside modern fundamentalism. Luther, Huss, Calvin, Zwingli, and other diligent scholars of the Reformation rediscovered faith and reformed the world's thinking about Jesus. Today that's once again the lost message of the church. God's promises are an important guarantee of what awaits a world of lost sinners. God lifted the spiritual nature of men by having the Bible written, making it available to anyone who wants to be transported to knowledge of the Saviour. But few today care to accept that truth. That's not the same thing as not reading it.

We are living in the last days, but the good news is that God promises in the Bible that he is still saving souls. Every believer needs to kindle a fire, compass himself about with sparks, walking in the light of his own fire, not allowing himself to be fooled into walking in the darkness that is everywhere in the churches today. "Get out of her," our Lord said. "Run to where God is."

His message for our times won't be found on TV or in most pulpits today. The humble message of this book is that God can be found speaking and teaching, only in his Word.

But, we see imperfectly. Jesus, the Jewish Messiah, Christ of the Greeks, Saviour of those who truly believe, came to earth as fully man, yet fully God. He most likely came in the year 7 BC, or precisely 2014 years ago this year. The year 1407 BC was a Jubilee year. It appears (based upon available computations, using biblical genealogies) to also have very likely been the year that the nation of Israel was finally led into the land of Canaan, the "promised land." If one accepts that every fifty years following that, brought another Jubilee in accord with God's dictum, counting by fifties would bring one to the Jubilee year of 7 BC according to the Hebraic calendar.

Why would anyone suppose that Christ would have been born in 7 BC? The Jubilee was observed at very precise times in God's calendar of Jewish activities. It also had a precise purpose. The times were established by God himself to guide his "chosen people." The first day of the seventh month of each forty-ninth year was to be a Sabbath—a reminder or memorial evidently, that the Jubilee was approaching. Our English Bible translation somewhat garbled God's message about that day. It speaks of "a memorial of blowing trumpets." But these words are not found in the Hebrew of the Old Testament. It calls only for a "holy gathering as a reminder signaled" (Leviticus 23:24–25, ILB). Where the translators got the idea of throwing in some trumpets is a mystery. They are not included in the Hebrew texts. It is often heard in the congregations that this was known as the feast of trumpets by the Israelites. That seems unlikely since they did not employ trumpets to announce it as some have been known to teach. Then, the tenth day of the seventh month was another Sabbath, a day of rest and sacrifice, called the Day of Atonement, a day on which all the people made offerings of fire to atone for their sins before God. There are no trumpets mentioned here either in the Hebrew text. On the fifteenth of that month, began a seven-day feast knows as the Feast of Tabernacles, sometimes called the Feast of Booths. The first and last days were Sabbaths. It would delight us all to be able to say that the shofar, or ram's horn, was blown to announce this feast, but the Bible just does not indicate that this occurred. But we do know that every fiftieth, or Jubilee year, according to Leviticus 25:9 (in the Hebrew), the shofar was blown! Our English Bibles call it a "trumpet," but a trumpet was a straight metal or animal horn, while a cornet (of metal), or shofar (of horn), was curved. Presumably, the shofar announced Jubilee once every fifty years, although we do not find any actual observance of this supposed requirement recorded in the Old Testament. The opening of the Jubilee was called the Day of Atonement, the tenth day of the first month of the Jubilee Year, when the shofar was to proclaim Jubilee by being blown "throughout all your land" (Leviticus 25:10). God wanted all the inhabitants to know it was the Jubilee year.

The theme of Jubilee was *liberty!* That would suggest that Christ spiritually *was* (is) the Jubilee! Christ came to pay with His life, for the sins of those He came to save. Also, he came during their observance of the Passover, and he was, in fact, spiritually the Passover lamb. He started his church on the very day of Jewish observance, seven Sabbaths after the offerings of the first fruits. It was known as the Feast of Weeks. Seven Sabbaths encompass about fifty days, so that feast is better known to Christians as Pentecost. It represented the end of the harvest of souls. His harvest began with Pentecost, where that of the Old Covenant left off.

So, it would seem that God is using the very days of remembrance and sacrifice to highlight the physical realities that those days represent! Does it not seem quite appropriate then, that God might well have planned to bring Jesus into the world of sinners on one of those special days? Jesus brought liberty to the world. He was the Jubilee! Why would God not have introduced Jesus on the Jubilee year since Christ came to give freedom from sin to the people he would save? God changed the weekly Sabbath from Saturday to Sunday—the day he created light, since Christ represented that light, on the day Jesus came out of the tomb as the light. This message is in each of the four Gospels but is little understood in the churches because it did not survive the translations into English of the King James Bible. Of course, it must be found in all the later "translations," which their producers swear are independent translations, mustn't it? As a matter of record, it's not there because they are, one and all, simply derivatives of the King James. There is a miry path through the history of Christendom.

At Christ's first coming, the leaders of the Jewish world were locked into their own defined concept of how the Messiah would perform, how he would busy himself, even what his physical appearance would be. Despite what their prophets told them, they were expecting a warrior king, something like a David, who would come to rescue his people from the rule of the despised Romans. That's what the leaders in their assemblies told them.

But when Jesus came, he came as the suffering servant, preaching a very different program from what had been anticipated. They had listened not to the prophets, but to the rabbis. They did not recognize the man whom the Prophet Isaiah said would come exactly as Christ Jesus came! So, they would not accept him any more than they would accept what their other prophets had to say. The prophets had for centuries not told the Jews what they wanted to hear, so the Jews sometimes murdered them. According to the Bible, murder seems to have been a somewhat familiar tool in the rabbinical bag of tricks. Some of the saddest verses in the Bible have to do with the very accurate predictions of the prophets of Israel and Judah. "He came unto his own, and his own received him not" (John 1:11). "The kingdom of God shall be taken away from you, and given to a nation bringing forth the fruits thereof" (Matthew 21:43). "What Israel sought so earnestly it did not obtain" (Romans 11:7, NIV). Yet, even with these lessons before them, theologians of today continue to insist the Jews are still God's special people!

But those who actually *study* the Bible, as opposed to simply reading through it in a year, should not fail to observe the facts! Jesus appears to be telling us to believe what the Bible says about Old Testament promises to the nation of Israel, not what we want it to say. We are obliged to temper what we think we know with everything the Bible is trying to tell us today concerning these final days. If the Bible is our witness, we most assuredly seem to be experiencing exactly what the Word of God is telling us we will experience in the end times. As we approach ever closer to the second advent of Christ, those who are confident they are among his elect had better consider updating their study. Otherwise, when he does come, not as most of the churches teach, but as God teaches, they could be found wanting. Jesus clearly declares that many who cry, "Lord, Lord," are actually unknown to God.

Men really have, when it comes right down to cases, a rather imperfect knowledge of just what the entire plan of God actually is! Most theologians, Bible teachers, and pastors will not accept the Bible's truth as reality. That's a hard thing to believe, but that does not make the truth a lie. The Bible tells us this repeatedly. Those who insist on a "rapture" preceding the Great Tribulation, for instance, just may have figured something out. But what will they do if it does not come out that way? How will they handle the rapture working out exactly as God says it will in the Bible? Is adding to or subtracting from God's book—in fact changing it—going to ingratiate those teachers with God? Will it be "cool" for those who have believed those false teachers not to have accepted what God's Word clearly says? That's up to God, but as a minimum it would seem such people are on pretty shaky ground. They have chosen a scenario not in the Bible and structured their beliefs about the end times in accord with that mythical scenario. They had to ignore a lot of New

Testament information to fabricate their reality. That does not seem to be something God would appreciate.

The Lord has written that his ways are different from our ways (Isaiah 55:8). The Bible does say that his judgments are unsearchable, his paths beyond tracing out (Romans 11:33). Recognizing what little we know of God, it would not seem wise attempting to limit him with theology of our own design, just as the ancient Israelites did.

Jesus insisted that as the end times progress, there would be a "great falling away." He's talking about people who have been renting a pew for much of a lifetime. There will, according to the Bible, be a crisis of faith. That alone would certainly be great tribulation, but that won't be alone. Jesus said, "Many will turn away from the faith," but it's going to be even worse than that. They "will betray and hate each other, and many false prophets will appear and deceive many people [...] the love of most will grow cold, but he who stands firm to the end will be saved" (Matthew 24:10–13). Will it feel like betrayal to a majority of churchgoers if the events do not work out in the fundamentalist pattern they are being taught, but instead reflect what the Bible teaches? Will some reading this be offended by a Messiah not acting as they were led to believe he would act, even if he acts precisely as he says he will in Scripture? It seems appropriate to ask why it's so very hard for so many people to actually believe what God has put into that book they insist that they trust.

While men remain on the earth, they see imperfectly, as "through a glass darkly," in the words of the Apostle Paul in 1 Corinthians 13:12. They understand only in part if Paul was correctly instructed by Jesus, and Christians probably ought to accept that he was. It is possible for believers to place all their trust in doctrines of a denomination or even in their pastor's teaching (since that's also denominational) rather than trusting implicitly in Jesus and the Bible he wrote. The first would likely work out in God's economy to be a form of idol worship.

Christians of every stripe supposedly know and affirm by

their acceptance that the entire Bible is true (unless it contains the five Apocrypha books). They also should know, if they have not been so instructed, that man's interpretation is always fallible! That is not to insist that it is always wrong, only that it is always apt to be wrong. It is good indeed to read and to study what the Bible says about final things and attempt to build understanding of them. It may be far less beneficial to become absolutely locked-in to what we have been taught about such things, even by men who claim to be delivering the biblical truth! Being super certain of outcomes sometimes has a way of confusing our ability to interpret what is actually happening. Perhaps, we should be equally prepared for surprise from our God, if that becomes his choice. One thing about God—he is sovereign!

In the last dozen or so years, several widely acclaimed books have been written in which the authors proved to their own satisfaction that Christ would return on a particular date or a certain year. The problem was they didn't prove their thesis to God's satisfaction. So, Jesus didn't show up! The difficulty lay in the fact that quite a few readers foolishly took action based upon the predictions. Many were harmed in one way or another by taking action based on books concerning a time which God stoutly maintains, "no man can know." There is another such book on the bookshelves right now predicting the end of the world in a very few years. Many will be harmed if that prediction, like all the others, fails to come true. Some will likely "fall away." This is precisely what is prophesied in the Bible.

There are several schools of thought active in the churches concerning how the so-called "Rapture" and the Tribulation will play out. Each is supposedly based on scriptural understanding. It might appear, however, that some are based very loosely, and in fact precariously, on that foundation. Irrespective of their viewpoints, the advocates of the several scenarios are likely sincere in their peculiar beliefs. Each has been able to convince some number of Christians that support for that position is found in Scripture. It would be more comforting to hear that each had found a position that supported Scripture. There is an old axiom that says that anything can be proven with Scripture. End-times theology is a prime exemplar of that idea. Our world is daily treading ever closer to that time when experience will be the final teacher. Experience is just around the corner for all of us.

It may now be appropriate for some of the die-hard advocates of one or another of the end-time scenarios to come forward and admit that man's knowledge is inadequate, since he sees through a glass darkly, to really say with certainty exactly how the end will come. Certainly, even without their assistance, God is equal to the task of delivering his chosen people, his elect, from whatever may come. It is within the realm of possibility for his people to remain content, whatever the circumstances (Philippians 4:11). It is high time those who call themselves by his name begin to move in the direction of becoming content. In God's lexicon, "content" appears to imply being content with what God has given in his Word.

That sort of contentment is part of what this book deals with, and what it contains comes almost exclusively from the Bible. That necessarily says that this book deals just as *excludingly* with the popular, fanciful "Christian" novels and with denominational creeds and confessions, with nursery rhymes and fairy tales, especially those "scientific" modes of study so popular with the seminaries and universities in guiding theology students *away* from God's exclusive truth.

This is not intended to be a harsh indictment of the "system." It is simply a declaration concerning the reality of our environment that is increasingly gaining momentum *against* the truths of the Bible. It is a statement concerning precisely the system that Christ has promised to return for the purpose of destroying! He would scarcely do that if the church system was healthy! Think about that for a moment. Now, think about it again!

Many who attend modern denominational religious services for an hour on Sundays before heading to the golf course, a picnic or the TV, have doubtless chosen not to recognize that Jesus is coming to clean up some specifics when he comes. What excuses are we to presume he will accept for a "Christian" not keeping his commandments? The whole system in which the denominations operate today is going to be erased. Does the example of Revelation chapter two suggest that God would destroy very healthy churches? It is logical to conclude that it does not.

The Bible says that his return will be on the last day, when the Bible also says the majority of people will plead with the rocks to fall on them to hide them from the terrible wrath of the God they have made so little of during their lives. They will be witnessing the end of it all! Weren't they assured they would be "caught up" before the tribulation came upon the church? Not by the Bible they weren't, and that's what God told his people to get familiar with!

If there was a presumption in the mind of this writer for even half a second that most people who read the Bible know anything much at all about the Bible, this book would not have been written. Actually, it should not have to be written at all. Reality is, however, that very few—very, very few who sit in church most Sundays, very few who man a pulpit on Sundays or a lectern at a seminary on weekdays, possess more than a small passing inclination of what that book contains. How could this possibly be true? Because they are human! They believe they are protected from damnation because they have "taken refuge" inside a building where they think God is supposed to hang out. That's what their teachers and pastors have told them. They don't need to study to learn what God himself has written down because their pastor knows all that and has taken care of them.

The preponderance of supposedly Christian literature on the bookshelves today bears little resemblance to biblical truth. Yes, that is a harsh indictment indeed. But, if you do not read it here, who will tell you? Who will tell you that the most popular reading among people who claim the faith just happens to be romance novels? Who will stand in the wall? Who will seal the breach? The Bible is absolutely not studied appropriately in most churches. Most people who attend church are not even aware of how to study the Bible! If there is one congregation to whom this does not apply, God will be pleasantly surprised.

Teachers of the Bible are warned in that book to be teachers of only the truth. This is no longer happening, and God has warned that such is precisely what will announce the end of time. If you are someone who does not think what was just written here is true, this book is exactly what you need to read.

That's because this book is written as a warning and as a way for some who have not encountered it in their congregations, to hear some of the truth of the Bible. The words printed upon these pages are not—are not—infallible. The Bible is. These pages are intended simply to mirror for you what the Bible has to say. You need to read the Bible. You need to study it. Use this book to lead yourself, with the urging of the Spirit, into the Scriptures wherein is truth. That's where you can find the truth concerning what God has to say about how He will personally bring down the final curtain on His creation.

WHY THIS BOOK?

THE BOOK YOU HAVE IN YOUR HAND IS ABOUT A VERY POPULAR topic of our day among people who attend church either to learn or to take Sunday naps. The topic has to do with what is known as the latter days, or the end times, or for the very stalwart, the last days.

It is fairly common knowledge that this subject is a "hot one," much emphasized of late, especially in the evangelical churches. Even before the series of novels by Jerry Jenkins and Tim LaHaye earned them a reported 200 million dollars, the subject of the "Rapture" was a popular one, and for very good reasons. "Rapture" is the name popularized by Jenkins and LaHaye but crafted originally by either speakers from the pulpit or seminarians. We can suppose the term made the telling of what Bible language calls "caught up" easier or perhaps more memorable for the targets of that story. As the story goes, when Jesus returns to claim his elect, they will be "caught up" by him into the clouds to be with him in his kingdom. Significantly, the believers will be taken from this world in a moment and delivered into heaven. Those whom he has not selected out of the herd to be his own will face a much less enjoyable future at the judgment seat, then in the "Lake of Fire."

Virtually all who call themselves by his name believe that some version of this scenario will play out at some undetermined future date. The only serious differences among the believers regarding the catching up of the saints are two, but they are enormous! One rather small group favors the biblical scenario, which recognizes the contributions of the New Testament. Everybody else likes one or another of several alternate, manmade versions. The most fundamental disagreement among Christians concerns when and where. "When" is in relation to the Great Tribulation spoken of in the Bible, and the "last day." "Where" concerns the various notions about which of the kingdoms the saints will be assigned to for eternity. How can people who read the same, or nearly the same Bible, differ so materially on such an important subject? This book concerns itself with answering that question without reliance on denominational doctrines or creeds. Rather, by relying solely upon what can be learned from what is contained in the Word of God. This is made possible by the simple recognition and acceptance of a biblically determined fact: that the closer this world approaches to the last day, the more that is being revealed to those who will earnestly seek God's meaning. It's called, "progressive revelation." We have passed the time when churchmen could simply learn and mindlessly regurgitate what their denominations declared decades ago to be their doctrines. To be fair, the interest in end-time theology by laymen has catapulted today into a near obsession, while doctrines of the denominations were formed decades, even centuries ago.

For the past dozen or so years the "premillennial" school of thought has dominated the thinking of the seminaries and is now the main theme issuing from nearly all the pulpits. Never mind there is virtually no support at all from the Bible for such thinking. The popular series of fables titled *Left Behind* has cemented the thinking of churchgoers and even theologians, much as popular ideas of Satan were formed. The pictures most people carry around under their hats about the devil and hell came not from the Bible, but from Dante Alighieri's book, "The Divine Comedy" published centuries ago. Like most evangelical churches, the one where the author received his early Christian instruction taught premillennial theory, which revolves around church members being excused by their pastors from participating in the "Great Tribulation."

But that was puzzling in a difficult way for a youngster. No support could be found in the textbook used in all Christian schools, including that for newly baptized church members. That schoolbook was the Bible, and it simply did not correlate with what was taught from the pulpit about the "catching up" of the saints. So, at least one student rebelled and went looking for instruction in other venues. After several false starts, each providing some valuable learning but no biblical correlation on this most important subject, the student eventually found his way into a Reformed congregation. Hallelujah! It turned out that others had experienced the same sort of make-believe doctrinal nonsense and had come to the same safe haven of learning. That was the beginning of a very fruitful experience and a recognition that King James had been eminently successful in championing a Bible that literate folks could not only read, but with study could understand. What the author had earlier perceived, but did not want to recognize, was that almost nobody, even in the seminaries, truly knew how to study the Word as God directed, nor cared to learn. That sounds odd, and to be sure, it was.

Now that is a difficult opinion to reveal, but it must be recognized as true and as operative in most of the churches if one hopes to actually glean from God's Word what he wants you to know. We realize many will not accept this premise and will label this book as having some kind of nasty bitterness or bias.

That will not bother the author one little bit so long as even a few readers understand the message. So the reader is encouraged to do himself a favor and read this text carefully, because it explains in modern terms what God put into the Bible but that has been interpreted poorly by teachers in most churches. There is important stuff in this book, and you are not likely to find it anywhere else, period! It is clear to the author that for the majority of "believers," where you stand depends on whom you believe, what your denomination has selected for you to believe, and what you want to believe, more than it does on what is actually contained in the Bible! Here is one simple proof of this contention: merely observe the nearly 2,000 versions of the Bible found in "Christian bookstores," written by men who wouldn't accept the original!

If that was not a valid observation, there could hardly be some 2,600 separate, distinct, corporations, registered as denominations, believing their interpretations to be the only true gospel. Therefore, in order to arrive at anything even near biblical truth, one must distance oneself from denominational doctrines and seminarian pronouncements. It turns out that academia is not where truth should be sought. The academicians have been pursuing fancy concepts for a thousand years, and we still have 2,600 different views of the truth! The fancy labels—hermeneutics, eschatology, etc., and their associated methodologies, do absolutely nothing to enhance a search for Bible understanding. By the way, for those who have gone unassaulted by the murmurings of academia, here's an example of the sort of idiocy the seminaries dish out.

They define *hermeneutics* as "the science of interpolation, especially that branch of theology that deals with the principles of scriptural interpolation." How's that for a meaningless and arrogant definition? Just think of it (if you care) as meaning "how to study the Bible." Now, the author of the book you are reading has two graduate degrees, wrote curriculum for a Southern Bible college, and taught in a university. He is able to spot a non-definition when he sees one, just as easily as can anyone else! But please don't think of him as "an academic." Basically, if for some idiotic reason you were to chase definitions, you'd likely wind up realizing that the colleges and seminaries don't want to admit that their so-called "science" of hermeneutics is incredibly slippery to pin a definition on. Being essentially indeterminate, it eludes description. So how can that be a science? That characterizes academe sufficiently for our purposes here. What is important is that you recognize that the seminaries and colleges of our day do not stray far from whatever their denomination's corporate officers have decided is their "truth." They have studied God's Word to death and cannot agree on anything, except to label whatever it is they are doing, a science! Perhaps "science" just pays better than just another "art"? If you think this is exaggerated, just hang around your local Bible school for a while.

The bottom line here is, before the reader is finished with this reading, she will, or he will, likely begin to recognize that some of the things taught in church, especially things having to do with the latter days, and especially the "Rapture," do not square with the Bible. The Bible is the sole direct reference for this book you're reading. That, when you consider it, was exactly the situation that drove the reformers from the iron grip of the Popes! So, when you come to that unusual recognition, you will have a dilemma. Is the Word of God final and binding authority for you, or is your pastor, or your denomination, or somebody else, the final authority? Only you can make that determination. Most people reading this probably have never been placed in the position of having to make that decision.

The author will pray that if someone reading this does not have it at the beginning, by the time he has finished this reading, he will have faith, not in his denomination, not even in his pastor, nor in church doctrine, and certainly not in this book or the man who wrote it, but in Almighty God! It is he, after all, who will make the final choices that will determine our destinies. The Holy Bible is where we need to place our trust, and as nearly as the author could manage, this book reflects what is contained there. So, the Lord also expects us to, "study to show thy self approved unto God, a workman who needs not to be ashamed, rightly dividing the word of truth" (2 Timothy 2:15).

Presumably, everyone who is among the elect of God believes in the coming judgment and the "catching up" of true believers in the end times by Christ. That belief puts us on semi-common ground. Unfortunately, each of us carries quite a load of denominational "baggage" that conditions what we think and believe about what the Bible says. Sometimes that actually moves what God has taught into second place or even into obscurity in somebody's life without that reality even being recognized. That could result in what God has to say in his Word becoming ineffectual to a person, and that's the last thing we want to have happen.

Most who read this book will be at least somewhat aware of one or more of the three major doctrinal positions concerning the end of time. They recognize the manmade arguments known as the premillennial, postmillennial, and amillennial theories, not contained in the Bible, but which have split the Protestant churches for more than a century. Some know them as pre, post, or a-tribulation scenarios. We will here pay homage to none since we cannot find that any is entirely supported in Scripture. We will, however, embellish just enough on these ideas to set the scene for the truth of the Bible that follows. We examine seriously only what is contained in God's Holy Word, the Bible, and those theories are not found there. We will, however, cover briefly what the fundamentalist churches teach in order to illustrate how those teachings differ from the biblical account of God's plan. None of the contents ahead comes from any source apart from Scripture.

Some may be a bit put off by what may appear to be the boldness of my assertions. That's okay, so long as the reader recognizes what is actually contained in the Word. To get that across is my only goal. But, if someone does find himself questioning what is contained here, I ask simply that you check me against the Bible. I ask such a reader to ask himself seriously, "Do I honestly want to know what God put into the Bible, or would I rather listen to my pastor, even if it turns out he is wrong?"

Please remember that the Bible is given freely, without prejudice or obligation. What this book contains are not my ideas or prejudices, but what the Bible actually says. So this is a Bible study about the end of the world. It is our hope that you will open yourself completely to what the Bible has to say and will check everything in this book against that authority. You should trust only the Bible, not this book, or its author, not your pastor or church, not any mere man or his doctrines. Trust the Bible, in which is contained the Word of Almighty God!

If the *Left Behind* series of fairy tales are where you got your ideas of the end times, as they are where many pastors got theirs, I earnestly hope and pray that you will allow the Bible to begin being your guide as you enter into this short journey of understanding. If to trust only in the Bible is not your wish, you may as well drop this book and enjoy a Spiderman comic or maybe read *Left Behind*.

If you have taken the step into continuing to read, feel blessed. You cannot now fail to come to understanding of this particular aspect of God's teaching. It is our earnest prayer that the reader will recognize that our gracious Lord is leading him through these pages. If you happen to have not said a prayer to ask God's blessing in this reading, it would be good to offer one now. My prayer is that your reading here will be both enlightening and enjoyable.

Some who just said their prayer are going to find, possibly for the very first time, some things that have been obscured up to now, by well-meaning but un-researched, and therefore ignorant, teaching. Before you object to what you just read, remember please that ignorant simply describes the fact of "not knowing."

Please be assured that what you will read here was developed through an inductive proof of Scripture with Scripture. Put another way, what is written here attempts to allow the Bible to prove the Bible by using passages from the Bible alone in most cases, and in the original languages, to define words and expressions found in Scripture. Most readers will probably never have encountered this form of biblical inquiry previously. But only in this way can we conceive of arriving at truth unfettered by man's interference, man's doctrines, or prior theological, but unbiblical, interpretations. You see, it is not uncommon to discover that some of the doctrines of some of the churches have never been tested thoroughly against Scripture before being inserted into confessions and creeds! It is healthy for you to doubt that assertion, but your doubt may not persist after you have digested what is contained between the covers of the book you are reading. Some will be shocked, even dismayed, at what they read here. Some will actually refuse to accept certain truths of the Bible because they have not been exposed to them previously. But everyone who bothers to check carefully what is contained here will find it to be straight from the Word of God. Be assured that none will be untouched by what is encountered here. We urge you to read with your Bible handy just in case you want to prove to yourself that what you are reading agrees entirely with God's Word. That's the only way to be certain that what you read was indeed, "given by inspiration of God, and profitable for doctrine, for reproof, for correction, for instruction in righteousness" (2 Timothy 3:16).

Once that has been established in mind and heart, definition can be found on a couple of other oft misrepresented prophesies somewhat closely connected to the entire controversy surrounding the so-called "Rapture" and "Millennial Theory."

In numerous paragraphs, we will discuss what you will find being termed "believers" or "true believers." These are common terms among evangelicals. For our purposes this will not simply mean someone who "knows" he is saved. It will instead refer to those whom God knows are saved, because he selected them prior to the foundation of the world (Romans 8:29–30, and Ephesians 1:5). So these terms refer not to folks who think they are saved, but to those who are actually saved. Another term for this group is *elect*.

The reason this book was written is a function of the recognition that protest characterized the Reformation. Protest today continues to affect the corporate churches. Protesting congregations have been in almost constant disagreement since the days of the early Reformers. That's why we have so many denominations, most of which agree sufficiently most of the time to fit into the classification system today as "evangelicals." The reason for the mushrooming of corporations into the 2,600-odd that exist today was mostly disagreement on church doctrines and what has been taught in the corporations. It's still protest! Without protest, there could never have been the nearly constant fragmenting that has characterized this mixed bag of protesters, most of whom are tentatively connected by the feeling of being evangelicals.

In reality, the fragmentation came mostly on the heels of what was *not* taught in the congregations! Most of the congregations follow not corporate doctrines, as appearances would suggest, but the teachings of specific men. They follow the teachings of Jerry Falwell, Jim Bakker, Pat Robertson, Paul Crouch, Tim LaHaye, Benny Hinn, Hal Lindsay, Hank Hannegraf, and others. "All," one might say, of the "big names" in evangelicalism today. Certainly they are the big moneymakers in TV evangelism. Most of them are multi-millionaire heads of huge congregations (corporations), but they are not theologians! Another characteristic of this crowd is that they do not always act like servants of God. All of them are also comfortable calling themselves "fundamentalists."

That's actually not a theologically oriented term, but instead, according to Christian writers who have studied these men, it is a geopolitical one! We will see that while these so-called and usually self-anointed, fundamentalists enjoy applying a theological aspect to this term for themselves, it is definitely not deserved as a descriptor of their theology. They are the leaders of what is known by detractors of Christianity in political circles as, "The Radical Right," or the "Radical Religious Right." Do not suppose, as many folks commonly do, that these derisive terms are applied consciously to all Christians. That would be a common, but mistaken, impression. The men at whom these descriptions are aimed want all Christians to believe they are included in such terminology by its originators. They want all Christians to feel assaulted by the same terminology. There is a specific political reason such descriptions were coined. Many will be surprised and possibly disbelieving when we show you in later chapters what that reason actually is.

But this book was conceived for the one express purpose of clarifying for those who do not know, what is actually contained in the Bible regarding the end of time and the so-called "Rapture," a term that does not originate in the holy text. It may be hard to believe until you follow along a bit further, but you will find that what is never taught among the congregations of probably thirty million evangelicals, all of whom have been told they are "born-again," is what the Bible actually has to say about the end times! If someone does not reach out to that large group that has only an earthly inspired idea, how will they know God's message concerning this subject in time for it to help them survive those times? Thankfully, God is still saving souls! It's not too late to fix it. Then there is also the author's burden to tell them the truth about where their heroes are leading them. There is a terrible lack of understanding in this country of what the big-money evangelists, in cahoots with big names in government, are really dedicated to and how it is reflected in fundamentalist thought and teaching.

So the book you are holding is not strictly an expository

short treatise on the truth of the rapture. Nor is it intended to be an exposé. It will bear no resemblance whatever to the teachings of fundamentalist evangelists that came spewing out in the past few years in the multi-million-dollar misinformation jackpot titled, *Left Behind.* Evangelicals treat those novels like candy, but they do not teach what God put into the Bible about the last days, at all! The novels did buoy up the secret cause of the "Radical Right," or more properly, the Christian Zionist movement. This was a significant part of their purpose for being written. The early chapters ahead will characterize and chronicle briefly the history of that now nearly 175-year-old political cause in this country. That will explain what fundamentalism really is.

So it turns out that we have here a book about America and its engineered slide into apostasy. Engineered by men and women whom their admirers consider both knowledgeable and faithful to the Bible. But it will also address the last days of the "late, great, planet earth" as that time is detailed by Hal Lindsey, but is treated quite differently in the King James Bible. The Lindsey book was pure fundamentalist, Zionist fantasy.

Every writer hopes his audience will respond warmly to his book. No doubt you exchanged legal tender for the privilege of carrying it out of a store. It seems only proper therefore, to hope you will enjoy it and can find something new or interesting in it. Perhaps even to be led to a new appreciation of the Bible. Then, of course, it is possible you may find satisfaction in something so simple as burning its pages for warmth! Whatever the purpose, we hope you find your particular preference for truth amply satisfied in reading the pages ahead.

May God grant you that fond wish and bless your reading as together we attempt to "rightly divide the word of truth."

THE NEED TO COORDINATE
DOCTRINES

IN THIS COUNTRY THERE IS A SORT OF AUTOMATING AND UNIT-
izing going on, of attitudes concerning faith. It trends toward
encouraging a feeling among those not paying attention, that
everybody who is a churchgoer is an evangelical Christian.

This presumes to reinforce the idea that the so-called "Conservative Protestant" denominations all turn out cookie-cutter
believers with similar, if not identical, beliefs concerning their
faith and concepts of biblical truth. That such ideas have no
foundation whatsoever is seen in the simple recognition that
there are some 2,600 separate and distinct sects, all believing
they alone hold the keys to the kingdom!

Little exists in the communicative media of our day to suggest that any outlook apart from fundamentalist conceptions of
religion, has validity. This is largely because, without the majority of people affected by it being aware, many denominations

have sold out to what seems to best be termed "Christian Zionism," wearing a disguise with the cozier, more recognizable title "fundamentalists."

If one were to turn for instance to the Internet site, beliefnet.com, a "Christian" discussion and teaching site, he would find, under the heading Faiths and Practices, a section titled, "What Conservative Protestants Believe." Here the reader is instructed that the "Conservative" appellation can apply to traditionalist, orthodox, fundamentalist, or evangelical denominations. On its surface, this sounds appealingly authoritative, while in reality being appallingly inaccurate. It goes on to say, "This is an umbrella term for Protestant denominations, or churches within denominations, which are Bible-centered, viewing the Holy Bible as the final and only authority, the inerrant Word of God, interpreted literally as law." It concludes that this collection of all conservatives believes that "On judgment day" Jesus Christ will resurrect the dead, reunite body and soul, and judge each for eternity in heaven, or on a restored, paradisiacal earth, or in hell.

The problem with such encapsulated, uninformed but widely accepted opinions, in addition to being grossly inaccurate, is they fail to recognize the important divisors involved, so they are of little real relevance in understanding the subject. This particular definition as an example is somewhat akin to what is contained in the Bible, but the Bible is not where fundamentalists and increasingly not where evangelicals get the doctrines they teach! There is more, but this should suffice to establish the point of this book. The vast majority of Protestants today consider themselves to be evangelical, while unwittingly and slavishly following the doctrines of a relative minority of highly visible leaders. The difficulty is that those leaders, who characterize themselves as fundamentalists, are in reality Zionist in application. Their religion is tied entirely to their personal political views, but that vast majority whom they influence are totally unaware of their agenda. They are immensely popular, and most are very wealthy and wield significant political influence, both in this country and, to a somewhat lesser degree, in the state of Israel.

The theological doctrines and eschatology of this extremely influential group exemplify the very real danger in depending upon doctrines not influenced by the Bible but by ideas external to the Bible. In this case, the manmade doctrines they employ directly contradict the Bible. The mid-nineteenth century ushered in the birth of fundamentalism as it is known today. It was built upon the premises of a belief system known as dispensationalism.

Most of what came out of the teaching upon which Protestant fundamentalism is built and that has greatly influenced evangelical doctrine today consists of gross and intentional misrepresentation of the Bible, which serves personal and political agendas. This has led in many Protestant seminaries to very errant teaching. That errancy now engulfs or influences most of Protestantism. Sadly, it concerns some of the most fundamental pillars of Protestant belief that were responsible for there being a non-Catholic world, and that have been buried by this phenomenon which cannot be ascribed to the work of God!

The zeal and sound teaching that characterized the reformers survived for about one hundred years then died away, as did interest in various parts of Scripture. Then, for about four hundred years, nobody put much emphasis into learning of, or teaching about, the last days. The word describing an emphasis on final things as a theological area of interest is *eschatology*. This word was not defined, not even "coined" apparently, until the mid-nineteenth century. Before that time there had never been a unified theology concerning such matters. It was just too far in the future to worry about. That suggests nobody was teaching the entire Bible, as God commanded. The general disinterest persisted up until about a decade ago in many Protestant denominations. Then the popularity of successful novels and movies with "Christian themes" ushered in a new awareness of things eschatological.

But, about a century and a half ago, the "scholars" believed they had it all figured out, so they dug eschatological trenches and hunkered down in them. That's where they remain today mostly, despite the fact that many doctrines have cried out for attention. But they have little time for resolving differences between what they earlier decided the Bible said, and what was taught by even earlier, undoubtedly more learned, theologians. In other words, they have been not in the record mode for the past half-century at least, but in playback. Consequently, what they needed to learn never became one of their priorities.

Once Bibles had become available to the very early Protestant thinkers, they recognized that the Popes had built a theology that serious scholars could not live with. So Protestant theologians spent their efforts on the more immediate need. That included subjects such as God's true doctrines, the seriousness of man's real position with respect to his Redeemer, realistic interpretations of the entire body of Scripture once the fiats of popery were removed, the role of Christ the Man and of Christ the God, and the true requirements of God's salvation plan. These and many more subjects required the more learned in the body to devote themselves to study and to the development of creeds, confessions, and doctrines for the competing portions of a fast-to-fracture Protestant church. So, as academicians do, the Protestant "nobles" busied themselves for more than a century, doing what some are still doing, rehashing, debating, and attempting to downplay their differences.

Meanwhile, some obvious needs of doctrines requisite to an informed appreciation of the end times have reared their impertinent heads. They are, in fact, just about all that is left to define, but there seem to be no theologians today who want to tackle progressive revelation. The "eschaton" actually amounts to an unveiling of what has already taken place, or been revealed. It is the Second Advent. Realistically, therefore, it amounts to an unveiling of what our Lord already set up during his first advent! The task then is really one of correctly relating one advent to the other.

Typically, when a theologian learns his Scriptures around age thirty, he folds up the used part of his brain and refuses ever to exercise it again. But there has recently come a reawakening to the need to exercise some grey matter. This is not an especially comfortable enterprise for the current crop of "nobles" who are used to reclining and rehashing the ideas of earlier theological thinkers! That is what the so-called "science" of theology has amounted to ever since the leaders of the Reformation died out.

Unfortunately, the majority of denominations have trapped themselves in doctrines concerning the end times that the Popes could more easily squeeze into their eschatology than can Protestants, who supposedly pride themselves on their doctrines being biblical. They built their ideas of God's revelation concerning "Israel" long before they ever had to face a systematic eschatology that could stand up to scrutiny. Making it doubly difficult are fundamentalists who have a private agenda that they want the church to wrap its arms around, and it pretty much has. How that affects what is being taught is the primary topic that this book busies itself about.

The research and writing that will be encountered in this book contains nothing inherently new. Every idea, every word, beyond purely historical detail, comes directly from the Bible. The author's intent in this book is to show as wide an audience as is made possible by the grace of our Lord, how far many of the doctrines most of their churches hold have deviated from the teachings of Jesus Christ. It is also determined to illustrate that some of the most widely taught and held doctrines of present Protestantism, including eschatological ideas in Protestant churches and families, have absolutely not come from a biblical basis!

That should suggest to many that this is not a time when God is very pleased with his eternal church. If Satan is dictating doctrine, then the time of the Great Tribulation must be upon the church! That possibility will be examined in some detail in the pages ahead. Those who need to be told that the Great Tribulation has seized the church have not been paying attention and likely have never been instructed adequately in the teachings of Jesus Christ.

The Internet description presented earlier typifies what is found almost anywhere a person who is curious enough to seek insight might look for definition. This makes such ill-considered examples actually very misleading to many people who may be trying to find a church that adheres to biblical teaching. So far as this writer knows, there is no such church in existence! That is entirely because the "Abomination of Desolation is standing in the Holy place," and almost no one has been allowed to recognize or been taught to deal with that present reality, which constitutes the most terrible "real and present danger" that could ever overtake the church, or mankind. What men call "the end times" is increasingly a large part of today's church culture. Everybody associated with study of the Bible or who attends a church today is probably more concerned about the future than anyone ever was up until just a few years ago. There is a very good reason why this should be so, and it is tied directly to fundamentalists' views of the end times.

A second outgrowth of the doctrines that we will be examining is that we will "unmask" to some extent just what it is these denominations believe, because all of its defined nature is held close to the vest by their seminarians and leaderships. These are the denominations that pride themselves on being "evangelicals." Almost anyone, this writer included, could easily believe he is one of these critters until he really gets a look inside at what that terminology actually means. The resultant effect it could have on the futures of a lot of people who think they know what God intends for his church is unknown. When an organization feels obliged to conceal from its loyal membership even one important aspect of its real doctrine, its real purpose, can it be serving the will of the membership? Even more important, can it be serving the will of God? That is a question some who read this book will have to struggle with after they read the entire unveiling of "fundamentalism" and its stepchild, "evangelicalism."

God revealed his love for the man of his creation by giving his beloved and only begotten Son to be born as a man and to die as a man (Romans 8:32). This was the only way a righteous God could save a remnant of sinful mankind, whom he early decided to love despite their sin. Jesus came as the life and the light of the world. It pleased the Father to freely give his chosen people (they are called "elect" in the Bible) all things through Jesus. Through him we have obtained the Holy Scriptures, which are our gift of the testimony of God concerning Christ, whose salvation story is everywhere in Scripture. "We have found him, of whom Moses in the law, and the prophets, did write" (John 1:45). It is he, the Christ, and his redemption plan in the Scriptures, "Of which salvation the prophets have inquired and searched diligently [...] searching what, or what manner of time the Spirit of Christ which was in them did signify, when it testified beforehand the sufferings of Christ, and the glory that should follow" (1 Peter 1: 10–11).

Jesus loved the church he established on earth. He did not want the true church to be in darkness concerning the things that would come upon her, or upon his plan for her redemption. Our Lord Jesus, therefore, revealed future events to the prophets by his Spirit. The last book in the Bible is titled "The Revelation of Jesus Christ." It opens with the promise that the book is "The Revelation of Jesus Christ, which God gave unto him, to show unto his servants things which must shortly come to pass" (Revelations 1:1). Christ sent that book by his own messenger to his servant, the Apostle John, who wrote what Christ himself "signified." What the book you are holding contains is the discussion of only a portion of the word of prophecy pertaining to events of our time. It is presented that you may be helped to understand the difference between wrongly and "rightly dividing" what has been revealed by Christ, in "the word of truth" (2 Timothy 2:15). This revelation comes either verbally, from Christ himself, or through his prophets. It consists however, of only prophecy contained in Scripture. The apostle says of the word of prophecy: "We have also a more sure word of prophecy; whereunto ye do well that ye take heed, as unto a light that shineth' in a dark place, until the day dawn, and the day star arise in your hearts" (2 Peter 1:19). He is speaking of the Bible and of Christ.

All prophecy in the Bible was originated by, or because of, Christ Jesus. Therefore, when we speak of prophecy, we can know it came from Jesus or from His Holy Spirit, no matter where in God's Word it appears. In New Testament times—the last days—the Prophet Joel tells us that every true believer will be a prophet. This is because in the New Testament to prophecy simply means to relate what the Bible says in order to edify, to exhort, and comfort others (1 Thessalonians 5:11). This allows those of God's people who are concerned to be a part of Christ's "Great Commission" to be armed with sufficient tools to accomplish that tasking.

It is our prayer that the self-same Spirit that guided holy men of old as they wrote the words and predictions of the Bible will also guide those fortunate enough to read it that they may partake in the blessing pronounced by the faithful and true witness. It is also to be desired that you will be blessed and edified in reading the interpretations of this book, that you may keep the things written here, as there; for the time is at hand (Revelations 1:3).

IT'S BEST TO START
AT THE BEGINNING

"IN THE BEGINNING CREATED GOD THE HEAVENS AND THE earth. And the earth was without form and empty, and darkness on the face of the deep." Thus begins God's history according to the *Hebrew* language version of what Moses wrote. But before the defined beginning of the Hebrew text was God. From analysis of disconnected snippets of text, God has shown to whosoever will seek his truth that he was not lax concerning the only thing on earth he would form in his image.

At the beginning of the beginning, God made a ball of goo! It was a big wad of empty! Our English-language Bible calls it a "void." Early English usage termed both the product of and the act of eliminating bodily wastes "void." Then the Hebrew text (in English) says (and "says" is a correct rendering since we are actually "hearing" the words of God when we read it), "And the Spirit of God was hovering over the face of the waters."

Notice how, from the beginning of the second sentence (in the Hebrew) as God dictated this to Moses, he placed himself in, rather than after, the action by almost imperceptibly (to many, including translators of most Bibles) adopting the present tense to describe the past action.

What was God, in the person of the Holy Spirit, doing? This action, not the light, as most theologians suppose, is the first act of God in the creation story! We cannot even be certain, if you consider it, that this action is to be included in the "first day"! But that isn't the important element for our consideration here either. Now don't feel you should also have considered this, because you have not yet been introduced to the thesis of this volume, without which (according to the rules of your high school English teacher) you cannot comfortably proceed. So, it is the duty of this book to now introduce you formally to the reason it is being written.

First of all, you are important. All of God's creatures are important to God's story, and that's what this book is about. Naturally, one cannot claim this to *be* God's story. That was wonderfully written and handed down to us long ago. It is proving to be, as more and more archaeological evidence is uncovered, the finest, most accurate history book ever written. Certainly it has been the most popular book in the world for nearly twenty centuries and a runaway bestseller for almost three. This book you are holding in your hands, however, is *about* God's story. It is written in the hope of bringing light to areas where some darkness may still linger. Some people have biblical misperceptions concerning certain areas in Scripture, usually because their teaching was inadequate. Usually this is due to the laxity, insecurity, lassitude, or, regrettably, self-interest of their teachers. It is our fervent desire that some who have not yet been introduced to the Bible truths may find some aspect of that truth illuminated here. That might persuade someone to journey expectantly to the source of all truth, the Holy Bible.

So this is about God's story "canteened" in the Bible. No,

this is not a misspelling of *contained*. The writer is painfully aware that his English teacher would not have approved of turning a noun into a verb. A canteen is something to carry water in. The word of Jesus Christ is the living water that brings redemption. The author likes to think of that water being stored for true believers in God's canteen, the Bible. More specifically, this book is designed to show you how to drink more deeply of that water. It can do that because some of that water of the Word has gone undiscovered by large segments of the human crowd who have been milling about, thinking they are redeemed from damnation when in fact they may not be! Some may discover pools of living water referred to here, lying previously undiscovered by them, within the Bible.

If for a moment you were to view humanity as a nice, big, flat, round pizza, there would be a giant, pie-shaped slice of churchgoers in that pizza who have never learned what the Bible actually says about some important subjects—salvation, for instance. What could be a subject of more intense interest? Their teachers have short-circuited their learning. If those teachers ever do read the Bible for its content, which only a pitiful few ever will, they should begin to question what they have been taught. Eventually many will either leave their chosen denominations voluntarily or be driven out.

This is happening consistently but quietly in the evangelical denominations. Their failures to teach all of God's Word are so transparent to those who truly want to *study* the Bible, not just browse through it. We have no wish to denigrate any denomination or creed, only to bring the truth of the Bible to the great multitude who have never been exposed to it in their churches. We are speaking here, of course, not of the eternal, heavenly church that Christ built, but of the external, or corporate, churches built and operated to the specifications of men.

"Now that sounds like a rather harsh condemnation," some may say. Some might contend that the Bible brings many harsh truths, numerous brutal condemnations that every true believer should be aware of, but that are never discussed in many congregations today. The first important truth in this book is that there is a famine of truth in a great many, if not all, congregations today! Please allow this book to show you what this statement means.

First of all, the author is neither young nor a zealot. He is quite aware, after some years as a Bible teacher of adults, that possibly the most diehard sucker who has ever believed the "Pitchman's" line is an evangelical Christian. Someone should do a study of that phenomenon. Some people who have not attended church for years and who have not read the Bible regularly at any time will become highly incensed if a messenger of truth troubles their waters! Many, even church members, will simply not trust the most fundamental Bible truths if they were taught, as many have been, something else in their early church days! Their tenacity can be staggering, and in one respect, that characteristic is wonderful, but it would be marvelous if such an attachment was directed at the true meaning of a Bible passage.

Then there are the lovely people, especially those from a liturgical background, who will believe nothing in the Bible that they have not been previously taught by someone from their particular flavor of congregation and denominational fragment.

Others who have never been introduced to certain Bible words in the original languages have difficulty accepting an interpretive difference from what they learned as a child, even when shown what was actually written in the Bible by God!

But the overall most obvious barrier to learning is for people to absolutely refuse to accept a concept that has not been taught to them previously. Sadly, it seems that many Christians have not gained their Bible understanding from the Word of God, so much as from the denominational bias of their earliest teachers.

These tendencies make their learning of some of the great

truths of the Bible difficult, if not impossible. It's the old dog, new tricks problem that can have sad consequences in some cases. The following are a couple of examples told by Bible teachers:

"In counseling one lovely lady in her late sixties about divorce, I prepared a three-page, typed lesson which precisely quoted everything I could find concerning divorce in the Bible and I provided some explanations. I did not bother her with parables or Old Testament passages concerning God divorcing Israel. I simply showed her the lessons contained in the words of Jesus and the Apostle Paul. I taught it to her then left the study paper with her.

I asked her a week later what she thought about it and if she had come to any conclusions. Her response was that she disregarded it since it talked so much about men and spoke little about women. She felt it was unfair, that God is love, and doesn't want people to be lonely, and that couldn't be the way he felt!" Here is another:

"Several years ago, I conducted a class for the residents of a large RV park. About six were regular attendees, and occasionally someone else would try us out and sometimes not return. I was not surprised that most were looking for a teacher from their own denominations despite none having been a regular attendee at church for years. One couple who came regularly asked for specific topical studies, and I obliged them since no one else objected. I learned from accommodating this one couple—actually just the wife—that when people nominate a subject for study, they really want only a refresher of what they heard thirty years earlier. When this lady learned from me that not every human being will be a resident of heaven, she became highly agitated. I had read directly from the Bible, which seemed to me a reasonable approach that made sense, but she was not impressed. When I showed her precisely what the Bible said in English, it did not help! She wouldn't believe it even when reading right out of the Bible. That was not what she was taught, and she was not going to accept it! She did not drop out of our study group, as I suspected she would, but she was skeptical after that, carefully dissecting everything I taught. I like to think she had begun learning."

Here is a third example: "A preacher from one of the dispensational churches comes to visit me at my house. He wants to welcome this newcomer to the community. Knowing that I studied God's Word in a sister congregation of another city a few years earlier and at the instigation of a dear brother and still close friend who preaches there, this brother hoped to coax me into his fold. His sheepfold, not the fold in the handkerchief I thought he was going to whip out and cry into when I taught him the Bible in my living room. We had a nearly three-hour Bible lesson, during which this minister of some thirty years preaching experience in a dispensational (fundamentalist) denomination lost his ability to discourse rationally, so confused was he by the Bible. To be honest, I did feel a twinge of regret, but what I told him came right out of parts of the Bible his denomination completely and deliberately ignores. That's why he was unable to handle discussing them."

On another occasion, when visited by another very friendly pastor, a teacher had answered the question, which he knew his visitor simply had to ask, "Why did you leave our denomination?" The answer was a simple one. "They did not teach all of the gospel and had a works gospel, rather than a gospel of grace, which the Bible presents." The teacher then asked his guest the simple question, "What do you tell someone who asks what he must do to become saved?" The questioner knew what the pastor's answer would be before he spoke. He regurgitated the standard fundamentalist response concerning believing, having faith, and for that particular denomination, a requirement to be baptized by immersion in water. Then the storyteller quietly demonstrated to him that, like almost all denominations, his did not teach the whole Word of God—the entire gospel! He was a bit taken back at that, probably feeling that he was in some sort of hostile, alien presence. But that's part of what evangelists are supposed to be able to handle. His accuser called him by name in as conciliatory a tone as could be mustered and asked him the following question. (For those reading this and who say they study the Bible, the writer will ask the same question.)

"What was God doing before he built the universe?" In all humility, my new friend admitted that he had no idea. I asked if he could recall the first two verses in Genesis chapter one (the same two verses with which, for your edification, this chapter you are reading began). It's okay if you want to turn back now to check the first page. Naturally, the preacher verbalized the two verses easily. "So, God, in the Spirit, was moving on the face of the waters," I said quietly. "Time had not yet begun, you see, since our celestial clock had yet to be assembled and correctly set for our position on the blob that was still waiting to be formed into something useful." He was embarrassed, and I was a bit sorry I had not maneuvered him a bit more lovingly. Then I dropped the other satin slipper.

I referred to the doctrine of election, noting that according to the Bible not everyone could be saved. His answer truly surprised me, not because I had not heard it often, but because I had never heard anyone I credited with serious knowledge of the Bible, coupled with evangelical experience say, "Oh, my God wouldn't do that! He loves everybody." I wilted a bit at the realization that some who have read the Bible all their lives have never truly studied it at all. They have simply read the Bible once, a thousand times, concentrating each time only on verses their denominations are interested in. So, I dutifully informed another sinner, ignorant of God's redemption plan, exactly where the truth was hiding from him. He already knew, and I knew that he knew. That's why I have little respect for that denomination. They refuse to bring the whole gospel of Christ to their adherents! They are knowingly then false prophets!"

The answer that went unmentioned in the true story above was the second part of the idea with which chapter one of this book began. It had to do with additional Bible information about what God busied himself with before he poured substance into the mold he carved for this world. For one thing we know from John chapter seventeen verse twenty-four that God spent time loving on his Son! Jesus himself said so in that verse, "for thou lovedst me before the foundation of the world." But more important to us, because it is a fundamental lynchpin of God's plan and purpose for man, is that God was busy choosing whom among all the people of the earth who would ever be created, he would elect for salvation, and whom he would not! Listen to what Paul said of that action in Ephesians 1:6–7, 10–11 (ILB):

> To the praise of the glory of his grace, wherein he hath bestowed favor on us in the beloved. In whom we have redemption through his blood, the forgiveness of sins, according to his good pleasure which he purposed in himself for stewardship of the fullness of the times to head up all things in Christ. [...] In whom also we have been chosen to an inheritance, being predestined according to the purpose of him who works all things after the counsel of his will.

There is predestination! God has not yet told us when that occurred, but he will. If we just back up to Ephesians 1:4 in the King James Bible, we encounter the words "According as he hath chosen us in him before the foundation of the world." There is the chosen part. But why would God do that? His reason comes in the very next phrase: "that we should be holy and without blame before him in love." In other words, God chose those he would save because he loved them even before he created them! That's a common refrain in the Bible, but one that lives out its life unconnected to the rest of the story. He also decided that once he elected us to salvation, he would consider us to be without sin as soon as we answer his call.

Now to cover the other part of this plan—the presentation of verse five in the Greek from the Interlinear Bible seems better than the English translation from the King James: "predestinating us to adoption through Jesus Christ to himself, according to the good pleasure of the will of him" (Ephesians 1:5, ILB). Then if that is not sufficient for us to understand when we have not been preaching all the important points of God's "good news," take a look at Romans 8:28–30 (below), which you will virtually never hear preached as a unit in any evangelical, dispensationalist, fundamentalist, church. They go by all or any of those names, at one time or another. They are also known (to themselves) as "mainstream."

> And we know that all things work together for good to them that love God, to them who are the called according to his purpose. For whom he did foreknow, he also did predestinate to be conformed to the image of his Son, that he might be the firstborn among many brethren. Moreover whom he did predestinate, them he also called; and whom he called, them he also justified, and whom he justified, them he also glorified.
>
> Romans 8:28–30

So, as anyone can see—that is, those who wish to see—God clearly says he had some things going before he began his work on the world.

So, actually, did Jesus. There was at least one aspect of Christ's work that was accomplished before he became Christ in the flesh. Check out 1 Peter 1:19–20 to get an idea about that. "But with the precious blood of Christ, as of a lamb without blemish and without spot: Who verily was foreordained before the foundation of the world, but was manifest in these last times for you." But many folks are not aware of Christ having been ordained to die on the cross long before any of us had any opportunity to get involved, or to get to know him! Listen now to the words of Revelation 13:8 where John speaks of Satan being worshipped in the last days: "And all that dwell upon the earth shall worship him, whose names are not written in the book of life of the Lamb slain from the foundation of the world." Note the capital letter on *Lamb*. This is Jesus, who had some things on his to-do list before he got involved in seeding all the lawns and planting trees at the beginning of the story. So that's what was told to the visiting preacher. He excused himself shortly after that, and although he had invited his host to Bible study with him prior to the dissertation above, he didn't mention it afterward. The author does not recount this experience to be smug, caustic, or haughty, but to illustrate an earlier point that this book was designed to make the truth clear to those who have not been exposed to the "whole truth and nothing but the truth" of the Bible. That includes, I am sorry to say, more than half of all who call themselves after his name. Also, it is Christ's choice that this is done in a loving way.

But many denominations will not talk about the part of God's program you just saw in black and ink, because they teach that men have an important part in their own salvation. Did you see even a bit part with your name on it in that playbill you just perused? Don't despair, neither did anyone else. That's because God does all—one hundred percent—of the work associated with salvation, and most of that work was accomplished long before your great-great grandparents were even introduced to each other. Now consider this question: would you be a little "put out" if you had laid out your invitation list, planned the party, sent your son out to die so all your guests could have a good time, then some clown came in off the street and tried to grab some of the credit for your party being so desirable? You'd be furious with him! Maybe lock him in the cellar. How do you think God feels about some of the sinners he is pretending are righteous, going about claiming to have been instrumental in the process for which his beloved Son suffered and died? That's a good thing to ponder if this is the first time you have heard this biblically, but not politically correct, story. Now, it is important that all this be qualified by saying that all those little one-line, daily Vacation-Bible-School Scriptures you learned about salvation "way back when" are not invalidated at all by what was just presented or by anything else you will read here. All and every Scripture God wrote is true and applicable to us.

Just consider this: if you start with the simple platitudes and parables that evangelicals begin their teaching with, you cannot rectify the meatier statements of God with them. But the wise man begins to learn where God began to teach. If you'll do that, you'll come to understanding of God's *process,* and his order of things, and you can be assured that it will come together into a meaningful whole. It cannot be done the other way! That way you'd wind up having to toss out a goodly share of the teachings from the Bible! A fine rule of thumb in decoding God's Word is to remember what God says in Second Timothy 3:16, that *all* verses of Scripture are important and are necessary to a full understanding. If some seem to contradict others or won't work together, you're missing something, and the something just might be the order in which you are considering them. We are not allowed by 2 Timothy 3:16 to ignore any passage of Scripture. If you find one that seems not to work, you may need to reorder your priorities! God breathed them all—every last one!

The foregoing discussion also serves as something of an informal introduction to the fourth chapter. So far as can be ascertained, that chapter follows immediately after this one. It deals with dispensationalism as a theological life choice for many denominations. Surprisingly, this is true despite its not being easily identifiable as being at all grounded in the Bible.

Once we deal as charitably with dispensational doctrine and its importance in today's world geopolitical climate as we are able, we can get to the important task of proving to you how desperately the fundamentalists need to reread their Bibles. What we will see in the following chapter is the problem that beset the churches in Galatia and what the apostle has to tell them. In Paul's day there was an understandable conspiracy among Jewish members of the Galatian churches (in what today we call "Turkey"), and some who came there precisely to abet that conspiracy. The whole thing resembled one of the same problems that bedevil parts of the church today. In a nutshell it was, and is, Jewish interpretation of Bible prophecy and their desire to impose those beliefs on Gentile believers. Naturally, Jews—even Messianic Jews, who have received the gift of the Holy Spirit—are Jews! They believe and so do the leaders of most (perhaps all) fundamentalist churches, despite what is contained in the Bible, that Jews are the beneficiaries of priority and privilege not accorded to Gentiles, in God's redemption plan. The actions of such folks in trying to advance these notions, were, and still are, called "Judaizing" by Christian religious scholars.

Any well-read Christian will react immediately to such teachings of Judaizers. Paul was no exception. He was in fact, the "point man" who led the struggle against the introduction of such heresies in the first-century church. As a matter of fact, when he discovered that some of the other apostles were sympathetic to such arguments, his reaction was severe and his challenge vigorous against the Jerusalem church (Galatians 2:12). Paul seemed to be the only teacher aware that even the appointed stewards of the gospel were susceptible to being led astray, at least temporarily (Galatians 2:13). It is no understatement to say that Paul almost single handedly saved the infant church and the gospel of Christ from perversion (Galatians 2:5). The teaching Paul contended about in the first century concerned circumcision. Today, the argument concerns the appropriate day of the week for Christians to worship. Neither topic is more important, or more damaging to the work of Christ, than the other. Both are attempts to force Jewish traditions and bad habits into the church that Christ founded because the "other folks" wouldn't accept the truth even when it was handed to them on a big, T-shaped stick! They are still "passing over" the truth of God's Bible, and they have been eminently successful at dragging down some who class themselves as Christians, into the lake of fire with them. If you think such comments are judgmental, you probably have not read the Bible carefully!

THE DISPENSATIONALISTS

LOTS OF PEOPLE THESE DAYS ARE VERY CONCERNED ABOUT THE future. Many view every rumor and every report of war, every tsunami, hurricane, or smoking volcano as evidence that the last day comes sometime in the middle of next week.

Evangelical Christians, of whom the bean counters boast 35 million, or 20 million, maybe more, depending on whom one reads, are fearful. These folks have been taught to fear what they ought to be welcoming, if in fact there was any evidence that it was imminent. They are worrying perhaps about what to do with all the good stuff they have purchased, from *Left Behind* series movies and videos and books and key rings and napkin holders and bumper stickers and framed paintings and pamphlets and sweatshirts and audio tapes and songbooks and stereoptigan slides and teddy bears, portraits of the real Jesus, and probably some stuff still at the wholesalers. Seriously, Tim LaHaye and his imaginary eschatology have buoyed up, and brought premillennium theology to the frontal lobes of an entire continent worth of craniums.

For about 150 years, the idea has been popular that all the true believers (the church, but there are conflicting definitions of its composition) will be taken bodily up to heaven if they are living when the rapture happens. This is in order to escape the terror of the closing of God's last chapter of earth history. Who wouldn't appreciate such a favor? Evangelicals suppose that there is even another modification to the scenario. They decided, presumably based upon Old Testament doctrines and entirely ignoring what the New Testament has to say, that this "catching up" of the church will occur prior to what is known as the "Great Tribulation." Their view that the Second Coming of Christ will precede the 1,000 years spoken of in Revelation 20, has tens of thousands of supporters, not one of whom can explain to you satisfactorily from the Bible why that is his fixation. In reality, most of it's adherents are such, only because that's what the TV preachers teach!

All this means that there are thousands of people who think they understand clearly, and can explain precisely, the events preceding the end of the world. But their various leaders promote a smorgasbord of variations on the theme—differing prophetic and propagandistic interpretations. Of course, struggling to get in on the immense profits that followed LaHaye's series of eminently saleable products, almost every church sect is promoting a book, video, seminar, or audio tape about the end times. These events combine to produce some weighty worries, which of course Christians are admonished in the Bible not to get themselves into! When will "Who has the truth?" become the battle cry? One can only hope that somewhere a light will go on and the evangelicals will recall that a Christian's view of any prophetic situation is supposed to reflect the gospel of Christ, the entire gospel of Christ, and only the gospel of Christ. Therein lies the rub. The prevalent ideas in the churches today about the end times fall generally into one of three sifting baskets. One basket holds the doctrines emergent if everything in God's Word prior to the book of Revelation is ignored. The second basket contains the accumulation of options contingent upon taking a long, theological stride from the book of Ezekiel to the present day. The third, and probably least popular next to never having heard of the Bible, is the view expressed above, namely, that you cannot follow God's lead by concentrating on any one part of prophecy. The entire gospel must be considered before coming up with a doctrine on anything that has anything to do with God.

So, it becomes appropriate to examine what sort of doctrine would brand someone a fundamentalist. This becomes a significant factor in examining the last days, because the evangelicals also call themselves fundamentalists. The other sects call them premillennialists, since their concentration concerning the "end times" is upon their belief that they will all be taken up into heaven before the Great Tribulation occurs. This brands them as "Pre-Trib," while the operative theology of their leadership is actually built upon their fundamental theological premise of "dispensationalism." My, what long names you have, grandmother!

One must learn to appreciate that Christians, especially the pre-tribulation rapture sort, go in for a lot of labels. That's probably because they don't like to get too immersed in the spiritual particulars their seminarians mumble on about. One man who attended a small Church of Christ in a big Western city a decade and more ago recalls the large charts the evangelist used to draw on bed sheets then hang on a cable across the building to exemplify the various dispensations his church believed in. The way he taught it, though, made everybody in his audience think he had found all this wonderful insight into God's plan all by himself. After all, he did draw all those humongous schematics on bed sheets by himself. Or so he claimed. Years later, at least one of his students recognized that the preacher had been a dispensationalist and that all those incredible diagrams had been done in textbooks long before his entry into the arena. One thing about evangelicals, they'll accept as much praise as you can find in your heart to heap on them.

What exactly is dispensationalism, and is it scriptural? Herendeen defines it as a, "system of prophetic interpretation." Quite a sparse defining of terms! But it is widely accepted today among the evangelical churches whose members consider themselves "fundamentalist Christians," but of course are not fundamental at all if they hold to dispensationalism. They see it as a "new light" from God concerning the interpretation of his Word. In other words it is "revealed prophesy," which we know God has not sent, because he warns in Revelation 22:18–19 that such will not come from him. Those who accept this erroneous, non-scriptural doctrine of course believe they are the only ones who perceive such a light. The idea of "new understanding," of course, destroys immediately and entirely the notion that such could be a fundamental Christian belief. As recently as fifty years ago, "fundamentalist" congregations would have known, understood, and practiced the limits imposed by Revelation 22:18–19 which preclude any "new light" from God apart from what is contained in the Bible.

In his third sentence, Herendeen changes his mind and calls dispensationalism a "system of teaching," indicating that the proponents of this approach to looking at prophecy are not quite certain just what they are actually propounding. Herendeen then proceeds to uncover his own nakedness as a prideful and arrogant academic, as he first condemns the "system" because it was "unknown to the spiritual giants of the past, and has never been incorporated into the creeds of any evangelical denominations." One would be hard-pressed to imagine a weaker opening to a discussion of a system for scriptural study! What congregation would admit to teaching doctrine not found in its denomination's creed, or allowing activity on its premises not in accord with that creed? About one deep breath later, the author confesses how great a lack of direction is apparent in the evangelical churches by saying of dispensationalism, "Its adherents seem, nevertheless, as convinced it is the teaching of Scripture as they are of the divine inspiration of the Bible." This comment is entirely valid, if the writings and declarations of leading fundamentalist-dispensationalists are considered seriously. So, though they are without direction in regard to dispensationalism, they are in unison when it comes to what they do believe about it, even if one teacher's dispensations are not another's. Perhaps he is digressing to fill up some pages, but Mr. Herendeen eventually gets around to accusing the evangelicals of "modernism for the orthodox." Some theologians would call such a departure, "beliefs utterly devoid of scriptural support," otherwise known as "false doctrine." One might wonder, in fact, where such candid descriptions have been hidden during the past decade as the *Left Behind* books swept all records for popularity clean away! Why have there been so few detractors? Doubtless because the evangelical bent of one sort or another comprises perhaps 80% of the Protestant church-going public, and no one in the popular media knows anything at all about prophecy apart from what they hear from that 80%. Then there are the Catholics, one supposes.

But why has no one in any seminary or university taken the "Left Behinders" to task? They have in fact left their behinds entirely exposed to any serious biblical scholar who might want to comment! Of course, it is possible most such persons do not much care what is in the popular press concerning Christendom. Alternatively, they may simply recognize that one cannot present truth to an evangelical believer and expect a reasoned response, so why bother? Several years ago it was reported that fully 80% of the professors of theology and of the Bible are atheists! They couldn't care less what you believe. In his 2002 book *Who Is This Jesus: Is He Risen?* the late Dr. D. James Kennedy, PhD, wrote (with Jerry Newcombe), "Men and women who train future would-be ministers of the gospel don't even believe the gospel themselves, and yet they dominate some of our most prestigious seminaries."[1] Kennedy goes on to relate that when he personally went through seminary, probably thirty-odd years ago, fully one half of his instructors did not consider the Bible to be the Word of God! He relates that, "Unbelief has grabbed some of the liberal denominations by the throat and is slowly destroying them from within, and nowhere is this clearer than at many of the liberal seminaries." He is speaking of evangelicals. It is public knowledge that members of the World Council of Churches, led by the United Methodists, are represented by homosexual and lesbian priests, preachers, and other leaders. Much of the corporate church structure of our day has been practicing make-believe Christianity for years, and everybody knows it except those sitting in their pews accepting the rubbish preached every Sunday.

The Holy Spirit is no longer any sort of necessity for a church to draw a membership. The do-it-yourself gospel is running loose in the congregations of America, and the people there don't even know it! Or maybe they like it that way. The point of these comments is to lead the reader to a recognition that what a denomination or congregation calls itself, or what a person calls himself, has little meaning in today's worship environment compared to what it would have meant sixty years ago. There are plenty of examples evident of big congregations who spend twenty million dollars on a new building for themselves to be entertained in and fifteen thousand dollars on their "missions" effort but call themselves "evangelical." Then the definitional ladder begins.

If a denomination views itself as evangelical, it becomes, by the popular definition, "fundamentalist," and that puts it in the camp of the "dispensationalists," who these days are all, or mostly all, premillennialists, which turns them into believers in a pre-tribulation rapture. Their disposition then naturally becomes one of support for the Zionists, making theirs a denomination of Christian Zionists. That is the one aspect of their slide into nomenclature that is problematical for their nation and which makes their master something other than the Bible. Of course, most of the members involved do not recognize that any of this is truly happening, mostly because few denominations today encourage Bible literacy.

If you had inquired of, let's say, several Baptist ministers of, for instance, the Southern stripe, shortly after the first LaHaye book came out what they thought of it, what might they have said? That was in fact part of a survey done at that time, and it is an excellent representation of the opinions of the vast majority of evangelical pastors. To a man, they said, "it was great." Then when asked "Where in the Bible is a pre-tribulation rapture discussed?" none had any idea whatsoever where that might be! If you are able to read this, we will presume that you have an understanding of just how representative the word "none" truly is! The only thing this might be said to indicate is that perhaps Bible teachers who do not carefully study what they teach will believe anything another evangelical with a new book tells them! Then too, if evangelical pastors are wanting in knowledge, perhaps the evangelicals have for too long now accepted ministerial candidates without determining that the candidates have the necessary motivation to be effective in the ministry field. It may also be a factor that salaries for pastors have come to be so generous, that increasingly many candidates may actually not be "called" to that profession by the head of the church, at all, but may be there for economic reasons, possibly coupled with reputation factors.

We are personally aware of at least one southern evangelical Bible college, which almost a decade ago hired a particular writer and university instructor to develop curriculum for them. The reason stated by the chancellor of that college was that none (there's that word again) of his professors—not one—was competent to develop courses of instruction! In every reputable university, even a brand-new instructor is typically expected to develop courseware if he has been designated to establish a new course. That is a skill fundamental to teaching, yet at least one college that was graduating ministry candidates could find not a single member of its faculty competent to accomplish this fundamental task. There is no reason to assume it was or is the only faculty with such a shortcoming.

But one among the many influences on the evangelical denominations in the past century has stood alone as an influence that has not built biblical knowledge into the evangelical community. In the early twentieth century, a new and much-esteemed Bible was introduced, which was decidedly the birth of dispensationalism being taught widely in evangelical circles. In 1909 C.I. Schofield first published his Reference Bible. This was the first of the genre that was to become immensely popularized as a "wonderful" study aid. But Schofield's ideas were by no means something new.

Liberal theology, or what some view as a "branch" of "religious thinking," was probably a natural outgrowth of the same factors, which spawned social and political liberalism. All were departures from the normative structure of man's world but not from God's. Just like other of men's activities, "liberal theology" is an oxymoron, precisely because it deals with the Creator. *Theos* is a Greek word signifying the supreme deity, according to *Strong's Concordance* of the Bible, word number 2316, from the Greek translation of the Interlinear Bible. We are told in Hebrews 13:8 that our Supreme Deity, God, who is also "Jesus Christ," if we call ourselves by his name, is "the same yesterday, today and forever." That would suggest that to liberalize his doctrine, regardless of the purpose, would not be in consonance with his personal theology. In other words, it is not a Christian doctrine or something permissible if one intends to retain the epithet "Christian"! That would be so, since in addition to it being necessarily a departure from the restricted thinking commanded in Christianity, it would also require a revised form of action—a different lifestyle—from that prescribed in the Bible. It would therefore fall under the list of departures from the normative prescribed for the followers of Christ. That puts it into the category of sin! Sin then would have entered into the church sometime in the mid 1800s to eventually spread its infection during the next century or so to nearly all so-called believers. That would explain the situation in the churches today if you consider it thoughtfully. Then realistically one can begin to understand why, with so many running around crying "Lord, Lord," our God insists there will be but a sliver off the forest, who will enter into the kingdom of heaven.

It is clear that liberal theology, according to those who study such things, had become dominant in what are known for some strange reason as the "mainstream churches" in the twentieth century. Another way to say that is that antichrist activity became standard fare for the majority of denominations during our lifetimes! Then the trackers of such matters decided that more conservative attitudes began to be seen again near the end of the last century. Wikipedia writers call these "moderate alternatives." But these "alternatives" are still alternatives to the Word of God, if they do not mirror it precisely! In some circles, that adjustment would, as what was adjusted, rate the term, "unbiblical."

But so far, we have not encountered an actual, understandable, definition of what dispensationalism really is! At the risk of offending some people (which books like this inevitably do) this writer will now attempt a death defying excursion into the nearly unknown realm of simple descriptions. Descriptions, that is, of something the theologians have never quite gotten their arms around. At least they have never explained it in a way you and I could understand. Attend now to my words as together we dispel confusion and ignorance. Here, without further ado, is the definition of dispensationalism in every day language, in it's unique essence. That is, after all, what separates it from biblical reality! This is not my definition, since human intellect cannot distill this thing into simple terms (apparently), I have borrowed the following from someone who ought to know. Charles Ryrie, who has a Bible named after him, and a book that explains the simple definition he has distilled down from about ten million words that have been expended in man's search for an explanation of this phenomenon. Ryrie (probably today's most well known dispensationalist apologist) says the very essence of dispensationalism is that it has established, [without any help whatever from the Bible] a "consistent ... and distinct understanding ... of "the distinction between Israel and the Church". [2] Ahem, uh ... excuse me, but uh, ok, so that's the essence, I mean ... that's the definition? So then, it's really kind of a non-definition, definition, thing, huh? Well, Ryrie ought to know. Is it any wonder those outside the field of the dispensationalists are unable to define what this thing is?

Now please do not misunderstand what you just read. What is written here does in no way suggest that the hard-line conservative Christians are any better at keeping Christ's commands than anybody else! "If we say that we have no sin, we deceive ourselves, and the truth is not in us" (1 John 1:8). The conservative, however, retains for his guidance the original statements of intent drafted by God if he does not succumb to the tendency, also brought by liberalism, to seek a Bible that allows liberal attitudes. Simply stated, nobody is perfect. A very few will be, on the last day. All the rest are going to whine, "Lord, all my life I was a _____ (fill in the denomination). How can you turn me away?" On that Day of Judgment, our Lord, the Christ Jesus, will say, "I never knew you: depart from me, ye that work iniquity" (Matthew 7:23). Then, every one of them will be known, not by a title, not by their idea of self-worth, not by how often they attended worship on Sunday, but by what our God will judge. He will judge their deeds. Then they will remember that Christ told them in John 14:15, "If ye love me, keep my commandments." There will be no question in their minds about what they did wrong. They will know!

"It's simple; just don't change, because I haven't!" God is saying. What he wrote down still goes, according to the rulebook he wrote for us. So, it would follow that neo-orthodoxy, neo-modernity, evangelicalism, process theology, and all the other new theologies, all—every one of them—fits into the same basket labeled by God, "Send to Hell." Every one of them is a departure from what Christ established. That makes every one of them, no matter what rationale someone applies to justify them, man-made theology. But you don't have to take this as authoritative; you can figure it out for yourself by simply examining some of the descriptives used to explain the liberal doctrines. Here is a list that constitutes a rough outline of "liberal Christianity" for you to examine:

- Its focus is individualistic, valuing subject experiences in religion above doctrines, church authority, or Scripture.

- It claims religion to be a community of individuals united by experiences, intuitions, needing a church only as a supportive framework in which new conceptions of deity can be explored.

- God, it claims, may remain immutable, but the "theist's" relationship, and his understanding of God, change with the times (history), invalidating the idea of fixed truths in theology. Each person's experience will reveal a new and novel aspect of God.

- It may see God as by nature, changing as his creation changes with time and circumstance, in a changing universe. It's the same sort of thing they claim as a model for our national constitution.

Even the hermeneutics are different, and in fact, liberal hermeneutics have been affecting the church for half a century. In case you don't know, hermeneutics are the method of interpreting the Bible. If you decide that you will interpret the Bible as a collection of factual, literal statements, that is then your method, or hermeneutic. Liberals tend to view Scripture as documentation of the scribe's, rather than God's, feelings and reactions to God at the time he was writing about and within the author's cultural and historical frame of reference. Starting there, they have built a proposition within which "religious concepts—the models we live with—require updating over time, or within social, political, even gender variations, which obviously, to the liberal, affect all reality. Pastors and other formally trained ministers who consider themselves to operate within the description of this theology already populate most mainline Protestant denominations today.

Given that we are still talking about that group described as dispensational believers, or fundamentalists, the reader may by now be wondering, based on what has so far been written, what then is an evangelical church? There are at least two ways to answer this question. One would be to tell it like it is, the other to tell it as those churches would. We will try to find accommodation with a dash up the middle! "Evangelical" as a descriptor, refers to a church typified (not necessarily accurately) by an emphasis on evangelism. Typically, its members also claim "an experience" of conversion. They often will recite, because there is also an emphasis on personal witness, the exact moment and circumstances of their having been "born-again." (Fifty years ago, the "born-again" terminology was a symbol of evangelicals.) They also feel deeply about the relevance of the Christian sort of faith to everyday living and to cultural issues. The term *evangelical* was coined in the late twentieth century in an effort to contrast themselves from those they considered liberals and those who were just "too conservative."

If theologians had to identify the distinguishing difference between dispensationalists and other Christians, their contrast would most often be characterized as dispensations versus covenants. The covenental brand of theology separates the Bible into two exclusive types of salvation opportunities or periods, called "covenants." They are of course, the "Old" and the "New," which are characterized by salvation through works in the first, as over against salvation through grace, in the latter. Simple.

Everything concerning Bible understanding is viewed as spring-
ing from one or the other of these governing categories.[3]

This is, of course, a gross over simplification, but how much
more understandable this is than the definition of dispensationalism we struggled with earlier.

The evangelical emphasis began in America with the Methodists of the eighteenth century when temperance, family orien-
tation, public morality, and such traits were the common stock
of Protestantism in this then still un-despoiled country. Piety
would likely have been a characteristic in those days. Meth-
odism these days is a different (and smelly compared to then)
kettle of fish.

Evangelicals advertise that they hold to the Bible as the
reliable and ultimate authority in matters of faith and practice.
They accept as factual the virgin birth of Christ, his Crucifixion, Resurrection, and Second Coming. These are all assertions.
The marriage of the denominationalists and the evangelicals (in
most churches) has now produced a variety of mutual understandings, all of which are quite agreeable to them. In a similar
fashion, the evangelicals have been grafted into the vine of the
fundamentalists, who until perhaps forty years ago were two
competing theologies. The rise of the televangelism monster
may have had an overall blending effect on Protestant theology for these three groups were not so very far apart that they
couldn't all be made to feel comfortably joined, once they swal-
lowed the cup of dispensationalist theology. At the same time,
some of liberalism and also of "charismatic-ism" colors certain
of their denominations as well.

The differences come increasingly to bear the more a person is "into" study of the Bible and dispensing of its contents
to others, as is Christ's charter for his church. Some, perhaps
many (we seem to hear that it is many), who had always thought
of themselves as evangelicals, have lately wondered whatever
happened to the foundations of truth that we grew up with in
our denominations. Many are leaving the churches and seek-

ing groups to fellowship with outside of the churches. This is at least in part because of the growing transparency of what is being taught in the denominations today. What even ten years ago were strongly-faithful-to-the-Bible churches are becoming increasingly, and worse, recognizably, apostate. Part of this certainly must be laid at the altar of televangelists with their "name it and claim it" doctrines, their glamorization of signs and wonders, "faith healings," and all their other visually saleable sideshows. Of course, without a noticeably "dumbed-down" audience, this factor would be greatly reduced.

But if they would, church leaders—pastors, deacons, teachers—could hold the line on theology, but they are rushing to join the liberals and to surpass them in liberality, hurrying toward the day their candlestick will be, if it has not already been, removed by God. Remember this: Christ told his disciples that judgment will begin with the churches! Perhaps what we see happening is why that will be.

PRE-TRIBULATION THINKING

A PRE-TRIBULATION RAPTURE,—THE SAINTS BEING "CAUGHT up" into the clouds with Jesus when he returns, just in time to protect them all from having to undergo what is known as the "Great Tribulation," spoken of in Matthew 24:21–22—is a very popular theory today among evangelical Christians. In fact, it may be the most popular theory among them. If, however, we analyze the arguments offered in support for such a belief, in light of what is contained in the collected writings known to Christians as "the Bible," we have a bit of difficulty correlating what the fundamentalists and evangelicals teach with what is presented in that particular book!

That's because the majority of Christians are being taught that should the great tribulation occur tomorrow, they will not have to suffer it if they are among the born-again ranks. That seems well and good, except for one small technicality that might have a decided effect on the scenario. That technicality is that the Bible does not appear to agree at all with this popular analysis of the tribulation.

Given the arguments outlined in the Bible and not having ever had a clear presentation of why fundamentalists believe what they believe about the tribulation and the rapture, we must join those who categorically declare that pre-tribulation-ism is contrary to the clear teachings accepted widely as God's infallible Word. The position supporting a rapture immediately prior to the tribulation simply is not among the teachings found in the Bible! Put simply, there is not a single shred of evidence to be found in the Bible to support such a contention.

The difficulty is that pre-tribulation arguments invariably (meaning there is no variation whatever) reveal a pattern of suppositions and vague theories presented entirely by men, which are imposed onto a biblical text without any exegetical justification whatever being either apparent or introduced by the proponents of such a belief! This leads to imposition of subtle meanings into words or phrases. These are meanings never intended by the Editor in Chief of the Bible! It also leads to either spiritualizing or to ignoring completely certain Bible passages that actually were intended to teach the unity of organization contained in God's plan for the end time. God's paradigm shows a sequence of events that flows out of a plan that is inviolate but that dispensationalism was dedicated to changing. In the Bible, there is order, in fundamentalism, disorder generated by an escapist fantasy that attempts to overturn God's dominion. This is but one example of errant meanderings through biblical exposition by the dispensationalist fundamentalists.

If someone were to examine chapter twenty in the book of Revelation, which premillennialists argue is conclusive proof for their ideas, it would be necessary to ask them, "What makes more sense as a method of interpretation?"

- To lift one single passage in a totally apocalyptic book, full of recognized non-literal symbolism, and call it a literal chronology of the second coming and what follows thereafter, despite this interpretation contradicting several other clear passages contained in the Gospels and Epistles, or

- To interpret Revelation 20 in recognition of, and agreement with, clear teachings found in the remainder of the New Testament?

The book of Revelation is, virtually every Bible scholar has recognized, not at all a literal description of God's planned future, but a representational description of a dream or vision! It is not a literal description of a thousand-year reign of Christ on this earth. Rather it summarizes, in a non-chronological dream sequence, the period between Christ's first advent and his second. This is a time during which Jesus comes to earth, dies, and is resurrected. His miraculous resurrection by God binds Satan in order that the gospel can go out, relatively unhindered, to all nations. Christ is King; he rules at the right hand of God. He always will, and his church will always be right there with him. That is entirely the gospel of Christ, whether the Jews like it or not. We can know that, but in order to know it, we must first believe the Bible is the actual Word of God, which it claims to be. It must rule the lives of those who are actual true, born-again believers. The Apostle John, author of the book of Revelation, uses a thousand years to express a really long period of time between the first and second comings of Christ. If one sets aside preconceptions in order to recognize what the Bible is actually trying to show him, he may recognize that both appearances of Christ are for the exclusive benefit of his church and of his gospel. They can, of course, also benefit any individual Jew, who becomes a believer in the gospel—the gospel that is God's *only* plan for the salvation of people he has personally chosen to populate his church.

In order to understand the Bible, and especially the book of Revelation, including chapter twenty, one must allow Scripture in one passage to translate Scripture in another passage. Revelation twenty becomes clear when we employ historical and didactic portions of Scripture in attempting to understand the spiritual and metaphoric or symbolic passages written by John. Christians should never seek to develop or find doctrine by engaging in flights of fancy concerning what they read in the Bible. But they must concentrate exclusively on what God clearly is attempting to teach.

JUDAISTIC INFLUENCE

ESPECIALLY IN THE EVANGELICAL CHURCHES OF TODAY THERE IS a growing failure—or perhaps an inability—to hold firm to the true gospel of the Bible. There seems not to be general recognition of the simple fact that the majority of fundamentalist, evangelical, and dispensational churches have forsaken the tried and true methods of yesteryear that produced both church growth and true believers who were willing to spread the gospel among their neighbors.

Where is the spirit of apostolic teaching and attitudes once so strong, once so common to the protestant ministry of Christ? Unlike the Apostle Paul, the denominations have become afraid to be steadfast, as was the early example of Peter when it came to his inability to stand against the influence of Judaism. It is happening all over again. The followers of Christ are supposed to learn from the Bible, how to stand strong for the Lord. But who today is paying any attention at all to that old Book? Certainly not the churches! Now we understand what was just written to be a terrible condemnation, but sometimes the Lord's truth is very difficult for us to accommodate. Some are already manning the lifeboats. Many who recognize what is going on in the corporate church structure today and who actually attempt to serve God, not their corporate leadership have already pulled the oars of separation from the sinking hulk that once was God's external church. Again, this is foretold in the Bible.

If someone, some day happens to pick up an old, discarded, King James Bible and happens to browse in it, perhaps he might stumble by chance, on a worn and dog-eared book titled, "The Epistle of the Apostle Paul to the Churches of Galatia." And would it not be some kind of coincidence if that old, useless Bible happened to open on chapter two of that book of Galatians? He might be moved by some strange coincidence to read about how a man of old, named Paul of Tarsus, stood alone, armed only with the sword of the Lord, and devotion to his Savior, as he confronted the work of Satan (Galatians 2:5) on a pitching and windswept deck that was the heresy of those who were not content to follow Jesus, but wanted to destroy his infant child, the first-century church. They were not content to follow only Christ's gospel, but wanted to add to it some of the trappings of their old religion, Judaism, with its reliance on the law under which only a scant handful of them were ever saved from the wrath of God. Paul did not bend to popular demand and single handedly saved Christ's church (with the backing of Christ). But now it is happening again, or perhaps still.

The disunity in the church is glaringly evident to anyone with sufficient neck muscles to look around him. It does not require much intellect to recognize that the true, eternal church must be in a sad state of recruitment also if the memberships of the corporate branches are any indicator! A fine example of exactly the sort of influences Paul argued against may be found today in what are called the "messianic" churches. These dear people do not recognize that to lay firm hold on Christ, they have been asked to put aside their "old" ways, along with the law their Messiah claims he fulfilled!

During the twentieth century the church—actually the organized churches (one can hardly affect one without impact to the other)—lost half a planet worth of ground! National Israel has just about totally captured the focus of the leadership of the evangelical churches and for a very unbiblical reason. This focus has turned their teaching into useless, nonsensical mush-headedness, because their minds are set on their political agenda. Of course this takes different forms depending on who the author or teacher or lobbyist happens to be, but all forms spring from a common and dangerous (to the church) ancestral root. You may right now be asking yourself, "What is he talking about?" Well, keep reading because you are about to find out. It is doubtful that you will accept what is being said here if you are a member of a local congregation, especially if you do not make it your habit to "study to show thyself approved unto God, a workman that needeth not to be ashamed, rightly dividing the word of truth" (2 Timothy 2:15).

Within the leaderships of quite a few of the big, financially dominant denominations, especially those who call themselves fundamentalists, or evangelical, or dispensational—depending upon which aspect of their beliefs they are discussing—there are some fundamental misconceptions. Their leaders do not talk about their core doctrines openly. That by itself should give their members pause!

The Apostle Paul faced a similar situation. He said that (1) the leaders had not correctly interpreted the Bible and (2) teachers were trying to prove their own suppositions and traditions with passages from the Bible. (3) The leaders and teachers were ignoring large segments of Scripture intentionally (or inadvertently) in their desire to teach their own views. Then, on top of that, it should surprise no thinking person who is even mildly familiar with the Bible that the sons of Israel almost never acted scripturally. The Jews as a people would never for long adhere to God's redemption plan. To generalize, they never had what one could say was an enviable record of applying the Word of God to their lives. They ignored their prophets or killed them as often as not.

Now it appears that the leadership of our corporate churches is following the Jewish design. The fundamental heresy operative today comes right out of, not the New Testament of Christ, but the Old Testament of Moses and later prophets. Men such as Jerry Falwell, Jim Bakker, Pat Robertson, Hal Lindsey, Jimmy Swaggart believe and teach, contrary to what Jesus has clearly given us in the Bible, that Jewish privilege, prestige, and priority with God are specified to be perpetual by scripture. They see the New Testament church as only a makeshift arrangement [but a very lucrative one if it is properly handled] by God (his providence). This second-thought arrangement (Matthew to Revelation) was thrown together, these stalwarts of the Bible believe, merely to get the Jews—the nation state of Israel and others—through the difficult times of the tribulation until a time when poor, overworked God could get it all organized. Then he will have the resources (one may suppose through congressional subsidies) to assemble his forces for Armageddon and to finally effect a Jewish solution to the almost insoluble problem of whom and how many of them to redeem! There is only a little bit of tongue-in-cheek exaggeration here.

If the reader has even a shadow of Thomas's syndrome about the facts here presented, or of the overall veracity of this thesis, please read several issues of *Friends of Israel* magazine, or *Israel My Heritage,* or any one of the several Jewish and "messianic Christian" religious magazines available today. You will see clearly that the leaders of such Jewish missionary-oriented writings, even when written by a supposed "Christian," are devoted to the future of Judaic, not Christian, traditions. These magazines are a monthly apology for the imperfections of the Jewish people! They repeatedly and enthusiastically quote justification after justification for thousands of years of disbelief by an entire people! What's wrong with this? What's wrong with Christian support of Jews? Nothing until it begins to come out of the leaders of Christian churches who insist that the truth lies somewhere other than in their Redeemer's voice. All believers need to be aware that the idea commonly taught in the "fundamentalist," "evangelical," and "dispensational" denominations—they are all of the same cloth—that there is to be a "millennial kingdom" here on Earth, comes from the Judaizers. They have also convinced themselves that one of the objects of that kingdom is the restoration of a literal temple in the earthly Jerusalem complete with feast days, with a revival of the Levitical priesthood accompanied by animal sacrifices! Some, in order to make this idea fit palatably with Christian beliefs, insist that there will be no animal sacrifices. If that's the case, why a priesthood when their primary role in Judaism was to conduct the sacrifices? The teachers (Rabbis) take care of the instruction and pastoral functions since the temple was shut down.

When you read this, does the trend mentioned here coincide with what you have been taught? If so, you are probably attending an evangelical denomination's services. Would it surprise you to learn that such an arrangement was not in Christ's agenda, but only in that of men who are quietly known as "Christian Zionists"? Because the evangelicals make up probably two thirds of the denominations of this century, nobody talks about these facts openly, apart from a diehard few who are considered "uninformed" by the big shots like Jerry Falwell and Pat Robertson. Do you find it interesting that evangelical leaders (Christian multimillionaires) always side with the State of Israel in political affairs between Israel's secular government and the very religious Palestinians? How about that they also agree, not with the gospel contained in the Bible, but that proclaimed by the religious Jews? They got their "Millennial Kingdom" idea not from Christ, but from the Torah.

Is there a big right-wing conspiracy? I prefer to think of it as a right-wingtip conspiracy since they have never come clean with the little people down in the pews. The revival of Old Testament Judaism actually is their interpretation of Bible prophecy, borrowed from the Jews. It just is not a correct one. Many self-styled "Christians" now believe fervently that Israel of the Near East will be brought back because John the Baptist and Jesus Christ, (both Old Testament prophets) refused to proclaim the Jewish model for a kingdom! The Jewish idea is that both of these prophets were killed because they did not foster the return of earthly power and glory—and importantly, privilege, for Israel. Christians accept these heresies without ever recalling that the Israelites never considered that Jesus was who the New Testament *and* their Old Testament say he was! In a moment you will see why it is that otherwise seemingly intelligent men who claim devotion to Jesus are actually working under thin cover, for Satan's, not God's Israel. Men being discussed here have a theoretical propensity that leads to their classification as "dispensationalists." Interestingly, all or virtually all of them represent evangelical churches. Being one who likes to slice all Bible history into bracketed historical times or "dispensations" for study leads one to the idea of a slice that needs a label, and they tacked "millennial kingdom" onto it. That terminology is not found in the Bible. Among the many denominations calling themselves "evangelical" are the Churches of Christ, Southern Baptists, Nazarenes, Churches of God, Disciples of Christ, all the so-called "charismatics," and numerous others. As for the Methodists, one cannot be certain they even use the term *Christian* any longer when they speak of their activities. They are rumored to be alone, way out against the left-field wall.

PITFALLS OF DISPENSATIONALISM

THE AUTHOR BECAME AWARE, WHEN FIRST HE HAPPENED UPON a "Reformed" church, only a scant seven years ago, that he was experiencing, for the first time in his life, an approach to examining biblical Scriptures, which was correct. It made sense. In late middle age, he finally was learning how to gain a real understanding of what God had been trying all along to impart.

That was when he recognized that it was men in the churches who were conscientiously keeping their charges from discovering the great truths of the Bible. He had often sensed it, but in that particular assembly he came to recognize the truth that seminaries mostly do not seek ministry candidates who are accomplished scholars. Rather, they recruit mainly from the membership base of their captive denomination young men and, increasingly nowadays, young women who will be pliable and accepting of their denomination's doctrines, no matter how little those doctrines reflect biblical truth. The very fact that they recruit women to preach (contrary to what is contained in 1 Timothy 2:11–12) is the first proof of this thesis, to be recognized here.

Such failing may account, at least in part, for not only the existence of, but the popularity and continued expansion of, the doctrine known as dispensationalism. The Apostle Paul, of course, argues in the Epistles that such false doctrines are often the intentional product of false prophets, errant teachers, and especially of those he called Judaizers. He was absolutely correct.

It is the last who make up the leadership of what we know today as fundamentalist Christians. Fundamentalists are typically a part of the evangelical movement but like to consider themselves separate. They are not separate at all from the perspective that they greatly influence doctrines of the evangelical community, which makes up a very large portion of modern Protestantism. At the influential, men-of-power level, evangelicals who subscribe to fundamentalist doctrines, including dispensationalism and premillennialism, are well-known figures. Many are TV evangelists and certainly leaders in forming attitudes and beliefs in the church, which ought to be in every case biblical. But in many cases doctrines of the fundamentalists and dispensationalists are not at all in conformance to the Bible. Many of the TV sort, for instance, champion a "name it and claim it" gospel and/or a gospel of works. Before huge crowds of church spectators every week, these salesmen perform the world's selling rituals and dances, rather than telling of God's plan and guidance found in the Bible. They employ the popular ruse of having people recite what they call the "sinner's prayer" and then announce that those who did that have just become saved by doing something on television! But the worst part seems to be (whether the remainder of Christendom wants to hear about it or not) that their motivations are largely personal benefit driven. In the readings that follow you will learn why this belief is widely shared among even those relatively few in the churches who recognize the motivations of fundamentalist leaders.

Their detractors like to allude to the fact that fundamentalism dates back only to about 1830, when a young Margaret McDonald supposedly had a vision. She was coached into divulging what was immediately accepted by men who were looking for new revelation as being from God. John Darby was one of that sort. Darby would later become known as the "Father of Dispensationalism." One might hope that the father of any Christian doctrine held by the church might be God! But God seems to have had little or nothing to do with having revealed dispensationalism to John Darby or with his revealing it to the fundamentalists, the turtles of the Galapagos, or anyone else. The fact that the Bible permits no new revelation from outside the existing Word of God seems not to have been any impediment to Darby and appears not to have caused any dispensationalist to wonder about its origin. The idea began to catch on in the late nineteenth century. Then in 1909 a man named C.I. Schofield introduced his Schofield Reference Bible to a world of waiting fundamentalists.

The sheer volume of existing information in scholarly writing and books opposing the whole concept of dispensationalism is astounding. Many theologians, pastors, and other knowledgeable Christian leaders wrote warnings in the last century about Darby and his unfounded ideas. Yet, no matter how well reasoned and how demonstratedly biblical such evidence against the authenticity of dispensationalism was and is, it has made virtually no inroads into the thinking of those who cling tenaciously to such doctrines, fundamentally unsupportable by the Bible.

The fundamentalists who support the dogma of dispensationalism claim that their ideas come exclusively from Old Testament prophecy. But interestingly, these luminaries who consider themselves to be Christians actually ignore intentionally what is contained in the New Testament and use as their authority only what they want to believe is contained in Old Testament prophecy.

But if they were interested in actually understanding the prophets, they should try studying some of the writings of the New Testament. A good place for them to begin their study would be Paul's epistle to the Galatians. Instead of only reading that letter or simply browsing through it, they will need to actually study the content carefully, and this they are not accustomed to doing. In Galatians they would find that the "church" described in the New Testament is the same one described in the Old Testament. In the New Testament, however, they will learn that the church, which Christ founded, is the fulfillment of *all* prophecy! That makes it—the New Testament church—the final phase of God's work of redemption on the earth.

In Galatians they will also discover just who it is that constitutes the true Israel, the one to whom the promises are all made. Then to them will be revealed that there really is no other Israel and absolutely no further fulfillment of prophecy. The ideas of the fundamentalists, that Jewish interpretations of prophesy take precedence over what God breathed and that Jewish priority and privilege take precedence over what God breathed into his plan for his church, sound great, sound really learned and well researched. They sound great-that is, until one actually reads what God wrote in the New Testament!

The problem Paul confronted in the Galatian believers was the conspiracy of the Jewish Christians who tried to impose on Gentile Christians Jewish interpretations of prophecy. They claimed that Jews who became true believers had priority and privilege, in God's scheme of things, over Gentile Christians. If you consider it, that was almost precisely what is being instigated today among the evangelical churches by the dispensationalist fundamentalists! In his day Paul repulsed such conspiratorial ideas with a fierce and unparalleled (in the church) severity. Despite Paul's best efforts, more recent attempts by numerous conservative, Reformed believers, and the language of New Testament prophecy inspired by the Son of God, whom the conspirators claim to follow, committed Zionist Christians have brought back the same erroneous doctrines with a vengeance.

The fact that popular and powerfully influential Christians today are directly encouraging such heresies should surprise no one who has made a scholarly effort to understand the Bible. There were parallels in Paul's day, when even some of the great men—stalwarts who learned at the feet of Jesus—were temporarily swept away from the true gospel by the pretensions of the Judaizer's claims to perpetual privilege and priority in God's economy. Even Peter, claimed by one cult to have been their first Pope, came under Paul's direct and forceful attack. He withdrew with his figurative tail between his legs. Paul's friend Barnabas, a staunch soldier of the gospel, also fell under the influence of the Judaizer's for a time until Paul drug him out of their control verbally. Of Peter, Paul says in Galatians 2:11(which is available even to fundamentalists),"I withstood him to the face because he was to be blamed." Peter relented, knowing he was guilty of dissimulation. Paul says of this episode, "Even Barnabas was carried away with their dissimulation" (Galatians 2:13). Webster defines *dissimulation* as "feigning, or hiding under a false appearance." It boils down to a *dishonest* representation of something and certainly is sometimes expressed as "lying." It amounted to false doctrine, intentional misinterpretation of the Bible, or what we know as heresy.

About this, Paul drew a line in the sand. He became the last human being on earth to stand between Judaistic heresy and the safety and veracity of Christ's church. Of the Jews who called themselves by Christ's name but who did not in fact follow Christ's teaching, Paul said, "To whom we gave place by subjection, no, not for an hour, that the truth of the Gospel might continue with you" (Galatians 2:5). Paul knew these men, whom he calls "false brethren" were attempting to "bring us into bondage" under the law.

In our day the same Jewish heresies have almost destroyed the proper theology of the evangelical denominations and any effective preaching of the gospel of Christ. Can it be that bad? Absolutely it can and is! Their errors—whether inadvertent or intentional—have taken different forms, but they are a product of the very same Judaistic root. That is the contention denied vigorously in the New Testament that Jewish privilege and priority are perpetual. From that misconception flows the idea that the New Testament church is, at best, simply a sort of makeshift lash-up by what they call "providence" (probably borrowed from humanistic roots). The temporary arrangement will be in effect only until God is able to get things worked out in a way to eventually achieve a solution to his problem of Jewish redemption, in Jewish style.

This is clearly seen in Jewish and especially so-called "Messianic Jewish" publications dealing with evangelization. They always quote Jewish leaders, Jewish traditions and beliefs, not Christian. They characteristically justify almost 2,000 years of Jewish refusal to believe in their Messiah as representing the Jewish expectation of a messianic, temporal kingdom here on earth, with a return to animal sacrifice, the priesthood, their own interpretation of prophecy. They cling to the mistaken observation that John the Baptizer and Jesus Christ both died because they failed to give the Jews the earthly kingdom they anticipated, where Jewish glory and power would be returned. Their error is in not understanding the prophecy God presents in the Bible. They never did understand or accept it, and the Bible claims they never will as a nation. God's salvation plan, unrecognized apparently by the fundamentalist churches as well as the Jews, was always an individualized procedure and in reality had never extended to an entire nation.

The dispensational approach to Bible exegesis has rendered what is happening today, significantly more subversive, more sinister, than was the beginning of the problem in the first century. That is so, for at least two reasons, of which the first is that there is no Paul around today to stop it in its tracks as the Apostle was able to do. Then also, it spread relatively rapidly throughout the majority of evangelical churches, while it became the center post of fundamentalist teaching, accepted widely in that narrower community. Its incidence was greatly abetted, beginning in 1830, by the willing acceptance of the new idea called dispensationalism, a concept found nowhere in the Bible. Dispenationalism began with a "vision" supposedly experienced by a young woman named Margaret MacDonald. Her idea energized a fellow by the name of John Darby to advertise it widely as his own development of "new revelation" outside the Bible. Already being accepted by some in the fundamentalist community, the spread of this doctrine was greatly accelerated and popularized in 1909 by Charles Ignacio Schofield in the notes of his Reference Bible. These notes popularized further the ideas of dispensationalism, evidently because the fundamentalists had little actual knowledge of the Bible. Also, of course, it played directly to the personal interest of their leadership.

Basically, the dispensationalists divided the Bible into a well-defined number of "ages" or "eras" (defined differently according to which sect was doing the defining). Some fundamentalists chose to use the original seven periods laid out by Schofield; others used between three and seven, seldom more. They all shared the common trait that they combined to exclude the Lord's church from all but a fragment of God's published Word. Jewish theory and teaching was predominant over what Jesus gave the church as his gospel. Then several different second comings and last judgments were invented. As a result of fundamentalist influences, the gospel taught today in evangelical congregations bears little resemblance to the New Testament gospel. It has been fundamental to dispensationalists to abolish the gospel Jesus taught for one that accommodates a premillennial tribulation. This is known as the "gospel of the kingdom," which will displace the gospel of grace when the church is removed out of the way. What was it the Apostle Paul said of those who would proclaim "another gospel"? Oh yes, it was, "Let him be accursed [...] though he be an angel from Heaven" (Galatians 1:8).

This idea of the "gospel of the kingdom" is so widely accepted today that it can be said to be at the root of all the new "denominations" that have sprung up out of evangelicalism in the past century. Virtually all are proclaiming one or another "gospel of the kingdom," and all or nearly all are built on a gospel of man's works. Nobody wants to admit to a gospel of works, so they use the orthodox-sounding title, "gospel of the kingdom." This title does in fact appear in the New Testament, but it is quite clear in those instances that the kingdom is not established in Jerusalem or any other geographical location. It is clearly established "within you," in all the true believers, as Jesus says quite clearly in Luke 17: 20–21. True believers—that is, people who understand the gospel declared by Jesus Christ—and even fundamentalists look askance at the "Kingdom Hall" of the Jehovah's Witnesses. But at the same time they too proclaim a different kingdom from that of God's Bible! What cinches the case is that the fundamentalist leadership does not notify their membership of their differences with the doctrines of the Bible.

With a bit of reflection, it becomes obvious there can be no fewer than three distinct and separate possible meanings for the term *kingdom,* in the Bible, and certainly there may be more. First would be the *realm,* or extent over which the king reigns. Second, might be the very *act,* or business of ruling. Third, could be the *people* who are ruled over.

When we study the Hebrew and Greek meanings in both languages associated with the "kingdom" of the Bible, we learn that the second meaning mentioned above is that which appears to be most used by the original writers. In the New Testament, we find the idea of the persons ruled over being often the meaning of "kingdom." We find this in both Revelation 1:6 and 5:10.

The realm of the kingdom of God is introduced in the Bible, after John the Baptist's ministry, when Jesus begins to build his own following. Our Lord's game plan was first to enroll the people of Israel in his kingdom, but the majority of its "proper heirs" declined and so were denied entry (Matthew 8:12). Only a few came forward in response to the Lord's call. These few became part of the kingdom. The sense of the kingdom at that time was that it was a present kingdom and yet extended into a secure future. The future portion of the kingdom was the place where eternal life would be lived in the presence of God, and at the same time it was the people in it.

Evangelicals are taught to understand that only those who "receive" (accept) God's rule will enter into the future kingdom. This presupposes that man, rather than God, is in charge of the salvation process. Men must, in other words, seek God's rule over their lives. This would be correct had the fact of election been included here. In reality, the Bible maintains that the only people who will seek God are individuals whom he has personally called to himself. It is these who will populate his kingdom when it takes on its future reality as the "Kingdom of Heaven." They can be Jews or Gentiles, but contrary to what the evangelicals believe, Christ's example nowhere suggests that he ever intended entire nations—Christian or Jew—to be born again, in a simultaneous "saving." *Called* en masse perhaps, but saved en masse is nowhere suggested in the Bible. Judgment day is treated in the Bible as an event for individuals who do not constitute the tiny remnant who were predestined by God to be citizens of his kingdom.

In the midst of this nearly worldwide unloosing of atheism and Satanism, which has now been going on for more than two complete generations of church families, evangelical testimony has been overwhelmed. Their theology has been almost completely destroyed, and it does not appear that they even recognize the magnitude of the changes within their own memberships. They are unable, even were they willing, to return to their roots.

But one may ask, "What do fundamentalist evangelicals say about what we have been discussing here?" They basically maintain they are misunderstood. Of course, they cannot claim a defense of the actual tenets of their newly invented beliefs. No Christian organization, no church, no individual of record claimed, for the first 1800 years of the true church, that dispensationalism even existed. No one claimed that any organized gospel but that of Christ existed, that the nation of Israel was slated to displace the church from the place of primary emphasis in the Bible! This is all new! It was literally dreamed up in 1830! Rome never brought this heresy. The Protestant Reformers never heard of anything remotely similar except from the first-century Jews. This was purely an invention of dispensationalists. These are people who reject the spiritual interpretation of Ezekiel 44:6–9. They insist that the Gentile in their kingdom must be circumcised in order to enter into God's sanctuary. It's a Jewish place in their cherished view. So, our Lord Jesus, reigning as they claim in a literal Jerusalem, must reign over the downgrade of his personal gospel, his own Kingdom, where the undoing of his Word is to be uppermost in God's priorities! Will he simply watch as animal sacrifices are reinstituted? How about the priesthood? Will Jesus then also be removed as high priest? What will God do with "spiritual Jerusalem," the final home of all who were saved by Christ during the New Testament times? What will God do while Jesus is looking after the rebuilt physical temple in the rebuilt physical Jerusalem? The Bible does, after all, indicate that the "New Jerusalem" is composed of the glorified saints whom he justified under the salvation plan so clearly outlined in the Bible. How, we are left to wonder, will Christ feel about being displaced by Moses?

It is clear that Paul's Epistle to the churches of Galatia was written for the express purpose of destroying this Judaistic "error" that we have been discussing here. Lest we be accused of overstating our case as Bible-believing Christians, we hope you will allow us to employ the Bible itself, and only the Bible, to now *prove* that case. When our case has been made, you will see that Paul's writing will not allow dispensationalist, fundamentalist, even much of evangelical, doctrine.

We begin, appropriately enough, with the first chapter in the King James Version of the book of Galatians, originally titled in the Greek, "Pros Galatius" (to the Galatians). Paul begins by showing clearly his credentials, his competence to speak with authority given to him directly by Jesus Christ. He is also clear in establishing right up front, the idea in the heads of the Galatians that the gospel which he preached, and which he received directly through specific revelation from Christ with no human intermediary, was in grave danger of being subverted. He lets them know, in essence, that he attended no seminary training by men, in Jerusalem or anywhere else. He got all his gospel teaching directly from God. He even makes it abundantly clear in Second Corinthians 2:12 that what Paul teaches is only a fraction of the divine wisdom that Paul received but was not permitted by God to divulge.

In chapter two of Galatians, Paul tells of his visit to the council of the church at Jerusalem, a meeting called specifically to deal with the issue of Judaistic disputes coming from Jews through Jews converted to Christianity. The same fundamental irritations are evident in the churches today. Converted "messianic Jews today, along with "seventh day" holdouts in several other styles of denominations, do their best to convince other believers and to indoctrinate nonbelievers in their belief that God wants them to worship on Saturday. "Just look," they say, "at the evidence in the New Testament of the church attending worship on Saturday." Or they point to the fact that Paul and other disciples visited the synagogues on Saturday. Well of course such evidence exists. First, until Saul came along, all the apostles were Jews "in the flesh!" At first Paul alone understood what it was to be a real Jew, in the manner intended by

Jesus. The apostles and most disciples were comfortable in the synagogues. This explains why so many were still in Jerusalem, long after Christ had sent them their "comforter." Second, all of them, including Paul, continued to witness first, or mainly, to the Jews! Paul alone really branched out early in his ministry, because that was his specific charge from the Holy Spirit. But everywhere he went, he first witnessed in the synagogues, and this was recorded clearly in the Bible. Paul's confrontation with Peter and the others at Jerusalem was concerned 100% with this issue! Paul had to kick Peter's behind (figuratively) in order to get "the Rock" back on the straight path.

If we will trouble ourselves to read carefully what is contained in the second chapter of the Epistle to the Galatians, we will see Paul's struggle to attain an unhindered liberty in Christ for Gentile converts. The apostle is here pleading with us today, to recognize that Christ has freed us from the curse of the law! It is the gospel of freedom, which is "the good news"! That liberty is to be unhindered by Jewish observances—any Jewish observances—of the sort that continued among the early Jewish believers, during the forty years of Jewish probation prior to the destruction of their temple. The Jews violated their probation! The Mosaic code, the priesthood, animal sacrifices, their connection with the temple, which represented their connection with God, all ended in AD 70. Yet many Christians today are still trying to drag back into prominence what God set out to destroy. Some Christians will just not accept the Bible as God presents it to them. That means, for those who do accept God's gospel untailored, that those who cling to what God displaced do not accept the covenant, whether they know it or not. To learn what they ought to be doing, these poor souls need only study (there's that word again), not just read once over lightly the biblical account of the evangelical council at Jerusalem under the superintendence of James, the younger brother of the Lord Jesus. This council was called specifically to address what has remained a problem to our day.

Paul and Barnabas disagreed about what a Gentile was supposed to do in order to become a Christian. With diligent study we will learn what Paul knew and taught throughout the Epistles. We will learn that we must do exactly nothing! Christ's gospel, as Paul taught it (and we can be certain that this is what Christ intended), is not a gospel of works, but one of unmerited grace and nothing more—zero, nada, ixnay—nothing else! A free gift from God finds as little acceptance by many in the churches today—acceptance without any performance factor attached to it, as it did in the first century. Paul's disagreement and that of the stalwart Barnabas, with men come from Judea to teach circumcision as a requisite male modification prior to salvation, was what generated the Jerusalem council. It was an outgrowth of Judaising busybodies who wanted to impose their will on men who had been already freed by Christ's justification from precisely that brand of will! We ought all to ask ourselves this question: if such was not the will of God, then whose will would it have been, and whose will is represented by such conduct today? We will hint for you that it is not our will—yours or mine. Beyond that, we will let you come to your own conclusion about who the chief figure working against Christ actually is.

So Paul and Barnabas arrive in Jerusalem (Acts 15). We learn in verse five who opposed their views and sent the troublemakers from Jerusalem to Galatia. Acts 15:5 says that it was "certain ones of the sect of the Pharisees who had believed." Paul is here speaking of men of the ruling class out of the temple or synagogues. They had been converted to, or at least influenced to investigate, Christ's gospel of grace, in preference to the law. They could not keep the law, so it had no power to save them from the lake of fire. Yet because of their conditioning under the Mosaic law, they were unable to completely put the law behind them, which meant they had not fully embraced the real Savior. This is still happening today in several denominations, including what are known as seven-day churches of several varieties and in the so-called Messianic Jewish churches, which many folks include among the list of Christian churches. They are not actually Christian, but still Jewish. This conclusion must be made since their rituals are mostly Jewish, and their chosen day of worship and celebration of feast days betrays their true fealty to the law. Jesus said, "If you love me you will keep *my* commandments" (emphasis added). Need our Lord have said, "Not those of Moses"?

At the council in Jerusalem, the Pharisees who were members of the Jerusalem church stood up to say of the Gentile Galatians: "It is necessary to circumcise them, and to direct them to observe the Law of Moses" (Acts 15:5). The second phrase would have sufficed to show their true colors. Circumcision is a part of the law. They could just as easily have asked for any of the various parts of the law instead of circumcision. Interestingly, no matter what the Gentiles had done—even if they had been circumcised and observed all of the law—they would not have been allowed to worship inside the temple in Jerusalem like the Jews! Judaism, you see, was an exclusionary arrangement, while true Christianity is an inclusive brotherhood with Christ. In short, the temple held men fast to man's ideas, almost never to those of God!

As a short side excursion, it is here appropriate to examine why so many apparently committed Christians fall short of trusting completely in the gospel of Christ. We are speaking here of the continuing insistence of many otherwise seemingly dedicated believers to hold to the Saturday Sabbath.

This mistake seems to fit into one of two possible categories. It can be simply one of refusal to turn loose of early teaching even for so persuasive a sponsor as Christ. Or it may reflect the seductiveness of newly discovered, curiously interesting ideas. Most of us are held captive by ideas gained in formative periods of our lives. One such period might be literal childhood, another, spiritual childhood as a "baby Christian," or as someone seeking wider understanding in a new environment, such as a newly found denomination. Then, of course, there is the ever-present influence of men like the Pharisees of Galatians—articulate and convincing spokesmen for a cause they believe in and which they have been, rightly or wrongly, tutored in since early childhood.

We suspect that nobody, including God, will be successful in developing within fundamentalist Christians a wider or more biblically correct understanding of the Bible, apart from someone advocating Old Testament doctrines. This simply has shown itself to be true, time and time again, in our humble experience. Like the Jews of old, these dear people today have been indoctrinated into an unshakable faith in the Law of Moses, and a limited knowledge of New Testament adjustments to that law by Jesus. This may be due in large measure to the inescapable fact that nearly 80% of university and seminary professors of Bible knowledge are atheists. But we left our discussion of chapter fifteen in the book of Acts and the Jerusalem Council unfinished, so let's return there.

After the Pharisees had their say regarding the law, the apostles and the elders who are not here identified by previous religious affiliation met to discuss the issue. There was "much debate," after which Peter stood up to address the council. Here are his words contained in the King James Version Bible:

> Brethren, you know that in the early days [of the church] God made a choice [...] and that [he] bore witness to them, giving them the Holy Spirit, just as he also did to us [the disciples, whom he chose from among the Jews.] [...] He made no distinction between us and them, cleansing their hearts by faith.
>
> Acts 15: 7–9

Then Peter continued, and here we will paraphrase for simplicity. "We believe they also are saved through the grace of the Lord Jesus, just like we are." (Acts 15:11) The Jerusalem council agreed and asked only of the Gentile converts (you and me) that they abstain from things (food) sacrificed to idols, from what is strangled, from blood, and from fornication (which in reality covers a lot of sins). The strangled rule is (presumably) because things strangled have not had the blood drained out.

Jesus had already made abundantly clear what he asked of his followers concerning the Mosaic laws. He in fact commands that the things which were only ceremonial laws, be put behind his followers, since they were simply "a shadow of things to come." The Apostle Paul says specifically that Jesus blotted out the ordinances, including rules concerning what and what not to eat, holy days, new moons (feasts), and the seventh-day Sabbath.

Again, these things were intended by God only as "shadows of things to come" (Colossians 2:16–17). The new Christian Sabbath was declared by God in all four of the Gospels (in the original language) in the biblical description of events at the empty tomb. It is a sad reality for many in the church who do not study in the original languages of the Bible that the translators of the English version of the Bible evidently could not comprehend the idea of a Sunday Sabbath, so were led in ignorance, to mistranslate those passages. Even a cursory examination of these passages in the Greek language shows that the Lord intended to set aside the shadow that was the Saturday Sabbath and have his church begin to observe the true Sabbath on the day Christ rose from the tomb.

But the point of the gospel-debilitating influence that has been dispensationalism, as applied by the fundamentalists, is once again that it has supported the Jewish conception of the Bible, rather than the message of Christ. It was, for instance, the influence of Saturday-Sabbath-insistent "Christians" informally aligned with the bootleggers and other criminal elements, and the Jewish lobby, who finally succeeded in abolishing the Sunday "Blue Laws" in this country. When these once federally sanctioned state restrictions on Sunday activities were removed, the decline of America began to accelerate dramatically. There was not a whimper heard from the evangelical community. We

Americans like to imagine that it was a secular government that erected the "wall of separation" in this country. Anyone who takes a good look at his history of American social change over the past century will easily recognize that was not actually the case at all. The churches had a heavy hand in erecting that wall. Mormons, who "formally" do not drink or gamble, disallow those activities in their own state but strongly support the small Nevada casinos and bars just across the state line. The fundamentalist Christians in, for example, the Texas panhandle, have always ensured that there was a "wet" county snuggled within the space of a short drive next to their "dry" home counties. Likewise, it would be self-delusion to assume the Southern Ku Klux Klan to have *not* been populated almost exclusively by "God-fearing" fundamentalists or evangelical churchmen. These would be the same men, in fact, who were founders of the dispensationalist, Southern Baptist Church, the Church of Christ, and others. They were also virtually all Democrats! Our history has been often manipulated in attempts to conceal God's truth. For whom would the cross-burning ministries have been held, the lynching sacraments been enjoyed, and the terrible treatment of black families been celebrated? It was of course, in large part, for black Christians!

The position of the Jerusalem church council in the first century, regarding its relationship to the Mosaic Law, is easily seen by simply seeking the verdict of the Old Testament prophets. It is not kept secret in the Bible, despite the fact that most evangelicals delude themselves into believing it's not really in there. Listen, if you will, to the words of the prophet Amos, who is being quoted in the book of Acts, as representative of all the prophets, in our sincere belief that there are no contradictory opinions in the Bible. Immediately after the words of James (above), confirming his belief that everyone is saved in precisely the same manner, Barnabas and Paul stood up, "declaring what miracles and wonders God had wrought among the Gentiles by them" (Acts 15:12). Then James took the floor again to speak from the writings of Amos. But as a prelude, listen carefully to what the brother of Jesus included among his own carefully chosen words: "Men and brethren, hearken unto me: Simeon [Simon Peter] hath declared how God at the first did visit the Gentiles, to take out of them a people for His name." James here means early in Christ's ministry when he says, "at the first." He is referring to Peter's recollection in verse seven, that God had sent him to Cornelius, the Roman Centurion (see Acts 10:17–48) who was a Gentile and who became saved by grace, not the law. In verse forty-three of that reconstruction, Peter gave witness that, speaking of Jesus: "To him give all the prophets witness, that through his name whosoever believeth in him shall receive remission of sins."

Notice that there was no distinction between how Jews and Gentiles are or were saved! This tells us that the words of James could just as well have referred to another time—any other time in biblical history. Seth, for instance, while he is not considered a prophet, was saved the same way New Testament Gentiles are—individually and by the grace of God, through the faith of Christ. Then there was Enoch, who "walked with God and was not; for God took him." Noah, like Seth and like Enoch, was a Gentile and was saved by God, because he walked with God. The same can be said of Methuselah, who also was not an Old Testament Jew! What then was he but a Gentile? Abraham himself was saved by the sacrifice of Christ and the grace of God before he ever became the first Hebrew. The point is that God has, and always had, but one salvation plan, under which every person ever saved was saved on an individual basis and in the same way as every other. Even before the time of Christ's ministry on earth, to which James was alluding, God saved *first* the Gentiles *and then* the Jews! That was always God's plan!

In chapters three and four of Galatians, Paul analyzes for future readers the nature and history of the true church of God. His first important conclusion is that the only true children of Abraham—the heirs to God's covenant with Abraham—who get the blessings of God and the promise, are the "true believers" among whom were a few Jews and a lot of Gentiles! "Know ye therefore that they which be of faith, the same are the children of Abraham" (Galatians 3:7). This is a statement of fundamental doctrine in the church of the first century. Paul's one sentence destroys the arguments of lesser believers of dispensationalism, premillennialism, and postmillennialism since it is foundational to all three of these fundamentalist belief systems that Jewish privilege along with a special Jewish future must be maintained. This is all hinged on their unbiblical insistence that the Abrahamic covenant was the exclusive property of the natural, i.e., Jewish seed (plural) of Abraham. In fact, dispensationalists must dismiss these two chapters in order to make their world come true.

You see, these chapters show clearly that this same "seed of Abraham" is in fact first Christ. He was the one who was to come to make only those who are Christ's, Abraham's seed and also heirs according to the promise! The promise includes no one else. Paul makes it clear that this same "seed" (singular) has abolished all distinctions based on birth, race, or privilege. That's because "there is neither Jew nor Greek, there is neither bond nor free, there is neither male nor female: for all are one in Christ Jesus" (Galatians 3:16, 28–29). But they must be *in,* or said another way, *of* Christ Jesus! There is another aspect of this business of the promise, which the dispensationalists make much of in attempts to show that the Jews remain "special." They never point out that the promise concerning Christ, who is the seed of Abraham, came some 430 years *before* God gave the law to Moses and the nation of Israel! They also don't want to be reminded that the law itself, with all the apparatus, the restrictions, temple, priests, and sacrifice, was given for just one reason according to the Apostle Paul, in Galatians 3:17–19. See it? It was added (only) "because of transgression"! It was the gap-filler and only until Christ came. But the fundamentalists want to turn God's program around to make Christ appear to be the gap-filler for the law.

In Acts 15:15, Amos is quoted as a representative to the council of all the prophets who ever lived. (Note the plural.) That quote is given as instruction in what? Obviously, in the correct use and interpretation of all related prophesies concerning the reference to the kingdom that Christ originally came to establish at his first coming! Among many other passages, this too establishes that his kingdom is spiritual, not Jewish or Gentile. It is of heaven and not of earth, just as Jesus said in John 18:36, "My kingdom is not of this world."

The "final answer" to the Judaizer's heresy was Paul's and held that Christ had abolished the earthly, temporal Jewish economy. In its place he set up an economy of the Holy Spirit, which transcends nations, things carnal or external to it. Also, Paul saw no break between Old and New Testament programs of God: "I through the law am dead to the law that I might live unto God. I am crucified with Christ; nevertheless I live" (Galatians 2:19–20).

So, the plan of our literalist brothers to restore Israel, the priesthood, and the temple, complete with animal sacrifices, which from their beginning were only a shadow of things to come, seems a little shaky, does it not? If those things were as the Bible indicates, only established as disciplinary measures to hold iniquity in check until the gospel could be established, why would God reinstitute them? Especially when one considers that the cost would be to recall the sin and transgression they were supposed to contain. Where then, does the heresy reside? We know for certain it does not reside with God. It was God, we must remember, who made the church that Jesus Christ established, the legitimate and natural successor to the "church" of the Old Testament.

Having recalled the facts of Scripture, must we not conclude that few chapters of God's Word have been so mistreated and so distorted by supposedly godly men serving a purpose other than God's as has the third chapter of Galatians? These men have endeavored to bend God's Word to say that, "The law was our schoolmaster to bring us to Christ." Have you heard that one in your church? They want you to believe that the Law of Moses is used in conversion to a belief in Christ by being driven through conviction of sin into the "happy clappy" arms of Christ. Whatever misguided tatters of truth may cling to this concept, it is not the argument of the Apostle Paul.

How can you know it is wrong? For openers, the mostly Gentile Galatians were never under the "schoolmaster." No Gentile ever was! The true function of that "schoolmaster" was the "dominion," if you will, of the law over the nation of Israel. That was for the sole purpose of preserving its function as the "church" of God until the "fullness of times." That meant until the time that Christ would come (his first advent) so that some of the believers among the Jews could be saved. Paul says, speaking of the Jews, "Before faith came we were kept under the law, shut up unto faith, the faith which should afterward be revealed."

For the reasons we have shown, it should give any thinking Christian serious pause when fundamentalists suggest that the "rudiments" of Mosaic law will once again, after 2000 years of Christ's reign, be reimposed on Jew and Gentile alike at Christ's second coming. This heresy, which baffles credence, can only be a tool that demonstrates Satan's dominance in the corporate churches today. Despite the thundering message of the Galatian and other Epistles, this doctrine so subversive of Christ's teaching, has gained what can be characterized only as a stranglehold on theological thought. It seeks to vindicate, it would seem, the roughly 2000 years of Jewish unbelief since their Messiah first came. The Epistle to the Galatians is crucial to proper exposition of God's Word being restored in the churches.

True Christians recognize that the true church, composed of both Jews and Gentiles, dates back to Seth. The "coming of faith" denotes the passage of the church from the economy of Moses to the teaching of Christ. It represents a moment in history when the regime of the law (represented by circumcision in the skin) passed away, to be succeeded by the regime of faith (represented by the circumcised heart). The "schoolmaster" handed over his office to the Son of God, and the church passed from its minority into its majority, or adult status. Chapter three of Galatians concludes with four verses comprising essentially the charter of the church in the New Testament era. They represent the authority for the claim that the church is the legitimate seed of Abraham, the true Israel, the true circumcision of the spirit rather than the flesh, the heir to the promises of privilege, and even the hope of Old Testament Israel. Here they are. Judge for yourself:

> For ye are all the children of God by faith in [of] Christ Jesus. For as many of you as have been baptized into Christ have put on Christ. There is neither Jew nor Greek, there is neither bond nor free, there is neither male nor female, for ye are all one in Christ Jesus. And if ye be Christ's, then ye are Abraham's seed, and heirs according to the promise.
>
> Galatians 3:26–29

This remarkable last sentence puts the cap on the Old Covenant. It abolishes the law, terminates the mission of the Jewish nation, ending their exclusivity relating to rights and privilege, and at the same time provides the key to understanding the writings and the prophets and the law of the Old Testament.

It ought properly to have, a century ago, provided the death knell to the heresy of dispensationalism that has filled God's church with the remnants of a legalism God himself dismantled. It is a heresy that seeks to reimpose in the future the restrictions and the temporal requirements, which Christ went to the cross to abolish once and for all. The so-called "gospel of the kingdom" is evidently supposed to cushion the blow. But it is a gospel of works, not of grace, so we can know it is not of God!

These claims, which become more outrageous the more they are considered, have nonetheless captured the imaginations of most of the fundamentalist and evangelical communities. We must conclude that this is due to the Bible being a stranger to them. Could ignorance be their goal, and precisely why evangelical leaders fail to teach what the Bible actually says?

WHICH KINGDOM OF WHAT?

PREACHING IN THE WILDERNESS, JOHN THE BAPTIST CALLED upon his listeners to "repent!" The reason he gave was that "the kingdom of heaven is at hand" (Matthew 3:2). Then when Jesus first began his ministry, he preached almost identically John's message, "Repent: for the kingdom of heaven is at hand" (Matthew 4:17). Then when our Lord decided to present his Sermon on the Mount, he began what we today know as "the Beatitudes" by saying, for all time and all seasons, "Blessed are the poor in spirit: for theirs is the kingdom of heaven" (Matthew 5:3).

But just what is this "kingdom of heaven"? The term appears thirty-two times in the book of Matthew, and as Matthew begins to run out of ink, new terminology seems to be the better habit of the writers who follow him. "Kingdom of God" starts haltingly in Matthew, appearing only twice in the early chapters, then seems to pick up steam in the later chapters, as the use of "kingdom of heaven" declines.

Are these separate entities, different meanings? Did Christ decide to change his lexicon, or are these two distinctly similar or distinctly different ways to say the same thing? Before beginning the search for an answer, we should acknowledge that sprinkled through the references in the book of Matthew to the two (or one) kingdoms above are some other "kingdoms." These are simply the use of the title "kingdom" by itself in a manner presupposing that the reader knows to what "kingdom" the speaker (or writer) is referring.

Now, some readers may become agitated, feeling they have "always" known what this usage means and that it can only mean what they believe it means. Why then, since this is so self-evident, even waste space on it in this book? But have these who "just know" and become agitated considered the alternatives for themselves lately? How about ever?

Experience shows that most Bible knowledge for the "average" churchgoer is almost totally the product of two factors. The first is denominational affiliation. The second is Sunday School memory. Have the agitated folks ever considered that one usage could mean the eternal church, or the corporate churches? Could another mean heaven and hell combined, since God controls both? Could it be the "barn" of the parable of the wheat and tares? Or might one refer to a "now" kingdom and the other to a "later" kingdom? Is the so-called "millennial kingdom" in view here? Then one might also ask another question: "Is hell Satan's kingdom after Judgment day?" You see, it really may not be so simple!

The Bible may hold all sorts of interesting intellectual exercises, prospects and projects, unless of course we already know all the answers. As a matter of interest to some, Bible teaching changed only marginally in most denominations over the past three hundred years. This, despite our Lord himself having suggested that there will be progressive revelation for those who seek it. One of the factors that make denominations stagnant is the absence of continuing inductive study by the vast majority of modern preachers. Yes, they typically continue to read the Bible, but that is not study. The Bible should be considered a living document, written by a living God! The worst professors in the university system are those who stopped learning in 1948 because they had learned all there was to know in their field. They have a PhD to prove it. Many people never learn that it's not uncommon for a pastor to be preaching today from the list of sermons he or someone else wrote in the 1960s. Far better it is that an old dog at Bible knowledge learn some new tricks than become stagnant. There is, for anyone who cares, more to learn today from your old Bible, than there was even twenty years ago—more in fact than there has ever been. This is true because God is now opening men's eyes to information he did not give them twenty or thirty years ago. Reading the same old lines, with the same old preconceived ideas, will not allow God to teach what has been hidden from view for the past 1950-odd years. To read the Bible is wonderful. To study the Bible is to grow in God's Word. Only arrogant pride knows all it needs to know about the Word of God, or anything else for that matter.

Looking in a concordance does not help to separate the various usages of the word "kingdom" by meaning. All the New Testament references to "kingdoms" of any sort are described by the same Greek word, *bas-il-i-ah* which in English suggests "a realm." Any attempt to discriminate among them, therefore, must be based upon usage of the word in the text. Looking through Matthew and comparing what we find there, then referencing other books where the word appears, leads to some inductive conclusions.

First, where we find the terminology "kingdom of heaven," we understand that heaven is not only God's creation, but is his home and as such is the "realm" he operates from. It is his possession and a place to be greatly desired for the future residence of men. It appears that if one simply says "heaven" without any embellishment as a kingdom, the passages mean precisely the same as they would with the embellishment. Despite this apparent lack of necessity, the words are retained in each of the Modern Language, Living, Revised Standard, New American Standard, and New International Version Bibles. This is evidently out of respect for the King James, from which they all "borrowed" their Scriptural foundations, while their publishers claimed they have been independently translated. If you ever want to prove to yourself that these Bibles are in fact not independent translations, simply compare what they have to say in Matthew 28:1 and the verses in the other three Gospels that cover the same event. They will all be identical. Then compare what the same verses say in the Greek of the Interlinear Bible. How would you explain that four different translators in more recent "independent" translations repeated the identical mistranslations of the King James? Maybe it's just a four-times-four-times-four-odds coincidence?

So, without hesitation and without remorse, it can be said that "heaven" would suffice for all the references in Matthew that contain the words "kingdom of heaven." We reserve the right, however, to not insist or ever suggest that the Bible's purpose would be better served by the trimming off of words! These words make reading the Bible more pleasurable than it would be without them. It is the very aura of God's words that make them clearly preferable. We have no argument against the words of the Bible, or the thoughts behind those words. The basic meaning is all that is being addressed here.

So, now to "kingdom of God." At this point we can assert comfortably that there is most certainly a strong, indissoluble connection between the two kingdoms we are researching, but their describers do not refer to quite the same thing. The kingdom of God is something we all know about but might be a bit squeamish about having to define publicly in ten words or less. Truth be told, we'd be squeamish to have to define it at all. As a matter of fact, the two sorts of kingdoms are considered to be essentially interchangeable definitions by most Christians. That's okay.

Kingdom of God in the Greek language was *basileia tou theou.*
It can be defined in one or more of three different ways. It is a
realm over which a monarch reigns, or it can be the people over
whom he reigns. Then, the *Zondervan Bible Dictionary* includes
also an archaic, seldom-considered usage in the English: "The
actual rule or reign itself" [4] The third meaning is important
to both the Hebrew and Greek languages. English is not sufficiently expressive to accommodate it, so it is seldom included
in the definition.

Those who have decided, as many theologians have, that the
kingdom of heaven is the same kingdom spoken of by the words
kingdom of God find a long trail of meaning which has to be
imagined and has many varied and interesting explanations and
avenues of approach. Such a pursuit into theological supposing
is not appropriate for this book. It suffices for our purposes, in
this non-graduate school of theology, to understand that the
kingdom of God has the three dimensions. If we cared to dig, we
could doubtless exhume at least one of each definitive excursion
into meanings, from a careful examination of Scriptures. Feel
free to do so if you desire. Those who wish not to do that will be
appropriately served by simply recognizing a couple of things.
First, the kingdom of God is the realm—the environment—in
which God's reign, his person, and his Son can be experienced.
Second, this realm is present for us today, future for us at some
time to be announced. That time is dependent upon the return
of Christ from the kingdom of heaven. You see, the kingdoms
do separate quite readily, almost of their own accord! Those
who believe the two are synonymous have to say "on the return
of Christ." They don't want to confuse the issue by saying where
he will come from. It's all kind of silly, but we ought to know
what we believe. But then there is the third, and we do not have
to ignore it unless we are very intellectual; then we deal with it
through worry and lots of big words. That's for academicians
who chew their nails. When we see the word *kingdom* alone,
it is often referring to the reign of Christ—his ruling of the

universe. The other meaning—his people—is found only in the book of Revelation. It appears twice: once in Revelation 1:6 and again in 5:10. Here the people are not his reign while they live in his earthly realm, but become so when they reign with him in his heavenly realm. When that happens there will be no question that the kingdom of heaven and the kingdom of God are one and the same.

However one may view this kingdom, there is general agreement that Jesus represents the kingdom of God, and when his people are "in" him, they are in the kingdom of God, where he is going to take care of them. That's all they really need to know. Anything more is for personal study. There is one other thing.

The various concept(s) of the kingdom of God set apart from each other those who believe in one of four views of God's kingdom. These "worldviews" are part of what has set the churches at odds with one another for about two centuries. They are:

1. premillennialism

2. dispensational premillennialism

3. amillennialism

4. postmillennialism

Just about everyone who has attended a congregation's meetings for more than a couple of years will be at least mildly familiar with one or more of these categories. The first two views probably dominate the thinking of most Christians of today, especially the so-called "evangelicals." That, of itself, testifies that most Christians of today may not be experienced thinkers. How such folks can read the Bible and continue thinking there is evidence for a belief in premillennialism is puzzling.

Perhaps a brief excursion into the biblical concept of what is commonly called the "Millennial Kingdom" will be beneficial for the readers of this book and relatively easy since we have already discussed kingdoms. In discussing this topic, we will be reading in the final book of the Bible, the book of John's Revelation. This is not an easy book to follow, chiefly because of all the hype and myths that follow it around. Most preachers seem to mostly take a hands-off attitude toward this book. It really is not as hard to read as many people think it is. One must simply read it for what it says, not what he has heard about it or thinks it says. You also have to recognize that it is not a front-to-back chronology as most think it is. But before you get into the millennium, it may be a good demonstration to you to look at the war on the earth that you've doubtless heard or read about—Armageddon, the last battle that you doubtless have all sorts of mental images about. There have been novels and Hollywood movies about the armies of the world clashing and killing millions of people. Some have even drawn out elaborate battle diagrams, supposing they can predict where these great armies will meet. But let's read it. Revelation chapter sixteen contains a brief explanation of the opening of the sixth vial. Here's what it contains in verses twelve through sixteen:

> And the sixth angel poured out his vial upon the great River Euphrates; and the water thereof was dried up, that the way of the kings of the east might be prepared.

This verse simply records that the river will dry up, so some "kings" from the "East" can cross on their way to the West. That's nothing terribly mysterious. Next we read:

> And I saw three unclean spirits like frogs come out of the mouth of the dragon, and out of the mouth of the beast, and out of the mouth of the false prophet.

In his dream, John saw nine "spirits." Then he said:

> For they are the spirits of demons, working miracles, which go forth unto the kings of the earth and of the whole world, to gather them to the battle of that great day of God Almighty.

John explains that the nine spirits are messengers who are sent to gather the kings who will cross the dry river so they can come to the big battle God is having. That suggests there will be nine kings crossing the river. All the nasty imagery we can just dispense with and read what is actually there for us to know. Verse fifteen is God announcing that he is coming. Then in the last verse to be considered here, John says, "And he gathered them together into a place called in the Hebrew tongue Armageddon" (Revelations 16:16).

So in summary, God dried up a river, sent some spirits for some kings who crossed the river, and God gathered the kings for a battle. At this point we are not certain whether the kings are for or against God, but "kings of the world" sounds adversarial, given our reading of earlier references in the Bible. "Of the world" generally describes satanic supporters.

The actual battle is entered in chapter nineteen where John sees Christ arrive on a white horse as the heavens open. He also sees a great army from heaven, come to support Christ. Earlier writers did not describe them as warriors, but we know these are the saved souls who have come with Christ on his return. We now find out what happens to the unsaved in John's dream. They too are an army, and the two forces clash. The actual battle is not described, but the good guys win! All of the bad guys are slain, and Satan is thrown into the lake of fire. The birds dine on all the carcasses.

Now here is where things can get a little confused. What follows the treatment of the second coming of Christ in the book of Revelation is the binding of Satan for 1000 years. Did we not just see Satan thrown into the lake of fire? Haven't we been taught to believe that is forever? Now Satan suddenly is to be thrown into the bottomless pit for one thousand years and is to be "bound"? Verse three of chapter twenty says an angel:

> cast him into the bottomless pit, and shut him up, and set a seal upon him, that he should deceive the nations no more, till the thousand years should be fulfilled: and after that he must be loosed a little season.

Following that, in the book of Revelation comes what is known as the Millennial Kingdom, or the millennial reign of Christ along with some saints who "live and reign with Christ a thousand years." This is the part of the Bible that generates the four millennium concepts discussed a couple of pages earlier in this chapter. Following the millennial reign (apparently), Satan is released, and his first activity is to deceive certain of the nations, then to round up his supporters for the war against Christ. But wait a minute—that doesn't work because we earlier saw the battle fought! This means that the sequences of Revelation are not presented chronologically, nor does their sequence agree with what we know from Matthew and other books that deal with the end of the world. So having recognized a discontinuity, we now must deal with it. We know there are no mistakes in God's Word, only lack of understanding on our part.

As we follow a logic train backward to a beginning, we arrive at the place in time occupied by the one whose kingdom we have been discussing. We know from reading the Bible that Christ limited Satan's activity with regard to the people who made up Christ's kingdom. Satan had, after the coming of Jesus on the scene, no power to foil Christ's work with true believers. He was, we could say, at least to some degree, "bound" by the Savior, and that important binding is to last until the end! That binding was effective at the cross. So, did Christ remove that restraint after 1000 years? Not if the Bible is correct. We know that it is the binding words of God, so it is correct. But there is an area of some "slack." We know that some of the numbers of the Bible are representative, rather than literal. What if the one thousand years was simply representative of the time between the cross and the return of Jesus, or some other event such as Satan taking over the churches? Could we then understand the meaning of this book, if there was not a literal thousand years placed in the middle of the sequence of events spoken of in Revelation? Indeed, we could, without taking any liberties at all with the actual events.

If the time between the cross and the Great Tribulation, for instance, is assumed to be the one thousand year period, the scenario of Revelation works very well! We must, of course, not be bound by the obviously non-sequential events presented. Here is the picture. Satan was in fact bound at the cross, so that he could not influence the salvation of true believers. We know that binding did not prevent Satan from wreaking a lot of havoc in the world because we are experiencing it. It is evident that this period we are living in is in fact the Great Tribulation. Since that reality has not yet been revealed in this book, it is simply mentioned as a part of the scenario of the book of Revelation.

When the period we are living in comes to an end, it will be because Christ will have returned. We can know Satan has been released because he is the reason for the tribulation. He is now out deceiving the nations, and he will lead them in the final battle between his armies and those of the Lord, when Christ returns in glory.

There is a lot of lead-in up to the battle at Armageddon, but little is actually said of it when it comes. At the seventh trumpet, the kingdoms of this world become the kingdoms of the Lord. That means he is victorious. At the pouring out of the seventh vial, there are noises, thunder, and lightning, along with a great earthquake that wrecks the world. The mountains disappear and every island as well. Then a great hailstorm comes from heaven on men. This must be the same time spoken of in Matthew 24, when the sun is darkened and the moon loses its light. The stars fall onto the earth, and the powers of heaven are shaken. This is the day of the second coming—the last day, when the earth is destroyed, and time is ended. This is judgment day, when Christ will sit on the great white throne of Revelation 20:11–15, the books will be opened, and the dead will stand before that throne. Christ will have already destroyed the earth and the heavens. Revelation 20:11 says that the "earth and the heaven have fled from the face of him who sits on that throne, and there was no place found for them." They are gone! So God will create a new heaven and a new earth (Revelation 21:1). And the new Jerusalem will descend out of that new heaven, and all things will be made new.

So, this book can be understood without too great an effort. There just has to be a reasonable amount of "want to" involved. What we have uncovered may later be found to need some correction, some adjustment, perhaps. But such is ever the case when it comes to Bible study. The important thing is that the effort to understand must be ongoing. No Bible scholar was ever 100% correct on everything. That's precisely why our Lord has left us the message of 2 Timothy 3:16: "All Scripture is given by inspiration of God and is profitable for doctrine, for reproof, for *correction*, for instruction in righteousness" (emphasis added). Don't ever be afraid to make a bold statement about Scripture if you have studied it, because if you are wrong that does not make you a false prophet. It makes you human, and somebody else will come along with a God-given correction. Do not be hesitant to accept correction. It usually comes from God! When the apostle wrote of "all Scripture being profitable for correction," think of the inductive study method and think how many passages you have to examine in order to prove what any one bit of God's Word may actually mean. Then reflect on this truth: not one preacher in 1,000 studies his Bible by the inductive study method. Most have never even tried it. You will be amazed, at some point, after you begin in earnest to "rightly divide" God's Word, how many respected "experts" are frequently wrong in what they teach. If this were not so, would there be 2,600 differing perceptions of God's Word, exemplified in there being that many denominations, all functioning in oblivion to some part of the Bible? The real reason so many disagree, is that few of them actually study the Bible carefully! May God bless your efforts to become enlightened in his Word.

FUNDAMENTALISM, BRIEFLY

THE BIBLE BOOK OF GALATIANS IS A BOOK OF PROBLEM SOLV-ing that has all the earmarks of applying graphically to the times we live in today. The Apostle Paul was dealing with particular problems brought into the congregations by people who were out to derail the gospel of Christ. It matters little to the potential outcomes whether such people are doing that sort of thing intentionally or unwittingly.

What it all boiled down to was that some just could not accept a gospel of pure grace without any works. One might hazard a guess that fully 80% of denominations today, because they have nobody with the understanding of a Paul in their midst, are following just exactly such failed gospels. As such, they are not doing the work of God, despite personal beliefs that they are committed to God's work.

The heresy came into the first-century church because of the difficulty of newness. Most of the true believers were Jews in the beginning, and like many so-called messianic believers do today, they held onto Jewish law and tradition concerning things the Lord meant for them to let go of. Paul was a voice crying in the wilderness in the finest tradition of John the Baptist. Paul even had to go head to head with Peter and other of the apostles in the Jerusalem church over issues stemming from the failure of some to discard the excess baggage of Judaism (Galatians 2:12). Paul's concern was very valid in that the baggage threatened to undo the teaching of the Christ, who alone was their salvation. Even the stalwart Barnabas was temporarily led astray by the seemingly reasonable arguments of the Judaizers.

But in the end, Paul triumphed over the forces at work in the church, which sought to turn back the hand of time to the days of reliance on the law—a reliance that Christ taught them to turn away from because such was the work of Satan. There has been no Paul to save the modern evangelical denominations from similar heresies. Anyone who really wants to understand not only what the Bible teaches, but what is the fatal failing of many presumed Christians today, ought to study the book of Galatians very, very carefully.

But turn your attention now from the lessons of the Galatian churches to the churches of our own day who, like Peter, have been led astray. The difference was that Peter learned his lesson, as did Barnabas, Titus, and the other apostles at Jerusalem. Paul stood firm. So must true believers in the gospel of Christ today stand firm despite what they may hear in their congregations that follow a grace-plus-works gospel. To hold firm to Christ is to lay aside the doctrines of the Old Testament that flow from the purely ceremonial laws of the Jews. These have no place in the New Testament churches. To accept the Messiah means to hold fast his teachings—the lessons of the Holy Bible. Christ's true followers have been set free from not only the bondage to sin, but also from the bondage of the ceremonial portions of the law! Because few Christians today really spend enough time in the Bible to become truly familiar with the commands of God, their collective views are often actually contrary to what is taught by the Bible. Many may not know, for instance, that the ceremonial laws that were fulfilled at the cross by Jesus Christ included, according to Colossians 2:16–17 what we are allowed to eat and drink, observance of Old Testament "Holy Days," new moons, the Saturday Sabbath. These things were only shadows of, or pointers to, "things to come." Christ superseded them as the Lamb of God who came to save sinners chosen by God for salvation. Also we have no requirement for circumcision. But "false brethren," Paul said, "[...] came in privily to spy out our liberty which we have in Christ Jesus." And their purpose according to Paul was to "bring us into bondage" (Galatians 2:4).

The church is very susceptible to false prophets in this day of widespread, rapid communication. The Bible says that those who know the truth are to take responsibility for stopping the spread of false gospels. Only those who are well versed in the truth of the Bible can stand against the bringing of falsehood by prophets of another god. The book of 2 John warns of what must be done. We will illustrate a case in point. Counterfeit gospels are being widely circulated to unsuspecting people in their homes. Typically, these "missionaries" of false gospels come in pairs, telling of a Jesus Christ who is not the Jesus of the Bible. Their Jesus is not God, but only a person free of sin. That removes the only qualified sin-bearer, yet they say they preach "Christianity"! No created being could ever survive the wrath of God on a cross so it would not be poured out at judgment day on those who believe. Only God could do that. Only God could have risen from the dead to assure our resurrection. So what is a follower of Christ to do? The answer is found in the Bible, where the apostle tells us that if anyone comes to your door whom you know to be one or two of these false prophets, "do not receive him" (2 John 10–11). That means don't open your door to Satan's emissaries. Don't open your door because John's warning continues, "for he who greets him shares in his evil deeds." Many readers will be surprised at these words.

There is another sort of false believer gaining increasing stature in the corporate churches daily. Fundamentally, this is not enjoyable to report, but if we are to be true to the Bible, we are commanded to bring the entire gospel—the entire truth of God's Word. It is obvious that many of what used to be "mainstream" denominations have fallen into the snare of being led by the body rather than by the head. Any congregation that allows a woman to preach, to pastor, or to have any sort of authority in their assembly has no commission in the work of God! That may sound harsh to some, but God has some harsh rules—harsh sounding—to those whose pride will not allow them to follow his agenda. There is a broadening secular social trend that has somehow dictated a role for women where God allows none in churches he commands. Fewer and fewer churches can be counted among God's faithful these days. They would rather appease one segment of their congregations than remain faithful to what God commands. Such churches have "run in vain" the Apostle Paul would say. Their service is of no value to God. That is, after all, what the following verses are saying. Listen now, as God speaks right out of the pages of the King James Bible. "I suffer not a woman to teach, nor usurp authority over the man, but to be in silence" (1 Timothy 2:11).

Now, some will definitely say this change is allowed because of the social customs of our time. That means they believe the Bible is out of date. That's sad, because it is, for them. But actually, the prohibition goes all the way back to Adam and Eve. Here's what our out-of-date, old-fashioned God has to say:

> For Adam was first formed, then Eve, and Adam was not deceived, but the woman being deceived was in the transgression. Notwithstanding she shall be saved in childbearing, if they continue in faith and charity and holiness with sobriety.
>
> 1 Timothy 2:15

Obviously, that verse begs understanding for most of us.

Here is what it actually says in the Greek passage the translators had to work with. This actually is a bit easier to follow!

> But the woman, being deceived, has come to be in transgression [however] she will be saved through childbearing [God needs the woman] if they remain in faith and love and holiness with sensibleness.

"Sensibleness" would seem to be demonstrated by following God's direction concerning woman's place in the church! Perhaps there are women who still believe the words, "Thou shalt not surely die," more than they believe the New Testament commands of Jesus. They remain deceived, it would seem. Can faith and holiness accompany disregard for what the Bible commands? Disregard seems to be a popular attitude these days.

Who was that masked prophet who said: "there can be no excuse so common it fails to mask the truth"? We believe it can be said that all of the useless and biblically nonsensical theology that abounds today, even though it takes many different forms depending on its author, comes from a common ancestral root. That root is *not* the God of the Bible!

That brings us to so-called fundamentalist theology. The problem that exists today is the same problem described by Paul in the gospels. Nothing has really changed in two millennia. Three ills are readily identifiable in the churches and seminaries today:

- The Bible is not correctly interpreted.

- Teachers attempt to prove their own traditions and suppositions with the Bible.

- The leaders are ignoring large segments of Scripture either intentionally or inadvertently.

There is also another shade of difficulty in the corporate churches of today. It reflects identically the problem Paul was having in the book of Galatians and other Epistles. The vast majority of teachers among the Jews were always unscriptural!

That made most of the people always unscriptural. It should surprise no thinking person today, especially one who has a modicum of Bible literacy, that Jews would not adhere to God's program—his salvation plan. Yet it is immensely popular among fundamentalists Christians today to listen attentively to what Jewish writers and teachers have to say about God's Word. They are especially interested in modern Jewish translations of prophetic writings from the Old Testament.

According to Jewish thinking (and fundamentalists are increasingly ignoring New Testament theology in favor of the Jewish "take"), privilege and priority for the "nation of Israel" are specified to be perpetual in the Bible. Of course, the Islamic people believe their status is at least a little more equal than Israel's. The Jews, and so now the fundamentalists, consider the church that Christ established to be simply a makeshift sort of temporary arrangement by "providence." The rest of us say "God." It was intended merely to get the Jews through the difficult time of tribulation (self-inspired) until a time when poor God could begin to get his act together and coordinate all his resources and assemble his forces. Assemble his forces for what? Why? To finally effect a solution the Jews could live with—a solution to the problem of whom and how many of them to redeem.

But he has to have a big battle first. If any reader has any doubt whatever of the veracity of what he just read, he may simply read almost any three issues of one or more of the several Jewish or so-called "messianic" Jewish magazines on the newsstands. Or he could read any of their several newsletters, all of which reach a wide audience among fundamentalist Christians in this country. Virtually all of the big names in fundamentalist and evangelical circles follow the Jewish political perspectives closely. The leaders of such groups devote themselves to the future of Jewish prophecy and traditions. Fundamentalists calling themselves Christians are in what seems ever-increasing numbers, expressing adherence to Jewish-inspired beliefs concerning the end times. Despite what is contained in the New Testament language, they believe in a coming "messianic" kingdom for Jews here on earth.

So what's wrong with that? If you have to ask, I'd like to recommend you read a few chapters in the book titled "the Bible." If you ask, it is likely you have no firm understanding of the prophesy contained in the New Testament, as proclaimed by Jesus. What the fundamentalists and increasingly the evangelicals, are buying into is Jewish teaching, not what Christ prophesied. Such is the stuff of the gospel of modern day Judaizers—the very people the epistles were written to warn church members against. We will see that they can be classed as "dispensationalists." It is the theoretical wandering into such beliefs that leads to the adoption of the Jewish idea of a so-called "Millennial Kingdom" by people who think they are committed Christians. Of course, they think of this kingdom as a monument to Christ and John the Baptizer, but they are sadly misled and have likely not considered the significance of the monument they want to erect. The idea of a kingdom on earth brushes aside almost 2,000 years of God's church as an interim measure! It accepts Christian gospels as something necessarily only partially true. It has decided on God's behalf that "Israel after the flesh" will inherit a kingdom of heaven right here on earth. So, according to those who hold such an idea, God was mistaken in trying to establish a place in heaven where he could implement his plan of "grace." Then, too, because their heaven will be for every Jew, God's idea of an individual salvation plan has to be scrapped as well. So it winds up, presumably, that the very Jews whom God would not allow into the Promised Land or would not allow inhabiting it perpetually, will be the end-time winners! Thankfully, we have the Jews to help God get everything straight.

As a matter of fact, there was a time when even some Reformed teachers gave a bit of credence to such erroneous arrangements. But their error was not one of being caught in the snare of dispensationalism. The earlier "postmillennial" teachings were not viewed as clashing with correct Bible prophecy, but of course they had to clash. As a consequence, that teaching was expunged from the Reformed churches.

But even that is not as subversive as is dispensationalism. The whole dispensational posture may be very popular, but it works sometimes surreptitiously, sometimes boldly, to pull down the true gospel of Christ. That is why it must be seen in its true light—as a tool of the force that opposes Christ. The premillennial doctrine that flooded this country in recent years from the *Left Behind* series of anti-Christ fiction, along with other dispensationalist books on the market, certainly serve as a case in point. The authors of such blatant non-biblical imaginings claim status as followers of Jesus Christ, despite writing novels distinctly at odds with what our Lord teaches. Millions of people were washed with distinctly dispensationalist beliefs, and as a result may never find their way to the path described by Christ. That constitutes working against God and the true gospel! Anyone who has studied the Word of God knows full well that such tales work contrary to biblical teaching. This is how we can know with certainty that men who write such things know full well they are not teaching what is biblical. They are essentially Judaizers who are substituting Jewish thought for what is contained in the New Testament—a book, it should be remembered, that God breathed his own words into. They are thus inventing a new Bible of their own design, with new versions of the "Second Coming," new "last judgments," etc. In place of God's Word, they are substituting their own made up "gospel of the kingdom," just as the workers for the watchtower god, the seventh-day visionary women, the Christadelphians, Mormons, Armstrongites, and others have done. Paul warns of this in Galatians chapter one. He argues against those in his day who would advance a new paradigm—"another gospel." He brings a prescriptive response to those who would bring a new gospel into the church: "Let him be accursed—though he be an archangel from heaven" (Galatians 1:8). We know of course that there will be many antichrists (1 John 2:18). But there is only one Christ and only one version of his Word, and that is contained in the Bible.

It has been said that the same "perversion" of Scripture that the Apostle Paul argued against twenty centuries ago is the precise root of all the various modern cults or sects that have sprung up around the umbrella of "evangelicalism" in the past century. Each has come claiming to alone hold the true gospel, when it has been plainly apparent that they were in reality bringing their own versions of a gospel. As far as this writer is able to determine, they all have shared a common character. All can be seen, even on cursory examination, to hold a doctrine of salvation by works! All have been represented by a common title: "gospel of the kingdom." Everyone has separated from another group, or has grown up separate, because of disagreements based upon one or two Scriptures upon which they mold their doctrines.

Yes, the Bible does indeed present the title the pretenders have all chosen. The "kingdom" of the Bible, however, is not the same one they claim to represent. The kingdom of the Bible is built upon the true gospel as preached by Christ and taught in the pages of the Bible. It is not in Jerusalem, or in Rome, or in any patch of earth. It is within each and every true believer. Jesus identifies it as being "within you" (Luke 17:20–21). He should know.

THE SCHOFIELD CHARADE

THE FUNDAMENTALISTS OWE A DEEP DEBT OF GRATITUDE TO C.I. Schofield, author of the Schofield Reference Bible. It could not be accurately termed a translation, since so much of it came right out of the mind of the man who dreamed it up.

It was a new Bible, much esteemed in the fundamentalist and later in the evangelical denominations. It came on the scene in America early in the twentieth century and is still widely used in certain circles today. First published in 1906, this was a work to be reckoned with. The second edition appeared in 1917, and many Schofield Bibles went "over there" with American doughboys in the great "war to end all wars." Many never returned. Many returned only when it was "over, over there." To this day, the copyright is so closely held that you will not see it credited, or hear it quoted, in *any* mainstream church literature. Don't you wonder why that was? Read on.

The new Bible was immediately well received. It was the first ever "study Bible" from which many varieties on sale today got their basic format. It is still a favorite of many evangelicals including the Nazarenes. According to Albertus Pieters (only one of Schofield's many detractors among conservative churchmen), C.I. Schofield, a reformed alcoholic and former Confederate soldier, practiced law for some three years.[5] "He then," Albertus Pieters says, and notice the verb usage, "*removed* himself from the practice of law and without any theological training whatever, became a pastor in the Congregational denomination."[5] Obviously somebody there believed he had some ability. Eighteen months later, according to Pieters, Schofield was ordained a minister in that denomination.

Later, believing that denomination to no longer be faithful to the "Great Doctrine" of the Christian faith, Schofield left the Congregationalists and moved into a southern Presbyterian church as minister. Interestingly, his biography makes no mention of his ever having served in a Presbyterian church. The author's research of applicable documents failed to disclose just what that "Great Doctrine" was.

Schofield does seem to have been the inventor of the "study" Bibles in such common use today. It appears that despite the tight copyright, all such Bibles have mimicked Schofield. Certainly, each is designed to teach specific denominational doctrines through the voluminous notes on virtually every page. It is mainly these notes of which readers must beware. They are explanatory, to be sure, but are slanted to develop specific beliefs in the reader, and they are not always biblical. This writer discovered that without having been told of the nature of such additions to the Bible. In studying with a friend who had a different sort of study Bible, it surprised both parties to discover that the notes we were using gave two completely different slants to the Scriptures, in two separate Bibles. Each was tailored to a different one of the 2,600 different belief systems such notes support. The author never again used a study Bible and definitely does not recommend their use by anyone who wants to learn the true gospel of Christ, unencumbered by its sectarian detractors. That gospel is contained only in the Holy writ.

Dr. Charles Trumbull, however, hesitates not at all to rank Schofield's Bible right alongside that of God's own creation. He calls the Schofield masterpiece, "A God-planned, God-guided, God-energized work." Obviously Trumbull considers the Schofield book divinely inspired, but he does not say why it was that God would have needed another Bible, in addition to the one he "breathed" to his prophets and apostles. One is left to wonder why God would breathe two different Bibles. God wrote his first Bible in parables and difficult-to-understand constructions, which Christ Jesus tells us was done intentionally so that many outside the remnant he elected to salvation, would be unable to understand it. Why would he then inspire someone like Schofield to craft another version with explanations of the difficult-to-understand portions? Simply stated, he would not!

One of the hermeneutical principles that have guided the leaders of the church through centuries of Bible study is that God will not violate his own laws! Yet in order to write a second Bible—to in fact add to what was contained in the first—would be a violation of the deliberate proscriptions that God placed in Revelation 22:18–19! God warns that the words of the Bible are not to be added to, or subtracted from! It hardly seems likely that God would curse himself in that way! It is likely that anyone who has studied the Bible will find no satisfaction at all in the pronouncements of Dr. Trumbull on Schofield's behalf. Schofield did, to be sure, give readers the first system of chain references and explanatory notes. But like all the study Bibles that followed after the Schofield, it was written to guide the reader into an acceptance of denominational doctrines, which varied from the intent of God in the original Hebrew and Greek language Holy Bible.

Despite its faults, the Schofield Bible found wide acceptance among believers who were not particularly well versed in what the Bible contained and among those who simply wanted to be spoon fed the Scriptures. Schofield was happy to oblige both groups. His has been called the "most influential single work—thrust into the religious life of America during the twentieth century." Of course, these are the words of one of Schofield's vocal supporters. Pieters, by the way, called these words of Kuizera, a "dagger-like" introduction, alluding no doubt to the use of the word, *thrust*.

The great problem with the Schofield Bible is that in the author's notes, he projects as biblically correct, a brand of millennialism which no Christian denomination has ever claimed in its creed! It was, in fact, a form of millennialism, which at the time the book was published, most of the wisest millennial proponents repudiated. Its detractors are quick to announce that in the "great standard doctrines of systematic theology" (to which all Protestant seminarians sufficiently agree) the book is found to be "decidedly good" (Pieters, pg.10). The disapproval of the barons of theology came in what has been termed Schofield's "Artificial and Extravagant typology" (pg.11). His "types" agree in meaning and intent as "symbolic language" of generalized theology. What the seminarians actually objected to was Schofield's overuse of such symbolic language. Their objections began in Genesis chapter one! There seemed, in the true Bible, little need for symbolic language in this area, which they saw as largely historic/literal true nature. But Schofield treated Eve as a "type" of the church—as the bride of Christ. Next, he had Enoch in the allegorical role of the church—the true believers on the last day, who are alive at the second coming of Christ. (This may in fact not be as farfetched as Schofield's detractors, who followed strictly a literalist, historical hermeneutic, imagined.) But then Schofield went on to describe Noah as representing the entire nation of Israel at the last day. Noah's family supposedly survived the days of the judgment of the Antichrist to be brought as an earthly people (just as they were previously) into the new heaven and the new earth of the millennium. He may actually have been one of the earliest advocates for, and a visible modeler of, the fundamentalist eschatology of today. Schofield built many allusions to the Israelites remaining God's special people into eternity. Schofield supposes they turn back to God (whom as a people they never served) after the church has been caught up to meet Christ in the air. That would essentially, as was mentioned earlier, wipe out the atoning sacrifice of Christ on the cross and make salvation no longer an individual process, as it was throughout the Bible from Genesis to Revelation, during the church age (or dispensation).

How this might work out, the Bible gives no clue and neither does Schofield. Between the appearance of Christ on the clouds and his calling of the elect and the raising of the dead in the twinkling of an eye, the entire nation of Israel alive and dead, presumably, will have a change of heart and decide that Jesus was who he claimed to be after all! That seems to constitute a significant modification of what is contained in the Bible. Is it scriptural then? If you can comprehend Schofield's intent, you have the beginnings of a picture of what the majority of dispensationalist, premillennialist, fundamentalist, evangelical, Israel-focused denominations today are teaching!

One who is very aware of this difficult-to-compose scenario, Dr. T.T. Shields, once said:

> "I readily recognize that the Schofield Bible is very popular with novices, that is those newly come to the faith, and also with many of longer Christian experience, who are but superficial students of Scripture. Ready-made clothes are everywhere popular with people of average size. On the same principle, ready-made religious ideas will always be popular, especially with those indisposed to the exertion of fitting their religious conceptions to an ever-increasing scriptural knowledge. That common human disposition very largely explains the popularity of the Schofield Bible." [6]

You are encouraged to go back and read this quotation again. It is heavy with truth.

Notice that his term, "superficial students of Scripture" must necessarily, in Shield's meaning, apply to such popular evangelical entertainers as Pat Robertson, Jerry Falwell, Paul Crouch, Jimmy Swaggert, and others among the expensive names in TV religion.

So, we come to the question that cannot be ignored—is dispensationalism scriptural? Can it be factored into the literal concepts and Spiritual imperatives of our King James Bibles? Before we can answer that question, we must first consider another. What exactly is dispensationalism? One theologian who follows a dispensational bent of sorts, I.C. Herendeen, describes it as "a system of prophetic interpretation." Swell, we knew that, but that bony framework needs to have muscle and sinew hung upon it if we are to make sense of it. Standing alone that's not much of a definition, but sadly it is not at all uncharacteristic of the sort of answers theologians are famous for. Let's retrace our earlier trail and say that it (this theory of prophecy) is widely accepted among evangelicals who consider themselves fundamentalists, most of whom also hold to dispensationalism.

They see this non-definition as a "new light" from God concerning interpretation of his Word, said Herendeen. Did you follow that? Does "a new light" then indicate that some super prophet received revelation straight from the man upstairs about this thing? Why was that not shared with the rest of the church? Actually, that declaration in itself immediately destroys any idea that these folks (like Herendeen) are actually living, breathing, and fundamentalists! As recently as fifty years ago, fundamentalists would have known of the limits strictly imposed by Revelation 22:18–19. They would have held that this passage precludes any "new light" from God, outside of the Bible pages. A sheer three sentences later, Herendeen corrects himself. He changes his mind and refers to dispensationalism as "a system of teaching." Still a lack of definition, but we can begin to suspect why that is.

In the next line he uncovers his own nakedness as a prideful and arrogant academic. He first condemns the "system" because this idea was "unknown to the spiritual giants of the past, and has never been incorporated into the creeds of any of the evangelical denominations." Or is he condemning the congregations who institute the teaching of doctrines not included in their creeds? Or do both stand condemned, possibly by the author and editor of the Bible? A weaker, more gelatinous opening for a teacher to employ can scarcely be imagined. One can but wonder how few of the denominations have ever updated their creeds to reflect what they actually teach or allow to occur on their corporate holdings. Herendeen, by the way, did not name his personal "giants."

Then he turns to an admission of how much lack of direction evangelicals have by saying, "Its adherents (still speaking of dispensationalism) seem, nevertheless, as convinced it is the teaching of Scripture as they are of the divine inspiration of the Bible." He is here backhandedly acknowledging that it is not scriptural! Lacking direction or not, we know two things about the evangelicals. First, they need to be taught what the Bible actually contains. That's neither new information, nor likely to ever occur. Second, they seem to be in unison when it comes to what they do believe, and biblical or not, they don't seem to much care!

But let's look at Mr. Herendeen just a bit more. As we continue to read his article, the man seems to turn from apologist to critic concerning his subject, dispensationalism. He eventually accuses the evangelical community of "modernism for the orthodox"—a nice euphemism for what we all know as "false doctrine." He then says their doctrine is "utterly devoid of scriptural support," and this writer begins to agree with him 100%. But at almost the same time, agreement morphs into curiosity. This writer wonders where such outspoken questioners have been for the past century and especially for the past decade, as the *Left Behind* books and movies and DVDs and napkin holders and neckties and world globes and dolls and children's books and things one can't possibly begin to imagine, have been so popular they sold like waffles? (Waffles because they were full of holes but nevertheless swept away all popularity records of the past, like a heretical tsunami.) Why was there no test of their veracity, as it properly ought to have come, by approbatory pronouncements or the opposite, by creaky-jointed old theologians in dank, smelly, seminary lofts? Nobody who knows said, "Boo! This is a joke!" Millions now have the fundamentalist make-believe doctrine of the end times clutched to their biblically ignorant bosoms.

Such ignorance can be attributed, at least in part, to the seemingly growing number of church attendees who are finding large parts of the Bible unprofitable for their attention. Why study it when dispensationally oriented pastors are teaching the premillennial inclination? What else is necessary knowledge? Many today are not even taught what Paul wrote in 2 Timothy 3:16 because that might cloud the issue. This is not to suggest that premillennialist teachers are necessarily emissaries of Satan. Not knowingly at least, but the result turns out to be the same. Consider for a moment how much of Scripture might new converts consider necessary to know, if they are taught they can rely on being "caught up" before all the heartache of the Great Tribulation begins? Of course, there is always the distinct possibility that Satan has already completed taking over all of the corporate churches and that all or most of the true believers have already left or been driven out. That will happen unless the author of the Bible was mistaken. What do you figure the odds of that to be? That was/will be the kickoff of the Great Tribulation of course. Personally, this writer believes we are already experiencing that unhappy time. But what if Satan's minions are indeed in charge of the entire dispensational clamor? What was it the Bible said in 2 Corinthians 11:15 about how Satan's workers would come into the church? Didn't it say they would, "be transformed as the ministers of righteousness"? Yes, it did, and it also says in the preceding verse that Satan himself will come "as an angel of light." Well, can you beat that? When Satan took over, his agents began to belittle the importance of great segments of God's truth. "It's not necessary," they say, "since we'll be outta here!" Since they look just like any other evangelist, Satan's boys will sound *so* faithful among fundamentalists, so loyal and fun among evangelicals, so knowledgeable of the Bible. Surely they must be correct about what they teach! But the really faithful teacher will bring the entire Word of God. He will denounce, as the Bible does, the degeneracy "they" call modernism, and Darwinism, and humanism, and freedom of choice, among other heretical beliefs. Can we trust those who come claiming that study of most of the Old Testament is not necessary? Ask the Bible. Can we trust to blindly follow fundamentalist assertions about Bible prophecy? Ask the Bible. A reader may ask how premillennialism goes along with what is known as dispensationalism. They are one and the same thing, and both are pure make-believe. They are the gospels of men, not of God.

Can we agree among us that there are no invalid Bible Scriptures? If there were, wouldn't the entire Bible then be suspect? Is it? Can you agree there are none? Those who cannot will not—do not—trust God, since he alone is the author of every jot and tittle we call "Bible." So then, we can agree that all of God's promises will be kept. So far he has an incredible record in that regard. Can we also agree that it would constitute heresy if we tried to assert that God made promises to Israel that do not apply to his church? In view here, of course, is the eternal, invisible church. We are reaching common ground if you have so agreed. Also, I commend you for your knowledge of the Bible.

Look now at Romans 15:4, where what we just agreed to, we can confirm. Then in verses eight and nine of that chapter, Jesus confirms, through Paul, that he came not to invalidate the law, not to cancel promises made under the law, but to confirm every promise made to the fathers under the law. Then, he next confirms his relationship also, with the Gentiles. He speaks of promises made in 2 Corinthians 7:1. What promises would those be? Here are the promises God made in the Old Testament that are repeated for the Gentile audience in 2 Corinthians 6:16–18.

"I will dwell in them, and walk in them; and I will be their God, and they shall be my people. "

Leviticus 26:12

"Wherefore come out from among them, and be ye separate, saith the Lord, and touch not the unclean; and I will receive you."

Isaiah 52:11

And will be a father unto you, and ye shall be my sons and daughters, saith the Lord Almighty.

2 Samuel 7:14

See also Jeremiah 31:9 and Hosea 1:9–10. Then recall that we are studying New Testament stuff!

The Holy Spirit assured New Testament saints that we have these promises (are beneficiaries of them). Since "Christ is ours, all things are ours" (1 Corinthians 3:22–23). The follower of Christ today should heed the lessons available in the writings of Paul the apostle. Let no man steal away your portion in the promises God made for your benefit. That would indeed be too great a loss to contemplate. Prove your teachers with direct reference to Scriptures. There is no other way to be certain you are in possession of the truth. Everyone teaching in a church does not necessarily bring the truth! A case in point is the Gospel of Matthew. It is true that each of the four Gospels has its own focus and that Matthew can be seen to be concerned mainly with Jews. But a fellow named A.C. Goebelein, in his "Gospel of Matthew" pages four and 142, teaches that it is entirely of and only for Jews. He says it has no application to the church of today. An interesting doctrine, to be certain, but that dog won't hunt! Goebelein is answered effectively in the booklet, "I was robbed" by Philip Mauro.[7] It is important to examine carefully what is labeled "dispensational truth." The following is a brief explanation of why that is so.

Many evangelical congregations have been taught that anyone who dares question dispensational doctrines is unsound and likely not saved at all. Consider the seemingly absurd postulate that many Bible schools and seminaries of this day may be teaching as the verified truth of God, something not only questionable, but that when you examine it, has not even a shaky scriptural leg to stand on! How could this be? It would be nice to be able to say more than "It just is!" If you think you are a Christian, please do not stop reading. I will attempt to prove to your satisfaction that what has just been phrased as an allegation, is God's truth, absolutely.

The preface of the following short proof is the thought that the desirable result of your reading this would be, in your case, a remedy for premillennialism—also known as dispensationalism—that, in fact, you would completely abandon and discard such doctrines altogether if indeed you have been taught them or are being taught them. Then, that you might return to the sound, scripturally valid doctrines from the Bible, held by all evangelical Christians until the closing years of the nineteenth century. It has been a general observation of Reformed theologians and teachers, that most, if not all, of the "great doctrines" of today's theological doctrines have come not from God-breathed Scripture, but from the pens of men.

Only last week, a teacher was explaining biblical "types" to a Bible class when a lady spoke up to inform everyone that her church taught that the sun represents Jesus Christ, the moon is the church, and the stars represent the individual believers. Any one of these might be found in Bible typology, but expressed as this lady heard, it was a pillar of dispensational teaching, and it is a wonderful example of how easily God-fearing Christians can be "tweaked" off the path God pointed out to them. That misrepresentation came directly out of the Schofield Bible. Do you see what's wrong with it? If not, please read it again, but more carefully this time. Is it not the individual true believers who populate the Lord's eternal church? Are they not one and the same? That's what the real Bible says! So much of what passes for biblical truth goes unproven by the listeners simply checking with the Bible. Of course, that's impossible to do if you are fond of using a counterfeit Bible. Many folks today are settling for new-age imitations of God's Word. Think about this: if it does not come out of what God put together for his followers, to assure they are following the correct leader, whose work is getting done by it? You can be assured it isn't God's work! The very idea of dispensation thinking, comes right out of the study notes of the Schofield Bible. On page 1,244, Schofield alludes to the dispensation of "the law," with its "pitiless severity" and all the appalling characteristics of "condemnation, death and the divine curse," which Schofield attributes to "the law"! (1245). He says these continued from the Old Testament "to the death of Jesus Christ," from Sinai to Calvary, from the exodus to the cross" (pg. 94). Oddly, the original Bible does not say any of that! What it does say in Luke 16:16, for instance, is that no less a scholar than Jesus Christ himself, asserts that "the law and the prophets were until John." He is referring to J. Baptist, Elizabeth's son, and confirming that C.I. Schofield was making up his doctrines as he went along. How does that old saying go? "When first we practice to deceive..." Wasn't it "oh what tangled webs we weave"? Why do you suppose men such as that want to change the truth of the Bible—money, attention, power? Obviously they are not—cannot be—serving the God of the Bible. They must know it.

Let's dangle in Schofield's tangled web just a bit longer. One can see, on page five of his novel, that the chief dispensationalist—nay the very inventor of that school of tangled thought—C.I. Schofield, wrote, "Seven such dispensations are distinguished in Scripture." Oddly, if you look, you can find not a single one! He must be using one of his own Bibles as his reference point. That amounts to proving a point exists, by defining it only in the body of the proof! His choice of seven is completely arbitrary, as is shown by two inescapable examples. First, there is no biblical support for his invention. Second, among dispensationalists themselves, the chief disagreement concerns the fact that some find only three dispensations, some four, others more.

But along with Scripture validity, we ought to check the use of English language terminology. According to the *Webster's Collegiate Dictionary* (and I apologize for using such a biased source), the word *dis-tin-guish,* a verb, literally to separate by pricking, "to perceive as being separate or different." The man didn't miss quite as far with his choice of words, as with Scripture, except that he used the word as a noun, and "pricking" is not found associated with it.

In fairness, real theologians have often considered the Scriptures to be distinguished by two major periods sometimes termed "dispensations." These would be the old and the new, referring of course to the periods of the law, and of grace, as relates to the primary and overriding purpose and message of the Bible—namely, salvation. The earlier agreed-upon titles of these periods have always been "covenant" or "testament," both biblically derived. Anyone is certainly free to divide for study, or for discussion, any number of eras or time periods mentioned in the Bible. There is, however, no biblical warrant whatever to say that such arbitrarily derived divisions are specified by biblical delineation. That simply is untrue. There simply is no such delineation in the Lord's Bible. This has been a characteristic problem for some of the evangelicals, almost from the first opening of Schofield's Bible in 1909. The reason for that is, they never have come to the slightest agreement among themselves on just how many of these nifty dispensations there actually ought to be. Who is to say? If pressed, you yourself might come up with nine or thirteen, maybe twenty-one—who knows what lurks in the hearts of men eager to change God's story? Don't think for a moment that these various sects ever came together in an attempt to agree upon a number! There has always been a wall of separation between them, composed of disparate doctrines, all supposedly derived from the same source—the same text.

But virtually all of them bought into the Schofield hoax. Nor have all of them claimed the same dispensations, even if the number claimed were the same. These disparities simply became another divisor between denominations. Just imagine how many separate denominations you could establish, just using number of claimed "dispensations" as your separator among sects all claiming the Bible as their authority! At last count (about five years ago) the Protestants had divided themselves into an almost unimaginable 2,600 different named and incorporated sects, based upon real or perceived variations in interpretation of Scripture and who knows what? One can but speculate on how many of that embarrassing total resulted directly from counting different numbers of "dispensations"! It is a sad fact of supposedly God-inspired Christendom that its followers cannot, or will not, agree on the basics of what they believe.

One is left to suppose that it is one of God's wonders, how in the world Christendom ever survived for some nineteen centuries or so before some academic coined the term *dispensationalism!* But as yet we have not asked ourselves how many times this term appears in the King James Bible that has been around since 1611. That's only 395 years. The Wycliffe Bible, first complete Bible in the English language, predated the King James by 231 years. Tyndale's English Bible followed that, in 1527. Then came the Coverdale Bible, translated from Latin and German in 1536. That was the year of Tyndale's death by strangling, compliments of the queen, who was a Roman Catholic. After that, followed the Matthews Bible a year later and the Geneva in 1560. The Word of God was completed sufficiently long ago for man to have adopted it as an unquestioned authority in his life. It will indeed be a miracle if he ever does!

The next credible Bible was known as the "Authorized Version," which was written for the common man and had been commissioned by King James, the son of Mary, Queen of Scots. It bears his name. So let's see how many times the word "dispensation" appears in the king's product. First, in the name of precise scholarship, let's attest to the Greek word *oikonomea* appearing four times, all in the New Testament. There is nothing even remotely alluding to "dispensation" in the Hebrew texts. But interesting about the word *oikonomia* are the various meanings ascribed to it (this great doctrinal title of Schofield's) by the original translators. Remember, as we step in this direction, this word has captured the imagination of the evangelical leadership to the extent that it has divided denominations, and been a watchword in their congregations for the better part of a century (and its Greek equivalent appears only four times).

The Greek word is spoken by the Apostle Paul in First Corinthians 9:17: "I have been entrusted with a 'oikonomia.'" The translators here decided the word best described the English word *commission*—the best fit for that statement, since Paul was referring to a God-given administering duty for himself. The same word next appears in Ephesians 3:2, where Paul is again speaking;, "You have heard of the 'oikonomia' of God's grace that was granted to me for you." In English, the word here describes "stewardship," because God assigned it to Paul. In Colossians 1:25 we find Paul speaking again, this time of an administering duty, "according to the divine 'oikonomia,' which has been granted me for you." The English word chosen here turned out to be the "office" of minister. It can be seen without much struggle that in each case Paul is alluding to arrangements made by God himself, on behalf of the church membership, for their redemption! Each refers to a part of God's redemptive plan for mankind. The Old Testament employed the law for preparing the way; the New Testament employed the concept of freely given grace, through the sacrifice of Christ. The New Testament, in fact, regards this as the finale of previous history! In each case God has assigned a duty to Paul.

But there is one last usage of the only Greek terminology

that would fit the English term *dispensation* in the opinions of the translators. Once again the Apostle Paul is speaking, this time in Ephesians 1:10, where we are going to encounter a somewhat different connotation than in the trio of previous verses. Different in that this time, God employs the Greek term *oikonomia* for what in English becomes a rather difficult passage to follow. The sense in this case is that the word applies to the initiator. Here we find that it is God's own "administration" rather than Paul's. It is God's office, God's stewardship: "That in the dispensation of the fullness of times he might gather together in one, all things in Christ, both which are in heaven, and which are on earth; in him." There is no doubt that what is in view here, is again God's salvation plan. God is personally engaged in bringing that plan to a conclusion in the fullness of time, by and through the divine intervention of Christ. Here only, is the sense of an allotment of time by God, being suggested.

So we see the use of one term being used to characterize four similar but different activities. Three are assigned by God to man, one taken on by God on man's behalf. Only one has any sense of an arrangement or assignment concerning the passing of time, and it is a serious stretch to conclude from it that God speaks of "dispensing" or allotting a specific interval of time. The word applies once to the assigning of stewardship, once to the giving of administering duty, once to a commission or designation of authority, and once to a segment of a plan. There is indeed a distinct separation in the way the one in authority manifested his grace under the Old and New Testaments. It is this difference to which Paul refers in the verses we examined in both Ephesians and Colossians.

The ideas generated by Schofield and presented in his study Bible, then eagerly broadcasted by the dispensationalist crowd—the evangelicals and fundamentalists—became the basis for premillennial doctrine in these same assemblies. Theirs is modernist theology, none of which is supported by Scripture. The theological use of the term *dispensation* in referring to some period of time in biblical history is unwarranted if the Bible is to be the test of theological doctrines. Such usage simply does not appear in Bible text. Interestingly, the Greek terminology *oikonomia* literally refers to a law, or the arrangement of a house. It has nothing to do with times or periods of time.

The central argument of Schofield, and the most easily dismissed with Scripture, makes the entire dispensational house come tumbling down. In view here, is Schofield's doctrine that is central to all his teaching, that John the Baptist and Jesus Christ were "offering" to the nation of Israel, the very earthly kingdom—the carnal kingdom—that had occupied the Jews' expectations of their Messiah for centuries! Then Schofield claims that, when such a kingdom was offered, the Jews rejected what they had so eagerly awaited! This rejection, then, according to dispensational (fundamentalist) theory, caused God to withdraw his offer and to postpone the coming of the kingdom until a later dispensation. It can be seen that God's activities were tied to, and jumped from, dispensation to dispensation. Some may not have recognized it, but this is preposterous!

Such an idea was not generated by anything, anywhere, in Scripture. Such a scenario is found nowhere in the Bible—any Bible—other than the one invented by Schofield. It is that Bible version, not God's, which so excited the evangelical community and that led to the widespread acceptance of the premillennial preference, rather than the scriptural version of God's truth. Can it be considered anything but an oddity that so large a segment of the Protestant community would not recognize that no such offer, no such dispensations, appear anywhere in God's Word?

They claimed this to be "newly discovered truth" back in the early days of Schofield's wholly apostate teaching. At the very same time, the evangelicals invented a completely new and miraculous process for rightly dividing the word of truth. The "new" method relies not at all on Scripture for its revelation, meaning of course that neither God nor his Bible is any longer their authority. Whatever is appealing to the senses or the attitudes within a denomination has evidently become acceptable. And, after all, isn't such a thing precisely what the Bible says will occur in the "end times"? Isn't this precisely the form humanism takes?

In the Bible, the transition to God's promised kingdom is promised to be far less than a smooth one. That's what the "Great Tribulation" is all about! The Bible shows us that it will be a nasty time for *only* his church! The tribulation is *for* the church, *in* the church, and as a matter of irony, *by* the church! It leads into the coming of judgment, which God assures us, *begins* in the corporate churches. Recall the words of Paul:

> Let no man deceive you by any means: for except there come a falling away first, and that man of sin be revealed, the son of perdition; Who opposeth and exalteth himself above all that is called God, showing himself that he is God.
>
> 2 Thessalonians 2:3–4

It's obvious that the "falling away" has been going on for some time. It is recorded that Jesus said, "For there shall arise false Christs and false prophets, and shall shew great signs and wonders" (Matthew 24:24). Remember the parable of the wheat and the tares? "But while men slept, his enemy came and sowed tares *among* the wheat, and went his way." (Matthew 13:25, emphasis added) The future is ominous. Lots of folks who go to church every Sunday are going to be surprised on that last day the Bible talks about when they cannot enter the marriage feast! "For many are called, but few are chosen" (Matthew 22:14). "Not everyone that saith to me, Lord, Lord, shall enter into the kingdom of heaven" (Matthew 7:21a). Many will say to me in that day, Lord, Lord, have we not prophesied in thy name?" (Matthew 7:22a). Then recall that the Lord tells us (again) why the above is so, saying,

> For such are false apostles, deceitful workers, transforming themselves into the apostles of Christ. And no marvel; for

Satan himself is transformed into an angel of light. Therefore it is no great thing if his ministers also be transformed as the ministers of righteousness; whose end shall be according to their works.

2 Corinthians 11:13–15

All of the above must be precisely the reason that God promised, "For the time is come that judgment must begin at the house of God" (1 Peter 4:17). So it should actually be no surprise that judgment will begin, or perhaps has begun already, with his corporate churches, which must be in view here. That is evident, because Peter alludes in the next phrase of that same sentence to judgment beginning "with us." So, when we recognize how much the churches have pulled away from reliance on the Bible, we can recognize why the language in the several passages quoted above appears there.

A Mr. Thomas Bolton of Australia, quoted in Herendeen, page nine, pointed out that "the kingdom" is mentioned in seventeen of the twenty-seven New Testament books. Of the 139 separate references in the Bible to "the kingdom," Schofield quotes only twenty-one, totally ignoring for purposes of his own, 118 verses! Why would a writer/editor ignore 118 passages where a subject is mentioned—any subject, when establishing a "new" doctrine concerning that very subject? One is permitted to feel secure that the reason would not have been that Schofield simply overlooked them. Two come especially to mind from among the missing passages - Romans 14:17 and 1 Corinthians 15:50. Here is what those two Bible verses have to say. First, Romans: "For the kingdom of God is not food and drink; but righteousness, and peace, and joy in the Holy Ghost." Then second, Corinthians says, "Now I say this brethren, that flesh and blood cannot inherit the kingdom of God; neither does corruption inherit incorruption." It would appear from these passages that in no way does the God of the original Bible envision that a "Kingdom of God" will be established here on earth. Personally, I would say he ought to be reasonably well informed on that subject. For some reason, however, that is not clear to the fundamentalists. It's obvious why Schofield wouldn't want the passages above in his book. He appears to have been correct about the fundamentalists being either too backward or too lazy to compare his book to the real Bible.

That seems obvious, at least from God's standpoint, and appears to mean it will not be a physical kingdom. The reason for the omissions becomes rather obvious in light of Romans 14:17, which does not sound at all like what the nation of Israel in the time of Jesus had in mind. It is also rather obvious that First Corinthians 15:30 would not fit well in the contrived version that is the Schofield Bible. How did the evangelicals buy into his deception so readily? It must simply be that the majority of them did not read much of the Bible!

THE MILLENNIUM

LIKE SO MANY TERMS WIDELY ACCEPTED BY CHURCHGOERS WITH-out questioning their origin, the term *millennium* appears nowhere in the English Bible commissioned by England's King James.

Modern dispensationalists teach a "millennium" that does not have its origin in Scripture. To be certain, there is mention of a time period of "a thousand years" in Revelation 20:2–3 during which Satan is restrained and thrown into the bottomless pit. It does not, however, appear there in the context that the pre-tribulation advocates advance at all. That particular Scripture makes no reference whatever to the nation of Israel or to a literal, earthly reign to come, of Christ on a throne located on earth in the literal city of Jerusalem.

So if that is the case, where in the world did Schofield's dispensationalists get their idea of a so-called "millennial kingdom"? If this subject is approached without pre-conception, it will be found that the "millennial" activities of Revelation 20 are taking place purely in the spiritual realm. The beings involved there are not earthly, not human beings. Notice that there are human souls mentioned in verse four, and they too are spirits. The dispensationalists imagine a "millennium" populated by living human beings, not spirit beings. That is obviously a figment of an overactive and not very biblically researched, imagination. One has simply to refer to God's Word to see this clearly. In Acts 3:24, for instance, Peter says the prophets of the Old Testament were not prophesying of an earthly millennium to come, but rather "these days." That's these days of the gospel—these days in which we are living and in which some of us in the churches are reading the Bible carefully, but most are not.

Many will read the notes of study Bibles such as the Schofield or tracts extracted from the Bible, but sifted through the views of men, and so-called "devotional books" presumed to have a basis in the Bible. But these same people often will not read God's Word at its source. The Schofield book (it's difficult to call it a Bible), which, if we are careful to learn what God has said, must surely be a satanic product. It is perhaps the best example of what infects the modern church. Many respected Bible teachers are fixed in their low opinions of study Bibles in general. This includes what are known as "reference Bibles." There is always much to deplore in them. The "notes" included at the bottoms of pages and disguised as being scriptural are designed, as we have shown, to steer the reader inexperienced in the Scriptures into what typically are nothing more than sectarian doctrines and preferences. Many readers accept these as biblical. Sometimes they are not even remotely biblical, as in the case of the Schofield book. Many modern Bibles are designed carefully to draw the reader into the doctrinal conclusions of a particular sect or cult and may not be at all consistent with what the Bible actually teaches.

It should concern every true believer that a book should exist in which corrupt words of fallible, mortal man are presented as an addendum or extension of the Word of God! This amounts to mixing the profane and vile with the precious.

Some reading this may be wondering just who the chief advocates of dispensational beliefs are. It is hard to know, because this is not one of those things that are widely broadcast. For certain, two of the earliest advocates for Schofield's personal doctrines were the Moody Bible Institute and the Dallas Theological Seminary. This is surprising only if we do not recall that it is widely recognized that at least 80% of theology professors today are admitted atheists! In the mid 1950s, the Dallas Theological Seminary and other seminaries and organizations friendly to the Schofield thesis began a softening and blurring process. Their intent was aimed at shaving off the obvious sharp disagreements with God's Word. They evidently felt it was important to downplay the distinctions between Paul's teaching in the Epistles and what they desired to be believed by unsuspecting non-scholars. They have been quite successful at turning the churches away from the truth of God's Word. The consequence is not surprising. The majority of the external church—the denominations swelled with pretenders—is without a clear sense of heavenly identity today! In his book *Israel's Messianic Kingdom*, M.J. Stanford called this process, "Kingdomization." It was quite intentional and quite unbiblical. J.B. Stoney wrote in the latter nineteenth century, "There is a tendency abroad to exaggerate the standing and state of the Old Testament saints in order to make little difference between the church and Israel, and thus the heavenly distinctiveness is weakened and lost. The aim of the enemy from a very early date was to draw the saints from their heavenly calling (see the book of Hebrews)." Stoney went on to say, "Once heaven as a present position and portion is surrendered, the great position and privilege of the Church, the body of Christ, is drained away." His words have come true.

M.J. Stanford felt, as have many others, that over time, dispensational distinctions have somewhat broken down. This outlook began in the seminaries and flowed naturally down to the churches. The result of this has been that in some of the evangelical churches, or at least in the minds of their membership, the church has become merely a phase of Israel's future millennium kingdom! This has been a slow but deliberate process by pastors and Bible teachers. There is a recognition in the pews, Stanford says, "that a present form of the theocratic kingdom is already established." If such is the case, believers are being deprived, by their own denominations and in collusion with their seminaries, of the knowledge and benefit of understanding their own heavenly status with the Son at the Father's right hand. This hardly constitutes teaching of a redemption based on grace. It certainly is not in agreement with the teaching of the church writ large. This would seem to make this movement a deliberate, knowledgeable, and salacious departure from God's written, biblical plan. In a very real sense this constitutes a fall from grace, from the sharply defined doctrines of the Apostle Paul and the dispensations he spoke of to an earthly, law-oriented realm—by the clergy! Under their teaching, grace must respect the law! That is indeed a frightening prospect, but we must remember God will not be mocked (Galatians 6:7). These people will reap what they have sown.

Comments on dispensationalism and its practitioners, by respected churchmen who have not taken Satan's bait, fill volumes. So much so in fact that it is surprising that the churches today know so little of its detractors. Lack of attentiveness likely explains this phenomenon. Painfully obvious also is the failure of scholarship among the ranks of churchmen.

Almost five decades ago, at about the time everything in our society was cracking from the horrendous infusion of liberalism and the influence of Hebraic doctrines, a fellow warned: "It has been a constant disposition on the part of certain writers to invent Old Testament saints with the same position, qualities, and standing as those which belong to the believers who comprise the Church." These were the words of Dr. Chafer, president of the Dallas Theological Seminary in the late 1940s. Chafer was concerned that Christians in quite a large number of denominations were no longer being taught that the Christian church alone will be partakers of the inheritance of the saints. Dr. Chafer knew what was happening.

Nearly seventy-five years ago, a Dr. Newell predicted that "Failure to rightly divide between kingdom and Church will lead to a wrong conception of the Bible, and a false interpretation of its truth." Among the first things this would lead to, in Newell's view, would be for churches to spiritualize the kingdom promises of the Old Testament and attempt to make them apply to the church of the New Testament. Newell's was a surprisingly accurate prediction, made keen foresight by the fact that what he was warning about was already happening in certain denominations! Sadly, men of Chafer's convictions are scarce in the seminaries today.

Then there was Dr. Donald Campbell, president of the Dallas Theological Seminary, who was not so opposed to dispensationalist views. Writing in 1985, he said, "The two opposite viewpoints of premillennialism and amillennialism are still with us." He continued, "still with us though some modifications are taking place. Some premillennialists now view the present 'church dispensation' as the first phase of the fulfillment of the promised messianic kingdom." Campbell felt that some believers were "now experiencing the spiritual blessings of the kingdom, such as the blessings of Israel's New Covenant." Israel's new covenant? Campbell did not get that idea from the Bible! His purpose is to lead people to believe the kingdom, in fact even the New Covenant, is *for Israel*. This man is supposed to represent the Bible! We should ask, "Whatever happened to the Christ of the New Covenant?" An honest scholar simply cannot find God saying anywhere in the Bible that there is a "New Covenant kingdom" for the nation of Israel. The Word of God is quite clear that the church *is* the New Covenant Israel.

This is one of our nation's most respected seminaries weighing in, and its representative is not quoting from the Bible! It is but one example, and a very good one, of the intellectual impoverishment of the church leadership today.

In order to illustrate that Campbell reflects a dramatic change in attitudes at the Dallas Theological Seminary, since the thirty-year period between when Dr. Chafer presided there in the late 1940s and when Dr. Darby was there sometime around 1910, let's look at what Darby had to say about this subject. Writing in the July/September 1988 *Bible Sac*, C.A. Blaising quoted Darby: "The eternal destinies of the two peoples, [Israel and the true believers who make up the church] now share the same sphere."

This would remove the absolute distinction between Israel and the church that had always been recognized in the Bible by learned theologians and by God. It is the very men, the supposedly "learned theologians," however, who have led large segments of the church on a new path of discernment concerning biblical intent. Darby didn't speak of dispensationalism, but he did assume some "sphere of sameness" that suddenly changed how the Bible was interpreted.

From the comments of these various men, we can to some extent read of the increasing strength over time, of their admissions of dispensational leanings. Traditional dispensationalism has never reflected the dispensations spoken of by the Apostle Paul. Its advocates have, of the necessity of their motive, always attempted to relate the church that Christ founded to their "New Covenant of Israel." They also have equated in a manner totally unwarranted scripturally the Old Testament nation of Israel to the present secular State of Israel. The two are neither biblically nor racially synonymous. The State of Israel is secular and was founded mainly by European, not by Semitic Jews of the Middle East! Dispensationalism has been progressively modified to suit whoever was "telling it," generally one or another of the luminaries at Dallas Theological Seminary. Then along came Karl Barth.

THE FATHER OF
EVANGELICALISM

B ORN IN BASEL, SWITZERLAND, IN 1886, KARL BARTH WAS
able TO claim the distinction of giving the Christian world
its first taste of evangelical theology. Educated in German universities, Karl Barth became a country pastor in Aargau, Switzerland. While he was in that capacity, Barth wrote his first
work, a revolutionary commentary on the book of Romans. He
became an overnight enigma. His fame spread across Europe,
and between 1935 and 1962 he served as professor of theology at
the University of Basel. In 1962, he first visited the United States
to deliver his now-famous four lectures on what he termed
evangelicalism. He lectured at both the Princeton Theological
Seminary and the University of Chicago. His theology, unlike
that of other liberal theologians and of many liberal denominations, did not make peace with the humanism that had become a
characteristic of most Western churches. Neither was his theol-

ogy man centered as was the theology of most of the big names in mid-twentieth-century theology. Barth centered his teaching entirely upon God's encounter with man, instead of the typical man's discovery of God. This resulted in something new for that time—a God, Christ, and Bible focus! His followers honor "Barthian thought." Because that sort of thinking begins with God, rather than man, many consider his evangelicalism to be "absolute" since the feelings and wishes of everyday man do not have a place in it. It is also a "modest" theology because it seeks constantly to understand and to speak of God and his gospel. As you can appreciate, what passed as Christian thought prior to Barth scarcely resembles at all what most Protestant sects teach today. It is hard for us today to appreciate the enormous difference.

Speaking of being studious concerning the pursuit of Christian knowledge, Karl Barth wrote: "Theological study consists […] in active participation in the work of that comprehensive community of teachers and learners which is found in the school of the immediate witness to the work and Word of God." What he is saying here, is "study the Bible." "To study theology," said Barth, "means not so much to examine exhaustively the work of earlier students of theology [as all universities do] as to become their fellow student." In introducing his evangelical theology, Barth explained that its qualifying attribute is the adjective, which "recalls both the New Testament and at the same time the reformation of the sixteenth century." He insisted that this was not only the style of the New Testament evangelists, apostles, and prophets, but was also the theology newly discovered in the Reformation. He insisted that his expression referred "primarily and decisively to the Bible." Sadly, it took but a few years for such a label to take on an entirely unintended personality. Today those who consider themselves to be described by Barth's theology (evangelicals) do not at all follow his precepts for adopting that character. This is easily seen in Barth's own assertion concerning his type of theology. In his very first lecture contained in his first book, *Evangelical Theology,* the teacher establishes (pg. 11) the character of this discipline by saying, "Evangelical theology will forfeit its object, it would belie and negate itself, if it wished to view, to understand, and to describe any one moment of the divine procession in "splendid isolation" from others." Yet this is precisely what twentieth-century evangelicalism did! It separated itself on the basis of one moment in the divine procession—the millennium! But everyone has forgotten the birth oratory of evangelicalism. This may have been why many of them began to characterize themselves as "fundamentalists." They could not function within the description of their own doctrines.

To show concretely that the originator of that theological bent would not recognize evangelical doctrines of today, simply consider but one of his statements: "The word spoken in the history of Israel [...] reaches its culmination in the history of Jesus Christ." Yet today's evangelicals insist that God will go to great lengths to reclaim the nation of Israel for himself and will do so in preference to the work of Jesus Christ!

Barth also said, "The ancient covenant, established with Abraham, Isaac and Jacob, proclaimed by Moses, and confirmed to David, becomes in Jesus Christ, a new covenant." In Jesus, you see, God finally finds a trustworthy human covenant partner! On page two of his book, Barth wrote, "Certainly what is fulfilled in the existence and appearance, in the work and word of Jesus of Nazareth, is the history of God and His Israel." Notice that the originator of evangelicalism recognized, as does the New Testament, that Jesus Christ *fulfilled* the history of Israel.

The history of Christ speaks of the realized unity of God and man. It is found in no other men. The fulfillment of Israel's history, according to Barth and virtually all of the Reformed theologians, is not its own continuation, but the indwelling of God in Jesus. "Israel was sent as God's mediator to the nations" (Barth 22). "The fact is, there is no history of Israel in itself and

for its own sake!" (23) Israel's history, you see, was the fulfillment of the name God gave to Isaac (Israel). It meant, "con-
tender against God," and that was precisely what Israel did all
through its history, with only a few exceptions.

Yet today, those who affect the title brought to them by Karl
Barth have a love affair with the idea of Israel. They see Israel
as being essential to their own survival. It is precisely their mistaken idea of God's intent and purpose for Israel that leads the
evangelicals into a dilemma—a catch 22 of religious belief.

Dispensationalists and other futurists realize that an honest analysis of biblical texts related to the timeline of biblical
events jeopardizes their prophetic views. Dispensationalists
have essentially given up on Christianity, believing it is not
faithful, at least to their non-Bible-based end times doctrines.
So, they have reverted to another concocted belief, this one that
the Jews will remain the favored breed. These people look just
like other Christians, but they believe that the modern state of
Israel is the reincarnation of the Israel of old—the Old Testament nation of Israel. If you recall, this was also a fatal mistake
of first-century Judaism. Those who refuse to study history,
especially Bible history, are doomed to repeat it.

The dispensationalists get their doctrines by employing a
literalist approach only to biblical interpretation. Philip Mauro
wrote, "It was the literalizing of Jewish prophesies concerning
the Messiah and His kingdom that led the Jews off into hopes
of the Messiah that were false. Literal interpretation of their
Scriptures blinded the Jews to their own Messiah."[8]

Premillenarians (because they are first dispensationalists)
incorrectly perceive that their doctrine was generally accepted
up until the 3rd century. According to Christian Historian Lewis
Berkhof, "The truth is that few of the well known writings of
that time mention it at all!"[9]

Mark Ames, writing in the New York Press, made the following observation, putting another color onto this clash of
doctrines: "When I pointed out to a Jewish cousin of mine

the insanity of this "alliance"—in which the Christian Zionists are using Jews in order to help God massacre them—he laughed." Then he said, "I know, they're a bunch of freaks and weirdoes. But we're just using them." So you see, the fundamentalist Christians and the Jews are using each other, and it affects the doctrine they cling to! [10] "The traditional interpretation of Galatians 6:16 conflicts with principles of interpretation associated with dispensationalism," says commentator Michael Marlowe. Galatians 6:16 says, "And as many as walk according to this rule [given in verse fifteen], peace be on them, and mercy, and upon the Israel of God."

It is clear from the context that the Israel of God spoken of consists of the New Testament believers, some of whom were formerly Jews.

Dispensationalists (fundamentalists) ignore the Bible proof of this truth and consider the Israel spoken of to be the nation of Israel. This is a biblically unsound interpretation. Mauro contends that "dispensationalists are interested in maintaining a sharp distinction between "Israel" and "the church" across a whole range of theological matters. They are not comfortable with the idea that here Paul is using the phrase "Israel of God" in a sense that includes Gentiles, because of their chosen contention that "the church" is always carefully distinguished from Israel in Scripture. Mauro is overly kind to dispensationalists on this point. Two Reconstructionist authors have written, "The church is one in the Old Testament and New, and the New Testament church is the fulfillment of all prophesy, the very last phase of God's redemptive work on earth."[11] An Independent Baptist pastor wrote, "Dispensationalism [...] is an extremely wobbly system built upon eclectic and cultic practices and literary thievery. It has been popularized in the last three decades by men of very questionable scholarship who have it has been discovered displayed dishonest practices."[12]

Another writer observed,

It's time to bring out into the open one of the largest political supports for Israel's political radicals, and debate how some religious leaders, particularly the Reverends Falwell and Robertson, push support for the most militant [...] in Israel and against the Israeli peace groups such as led by the murdered Yitzhak Rabin. Many fundamentalist leaders have crossed the line from forecasting Armageddon to trying to bring it about. Their alliance with Zionist radicals is very two sided, each thinks it is using the other.[13]

In the Bible there is found no warrant, no necessity for special treatment of any land or city. The Bible's new Jerusalem is a concept of a city which comes from God, and he transcends any limitations of the physical world. That city is not a physical entity, but is composed of the spirits (souls) of all true believers. That is, his church.

Why would the prime minister of Israel make a statement in a gathering of 3,000 Christians like, "The State of Israel has no better friends than American evangelicals"? Why would he not say "the American people" or "the American government"? Gary Bauer, longtime president of The Family Research Council, explained it well in saying of Christians who believed as he did, "Many evangelicals believe that the land of Israel is covenant land that was promised by God to the Jewish people." [14] He was, of course, speaking primarily of fundamentalist dispensationalists. Bauer was later described by the *Jerusalem Post* as "a better spokesman for Israel than some Israeli diplomats." The fundamentalists simply ignore large portions of Scripture if these happen not to support their concept of the future of Israel. One of the passages evidently unaccepted by the dispensationalists is highlighted by author David B. Curtis in his book, *Who Is the Israel of God?* Curtis employs but a single passage to show that the state of Israel is not the inheritor of God's kingdom. He points out that there are two distinct and readily identifiable Israels (Romans 9:6). There is ethnic, physical, secular, national

Israel, and there is the true, spiritual Israel composed of the children of the promise—of election.

Jack Van DeVenter wrote, in *Israel and the Church,* of the single most objectionable idea to the rest of Christendom in fundamentalist philosophy: "Despite Christ's ultimate sacrifice as the 'Lamb of God' who takes away the sin of the world, dispensationalism teaches that the (Jewish) sacrificial system will be reinstituted." This not only relegates Christ to relative unimportance, but it also removes the whole idea of individual, personal salvation by grace! This, in favor of people who just happen to live in the state of Israel. That turns Christianity into a temporary expedient. There is no suggestion in the Bible for such an arrangement in the future. If we happen to believe in God's Word, such ideas become patently unacceptable propositions. Fundamentalists evidently don't have that problem!

If we read the Bible carefully, it becomes obvious that throughout all of redemptive history, God selected, then embraced, only one people whom he adopted as special and chosen to share in the inheritance of his only begotten son, Christ Jesus. He preselected each of these chosen individuals before the foundation of the world (Ephesians 1:4) so God would have and Christ would have certain, selected, special people to sing their praises through eternity.

An odd situation developed on the author's way to a Bible bookstore in Branson, Missouri, several years ago, during a cold, snowy Christmas season. Now, we know God is not speaking directly to us today or bringing signs, dreams, or weird non-understandable voices in order to communicate with us. Those things do seem to be experienced by some who think they are true believers, but we can be assured it's not coming from God, because he told us in the book of Revelations that wasn't going to be in his program. But something whispered that crisp morning in December, the thought: *How little have the expectations of some people today changed from the expectations of first-century Jews!* The author does not remember what was going on that day to cause that thought to occupy his mind. Maybe something in the Bible bookstore where he was standing reminded him that some people are still determined to have the physical king and his kingdom that the Jews never accepted, even though he spent three years trying to talk sense to them. They just have trouble, it seems, comprehending the difference in God's economy between the physical and the spiritual. Jesus even said (and he is God), "My kingdom is not of this world." Some people just do not listen. The Bible says God has not given them ears to hear.

John N. Darby, father of dispensationalism, proved his brainchild lacked a brain. It is filled with error and heresy, not prophecy from God. His followers insist that redemption remains unfulfilled despite Jesus going to the cross. Evidently, in their view, God can fail!

There is one kingdom predicted (promised) by the prophets. There was one kingdom in the words of Jesus. There was one kingdom that began at Pentecost and will be brought to fullness at the "Parousia"—the presence, or second coming of Christ. All these are spoken of in the God-breathed words of his Bible. One reality of our world ought to be considered. For many decades the book of Revelation was largely ignored in the seminaries and in the pulpits. It was left to the fundamentalists among the evangelical community to interpret. That's why we now have so widespread an apocalyptic interpretation. That is, after all, fuel for a very lucrative prophesy industry, of which the *Left Behind* series of fairy tales is but one example.

Today, Karl Barth would not recognize evangelicalism and especially its most radical branch, fundamentalism (the camouflage of dispensationalism), he would find in this country. It is no longer the system of study he initiated. He would in fact be alarmed at the direction it has taken.

During the twentieth century, and to date in the twenty-first, the populations of perhaps half, if not more, of all Christian churches have been told repeatedly from the pulpits and in countless books that "God has an unconditional and abiding love for Old Testament Israel." What they in fact mean by that is "God's love is directed toward a particular, racially 'correct' people descended from Abraham." This is said to pertain regardless of that people's faith or obedience to God's plan, and in fact despite what the Bible says. In short, what is being taught in evangelical circles is that membership in "Israel" has nothing whatever to do with faith but is a purely racial matter. A person with even a basic comprehension of the biblical salvation plan recognizes at once that this is absolutely contrary to what God has written in the Bible for his chosen followers to understand. But evangelicals haven't figured that out. Such foundationless teachings are proof that a great segment of "the church" has not even a fundamental, basic comprehension concerning what the Bible insists is God's plan of redemption. How could they have gone so far astray? For one thing, it was purposeful. That means that Jesus was 100% accurate when he said that in the last days many would come who will lead astray even the very elect unless they pay very close attention to his Word. The trouble is few will ever do that. They go about reinforcing each other's ignorance of biblical exegesis.

Most of the many people who use the Schofield Reference Bible, and who are exposed repeatedly to dispensation-oriented teaching, will be in this group. They will know very little about the actual content and meaning of the true Bible, nor are they aware at all of historic, Reformational, nor Covenantal Reformed theologies in particular. They will never have encountered the *Westminster Confession of Faith* or the *Heidelberg Catechism*. In short, they may have never been exposed to the actual teachings of the one true God at all!

Dispensationalism was incubated by the teachings of John Darby, spread by exposure in the Schofield Bible and the "evangelical" movement of the past century. Stephen Sizer wrote,

> Until the rise of the novel theology of Christian Zionism, unlike the Jews, Christians have never looked to, or expected

the temple in Jerusalem to be rebuilt. Christians today are being forced to choose between two competing theologies. The one is based on the shadows of the Old Testament, the other based on what appears to be the reality of the New Testament. The focus of the Christian Zionist is upon the land and the Jews, excluding the entire New Testament revelation. The Bible assures anyone willing to read and believe it, that the story of God and Jesus Christ is one that is inclusive, and centers on the Lamb of God. The Bible that God dictated focuses on a New Covenant, a New Israel, a New Jerusalem and a new universe. In this view, God is a remodeler of all that went before. The other, because of its focus on the end of time, is an "Armageddon Theology." Armageddon because rather than accepting the biblical description of an "inclusive theology" of justice, peace and reconciliation of man to God, the Zionist ideal represents a theological endorsement for ethnic cleansing and exclusion of people for reasons God has repeatedly denied in His Word. To be sure, millennialism is a misguided belief system.

Why would Sizer choose the word *misguided?* In part at least because it appears to be an ethnic-based salvation belief system following the Great Tribulation. It returns to Old Testament theology of the nation of Israel, a system that God displaced for the new. Despite the Bible declaring that old system never worked, dispensationalists would return to that system. They completely ignore God's announcement, early in the New Covenant years, that there had always been but a single redemption plan throughout both Testament times. That single plan, according to the Bible, will continue until the last day. It is the plan presented by Jesus Christ and later by his disciples. It is ever and only a wholly personal and individual salvation expectation repeated again and again in the New Testament of God.

But after the coming of the Schofield Bible, which we introduced in a previous chapter, twenty to thirty million people who believe they are Christians no longer accept God's plan of redemption. They like the idea of Zionism better than what God has to say.

In the Bible book of Romans, specifically verses twenty-four through twenty-seven of chapter eleven, the Apostle Paul is discussing the nation of Israel. Notice, however, that the apostle's interest is not concerned with race, creed, ethnicity, sex, or anything apart from the Israelite as an individual, thinking human being. Our example here is one of an apostle of Jesus Christ speaking of Old Covenant people but expressing only New Covenant redemption!

We can examine such a simple thing as the word *meet*, which pre-tribulation rapturists would have us believe is a critical designator of theology. They associate this word, this verb, with Jesus reversing his direction of travel while on his way to earth on the clouds, as described in Revelation 1:7, Matthew 26:64, Mark 13:26, and elsewhere. Except there is no mention of such a reversal in Scripture! But, he certainly would have had to do that in order to lead the newly raptured evangelicals back with him to heaven. Then, he has to reverse himself again to go down to Jerusalem in Palestine to rule there, while Great Tribulation is pummeling the true church, and the earth, according to the Bible, is under destruction by the wrath of God. Then, somehow in the midst of these competing activities, Christ must rush off to fight the battle of Armageddon, which the Zionists insist has to be a physical battle between God and his enemies. So, to an evangelical, the word *meet* must mean to reverse direction and to return along a route just traveled to join those who are being met. Then the second *meet* must mean something else, *n'est-ce pas?*

All that as it may be, why not simply divide the word of truth rightly, without inventing any new dispensations or even a new denomination? The Greek word that the translators chose to call "meet" as found in First Thessalonians 4:17, is *apantesis*. It's a word that occurs only four times in Scripture. Other Greek verbs are chosen by the translators for nineteen other passages where they chose the English word *meet* to express variously, worthy, together with, valuable, encounter, and "meet" with. But in each case when *apantesis* is used, the meaning is actually not exactly to "meet," although that could adequately represent the intended meaning in each case. What apparently is more appropriate in each case, however, would be a "friendly encounter"! In none of the nineteen Greek verbs translated "meet" in the King James Bible, is there a hint of turning around, reversing direction, or going back. That idea could not have come from the Bible! This appears to be entirely one of those occasions in which someone desires to make the Bible reflect some preconceived meaning that has nothing to do with the actual Word of God. Schofield simply said that's what it meant, and 100 years worth of people in the pews and pulpits, too lazy to read the Bible for themselves, believed him. It actually should surprise no one that the true meaning is remarkably like the true gospel says it is. But false doctrines are being manufactured all around us every day, and entire congregations keep believing them. That is why God has ended the "Church Age" and ordered his true followers to "get out of her." The true gospel—the "Good News"—is that Christ shall appear on the clouds, meet the elect in the clouds, after which he will clean up the mess made by Satan, including the altercation at Armageddon, before returning to wherever the judgment seat will be located. His last act on earth will be to destroy it, just as the Bible reveals!

After reading Mauro and other writer's condemnations of dispensationalism, fundamentalism, and premillennialism with Bible truths, a reader ought to ask himself a question. What advantages does he personally have over those who pass themselves off as teachers of the truth in many churches today? His answer to himself might well be, they are simply the employees of corporations masquerading as churches.

His advantages are at least three, in most cases, if he is a true believer. First: he is not one of them! Second: he no longer has to be a member of a denomination. He is free not to apologize for, or to have to bend, God's truth. Third: he no longer has to be encumbered by the fake humility and feigned knowledge of the leadership of a church. Therefore, he is free to read and interpret his Bible with the Lord's guidance, as best he can, and to recount truthfully what he has read. He can always endeavor to follow God's lead and is free to pray for those who follow another path, disregarding the Word of God.

The Schofield Bible was replete with comments by the author, which were assumed by many gullible readers to be an integral part of the Bible. These notes were in fact compiled entirely by the author to influence an entire generation of Bible-believing Christians to accept his personal premises. He was very successful. Remember this was the first Bible ever to have its own "notes" to explain Scripture, and to "guide" the reader to the author's brand of truth. It became an immediate hit in the unsuspecting churches, and a special treat for lazy readers. That meant it was an immediate favorite of fundamentalists and evangelicals.

Many new churchgoers today are encouraged by pastors to pick up a "study Bible," not suspecting at all that such a publication is going to be chock full of one sort of sectarian slant or another. Every pastor, however, stands ready to point the new member to what is considered to be "the best" Bible to acquire for Nazarenes, or Baptists, Presbyterians, etc.

But what was it that was so different about Mr. Schofield's ideas and his Bible? Simply stated, he was the first to advocate, in the pages of a Bible, his own views instead of God's program! For instance, on page five, the chief dispensationalist of his time stated, "Seven such dispensations are distinguished in Scripture." Had he been a bit more circumspect, he might have said, "can be distinguished *from* Scripture." Some strict interpretation commentaries immediately condemned him as a heretic. Actually, no one ever "distinguished even one dispensation in Scripture." Added to that, while the number seven correlates with many numerically significant references of the

Bible, Schofield's use of it is totally arbitrary. This is attested to by the fact that other dispensationalists have come up with different numbers of time periods to label as "dispensations." It's a marvelous word, *dispensation*. It makes one who uses it feel, well, almost erudite. And after all, that was then a totally new concept (dispensation, not erudition).

That was because almost nobody could find any scriptural support for his dispensations, and when they tried to apply Schofield's method, they came up with four, five, three, or only two dispensations. Let's find out from Mr. Webster exactly what Schofield might have meant by "distinguished"—maybe that was the problem. Mr. Webster's heirs say, "Dis-tin-guish, a verb, literally to separate by pricking, 1. To perceive as being separate or different." It certainly would appear that Mr. Schofield missed about as far with his verb as he did with his mischaracterization of Scripture.

Of course, in reality, God did divide the Scriptures into two natural divisions, which in essence are time separated as well as being separated buy two sequential, but overlapping, covenants. Really, that had always been sufficient to everyone who made a life out of studying those two covenants. Certainly, one's individual study methods are in no way restricted as concerns dividing time periods for clarification. There is, however, no biblical warrant whatever to label such divisions so as to make them appear to be delineated scripturally. There simply is none. This has gotten to be a problem for the evangelical, fundamental, and dispensational denominations. The problem is that they ever accepted such a division of the Bible in the first place. But that's not the problem they recognize. What they struggle with is that they cannot agree on how many unscriptural dispensations to teach! So, in fact, Schofield has turned out to be not only a teacher of unbiblical falsehood, he has been an element of divisiveness among those who have hoisted him up on a pole as their icon.

But what's new? They agree on very few aspects of God's

Word either! There are more sufficient, disparate, doctrines to separate this "branch" of what they all claim is God's true church. Just about the only common thing they can point to is that they all happened to buy into the Schofield heresies, and that fact conditioned what they believe without biblical support. Although they all claim the dispensationalist "handle," they do not all claim the same dispensations. So, dispensations became just another delineator of their differences. But then, Protestants have always been divisive, giving the Romish worshippers ample reason to perceive them as a band of purposeless vagabonds simply wandering in the wilderness of their own ignorance. Protestants, in case someone hadn't noticed, have divided themselves at latest count into 2,600 separate sects, each claiming biblical authority for only their special point of view. Of course, that report is now a week old, so there may be more. One can only hazard a guess how many of that grand and embarrassing number were caused exclusively by differing counts of dispensations. It is a sad commentary on the current state of Christendom that all these people who claim to answer to the same Redeemer cannot find a way to agree among themselves.

The ideas espoused in the Schofield Reference Bible, have ultimately been a greater influence on the evangelicals than have the words of God that Schofield also appended to his own words. Today, those who have been romanced into what we now call "dispensationalism" eagerly broadcast his ideas. Schofield's influence has literally become modern evangelism, modern theology. Many churchmen saw this coming and worried about it but could not stem the tide sweeping over the church, despite their numerous books, tracts and articles written early in the twentieth century. Premillennialism is everywhere broadcast as "fundamental" Christianity, and so the evangelicals gave themselves another label. These two nominal descriptors could not be more popular if God had included them in Scripture. Many who have not been saved, but have found their way into churches, along with many who are saved, are being misled on many "vital doctrines," which are not of God. Fortunately, some are leaving the corporate churches to seek for the true Word of God elsewhere. They will find it only in the Bible.

The central argument of Schofield has turned out to be most easily disposed of with Scripture, if anyone cares to do so. It is, therefore, actually the very argument that makes Schofield's entire thesis of dispensationalism come tumbling down. That would be Schofield's central doctrine, that John the Baptist and Christ were both "offering" to the Jews the very earthly kingdom, the carnal kingdom that occupied the Jews' expectations of their Messiah. This, is shown in the Bible to be patently false; yet, fundamentalists believe it and teach a gospel that reflects this belief. They also teach that when such a kingdom was offered, the Jews rejected it. Never mind though, because the fundamentalists are teaching that just such a kingdom for the Jews here on earth is part of God's plan for the future. They have concluded that the rejection of his offer by the Jews caused Christ to "withdraw" his offer and to "postpone" the coming of the kingdom until a later date. Actually, a later dispensation! One has to totally ignore a great many scriptural passages to come up with that analysis. But the dispensationalists—the fundamentalists—the evangelicals—are able to ignore God's words with aplomb easily equal to the nation of Israel, or even the popes! The only Bible in which such a plan is found is that of Dr. Schofield, and many who profess to be servants of God have chosen to believe Schofield, rather than Christ. Many still use Schofield's Bible.

Can it be that over the past century so many who profess to follow God can actually recognize that no such offer as Schofield proffered, actually appears in Scripture? They would then have to recognize no such dispensation can exist, yet still celebrate their attachment to the doctrine of a man as dogmatically as they do, wouldn't they? Yes, evidently nothing is too outrageous for these people. They claimed his to be "newly discovered truth" back in the early twentieth century. They discovered "revealed truth" external to the Bible but inherent in the book of Schofield!

Can there be any reason why someone wishing to establish the idea that God will set up an earthly kingdom, in which Jesus reigns over the Jews who murdered him, would not want to use these verses as support for his contention? How about why he would instead pretend they never existed? Surely no one would accuse Dr. Schofield of "stacking the deck", would he? Certainly, the good doctor wouldn't have tried to ignore the facts of Scripture. Surely the Jews will all magically develop love for the Holy Ghost sometime just before judgment. Odd the Bible doesn't recognize such a possibility, hmmm? There has always been so much peace and agreement among the Jews. Well, even if there wasn't, God could surely change his mind about them. But how do they get around the "flesh and blood" part? The evangelicals must be asking themselves that question. You see, this kingdom has to consist of the actual modern nation of Israel, not their souls only. That's a problem, but we can just ignore it. We have already ignored the fact that God says that when Jesus returns it will be the "last day." Already that doesn't fit smoothly into a "Pre-trib" rapture; but we've ignored those little discrepancies so far, and nobody on our team even noticed.

One can hardly miss the fact that just the two passages above, standing alone and coming from God, very effectively sink Dr. Schofield's rubber ducky. Why can the fundamentalists not see it? The answer is they do not want to see it. God has simply not given them eyes to see! We will get to that explanation in due time.

In the Bible book of Romans, specifically chapter eleven, verses twenty-four through twenty-seven, the Apostle Paul is, admittedly, discussing the nation of Israel. But let's examine closely, what he is actually saying. We see that his interest is not focused upon race, creed, gender, or anything else that can be shared by an entire nation. He is speaking of the Israelite as an individual! Here then, is the Apostle, speaking of an Old Covenant people, but he is expressing only New Covenant redemption!

PAUL AND THE JUDAIZERS

WE HAVE INCLUDED HERE A STORY FROM THE BIBLE THAT MAY assist to show the reader what is important for a Christian, or for a Jew, to recognize as the truth of God's Word. This story has to do with what in the Bible was considered "Judaizing," or teachings heretical to the true gospel of Christ and, therefore, also to Christianity.

Today, a portion of what still comes out of Judaizing is termed, "Christian Sabbatarianism." It has that name because theologians are a peculiar breed given to inventing two-dollar words to express what are sometimes only two-bit ideas. If that concept gives you pause, simply consider the name they made up for themselves. They could use the label "Bible Scholar" or even "Bible Schooler," since they haunt the halls of academia. But they designed their own label, "Theologian!" Very regal sounding isn't it? *Theos* refers to God, and *logia* has to do with the Greek word *logos*, which in English sounds like it might refer to logic, but it does not! It means "word." So they deal in

God's Word. A lot of them want us to think that *logia* is the root word for *logic,* but logic is sadly lacking in today's theology crowd. It will be my prayer that the reader will recognize this is presented somewhere around half in jest.

But we began by discussing "Sabbatarianism." This simply is a fourteen-letter word meaning "holding to a doctrine of the Saturday Sabbath," which is only a seven-letter word.

In his Epistle to the Galatians, Paul certainly speaks seriously about the problem that was besetting the Galatian churches, though he chose not to put a label on it. There is no barrier to us doing that. It was the problem of mixing Judaizers among Christians. Well, at least it was Judaizing among people worshipping in churches designed for Christians. The same thing is happening in some of the denominations today, but it has a slightly different twist.

In Paul's time, Judaizing took the form of a conspiracy among some of the converts from Judaism, or among some who only appeared to be converts, to impose Jewish interpretations of Bible prophecy on Gentile believers. Simply stated, they felt that Judaism still had viable answers for those who serve Christ. That, of course, was despite Christ having turned his back on the nation of Israel. Paul's reaction makes for great reading. He would be led to challenge the church in Jerusalem and Peter personally over this issue. Paul took a stand that some felt was rather severe in its reaction. He stood his ground alone, with no other apostle supporting his position originally. The result was that the infant Christian church everywhere was saved from the influence that sought to destroy it. We know that even Barnabas, one of the true stalwarts of the gospel, was led astray for a time by this same influence, and as a matter of fact, so, apparently, was Peter.

Because of an illness while on his second missionary journey, Paul had spent some time among the people of the region of Galatia. This would have been just about in the midst of the region we know today as the nation—actually the Republic—of

Turkey. Paul had become very kindly disposed toward the people who would become known later as the Gauls, the founders of modern France. They were also called the Celts. They were a somewhat simple, fickle people. For that reason, once Paul had taught them, then continued on his missionary journey, they became easy prey to invaders whose mission it was to bend them toward Judaism. Most of the first-century churches suffered but survived such assaults from time to time. That was only natural, since Judaism was every bit as evangelical as was early Christianity and had lost many proselytes as well as Hebrews to the ravages of the traveling preachers of Christ. They wanted to get them back. We must never forget that in organized religion there is always an unspoken financial and power agenda.

It is obvious that the "circuit riders" of Jewry did not have to work especially hard to discredit Paul's previous teaching to the gullible Galatians. One of their tactics was to tell them Paul was simply an evangelist from the Antioch church, which was in fact not entirely false. But telling them Paul was not an apostle was false. As a consequence of not being very well grounded in Christian doctrines, people of any age could be rather easily led to accept specious or fanciful stories and to exchange the truth for a lie. The Galatians accepted the premise of some of these raiders in their midst, that the benefits of the gospel could be theirs, only by first complying with the requirements of the Judaic law—specifically with the Hebrew requirement for circumcision.

What sounded like logic to the simple Galatians who had not been advantaged by any continuing teaching to strengthen their knowledge, and whose Old Testament knowledge was thin, appeals to many in the church today. The case goes like this: "The law could not have been set aside! It was, after all, a divine institution, not a temporary expedient. It was and is, binding on anyone who wishes to be in God's will. It was therefore never abrogated as some of the Christians teach." The Judaizers themselves, like many Christians today, had imperfect knowledge of the covenant and its relationship to the law. The average Christian of today has been taught, and recognizes, that Christ both fulfilled the law and abrogated it. But it is doubtful if many could explain the relationship between the law and the Abrahamic covenant. Paul shows us how that works in the book of Galatians, so we are going to touch on that relationship a bit in this book.

This in no way constitutes a sufficiency as regards Christian knowledge of this or any other subject. There is no source of truth apart from the Word of God. For that reason, what is intended here is to prepare you for the remainder of this book, and I hope to interest you by this reading, to read carefully the entire book of Galatians in the Bible. You are here urged to trust no teaching except that from the Word of God. Trust only and completely what you thoroughly study in the Bible! Trust no man, but trust Christ implicitly. Christ was the only man who ever walked this world, who was always correct. He never once had to say, "Oh, excuse me, I was wrong about what I told you."

We can know pretty much what the spurious teachings were that beset the Galatian churches, from what Paul teaches them by way of correction in his Epistle. What you will read here is not intended to be presented in the order of the Epistle, so don't look for verse one here. To begin, it must be said: if the law and the works it required, have any claims at all upon true believing Christians, and if these works must be performed before those Christians can be saved, then, as Paul writes, Jesus Christ was, and is, of himself, insufficient and ineffective in God's economy! We know full well that this is just not the case. But some who have been made to think they are true believers do not understand this fully. The very reason we have been freed from the law is exactly the sufficiency of Christ. "For the law was given by Moses," according to John, "but grace and truth came by Jesus Christ" (John 1:17).

Then, Paul teaches the Galatians along with the rest of us, that only the people who accept the promise, and not those who believe in and cling to the law, are children of Abraham and walk in freedom. The Judaizers taught the Galatians that Christ observed the law. That part was true. Our Lord lived under the law, but he also fulfilled that law, to make us free from the influence of the law, entirely free (as concerns salvation). But you know what? Without the heresy of those Judaizers, we wouldn't have this wonderful epistle rich with the teaching of the apostle. We should thank God for the Judaizers, and then we should read the epistle ourselves. Next, we should go out to personally help ensure such teachings never creep into congregations today. Paul's position was obviously something like this: if Christianity is to become the universal religion and not a mere Jewish sect, then religion must be spiritual and not mere ritual. If union with Christ really means emancipation from bondage of every kind, then once and for all it was time for Paul to make clear to the Galatians, to the church at Jerusalem, and to those of us who read what he has written the true biblical relationship of Christ to the law.

So you ought to read the book of Galatians, and read it without referring to any reference notes that might be in your Bible, to any Bible commentaries—even the "good" ones, or to any other reference book. Why would you want to limit your search? Because every one of those books, from D. James Kennedy to Matthew Henry, has a denominational bias that often contends with the truth of the Bible. Let us illustrate something. Let's pretend the reader is a practicing Baptist (any denomination's name could be inserted). Would his pastor be comfortable if he were studying the Lord's Supper under a Catholic priest? How about a Jehovah's Witness? Maybe a Mormon bishop? Christian Scientist? You see, every denomination is more jealous of its own teaching than it is about the Word of God! It's true. Why do you think most have some sort of "What We Believe" document for you to take home? If a passage refers you to a Scripture, why is the "What We Believe" necessary? Why also do many of the "big churches" publish their own versions of the Bible, typically with study notes at the bottom of every page?

The proliferation of Bibles that crowd the Bible bookstore shelves today began among the dispensationalists back in the nineteenth century. This was considered necessary in order to convince their members that God did not mean what the Bible actually says, but rather what they said it meant. Their failure to hold firm to the true and to the entire Word of God has caused the evangelical churches to become Judaizers of a sort. In a sense they follow Peter rather than Paul. Recall that Paul stood firm against the influence of the Judaizers when Peter and most of the other apostles caved in to it. Today, the very fact of the existence of "messianic" congregations who have separated themselves from the rest of Christianity, is mute testimony to what we are talking about here. These nice people think they are serving Christ, when in fact they are clinging to their Jewish traditions, some of which were antithetical to Christianity in Christ's day. Because Christ is not physically present, are those high places now in accord with Christianity? As an example, the Bible teaches a Sunday Sabbath that began on Resurrection Sunday, yet the "messianics" cling to the Jewish Shabbat (along with some others who are, without recognizing it, in rebellion to the living Christ).

But the self-removed evangelicals—removed from adherence to the Bible's gospel—are the greater danger. Jewish-style heresies have essentially taken over their thinking—at least that of their top leadership. This tendency has turned their theology into nonsensical teaching that is useless to God. This has taken different forms, depending on whom the author of their gospel is, but all forms spring from a common ancestral root. That root is self-interest. This results ultimately in several problems for their denominations. First, parts of the Bible are not being correctly interpreted, so they cannot be taught correctly. Second, this results in their teachers trying to prove scripturally their own suppositions or traditions. They have to bend the Bible to do that. Third, their "spin," based on a senseless hermeneutic imposed by the seminaries, requires them to ignore large segments of Scripture, either purposely or inadvertently.

The fundamental heresy that colors everything the evangelical believes, comes from what makes his denomination different from others. The difference is defined in his being a so-called fundamentalist. That means he believes that in the end days, God will essentially throw out all the work of Jesus and his church, and will return to an eternal attachment with everyone in the current State of Israel, all of whom will magically become believers on the last day. Evangelical leadership does not find it expedient to frame it quite that simply, or to mention that sort of stuff at all in the congregations. We will get to the variations on that theme and its importance, but for now let's not get bogged down in the details just yet. The very term *evangelical* is quite interesting. If you asked someone who calls herself by that epithet, it is likely she will be unable to succinctly define what it means. We know that the "evangelist" of the Bible fell into a particular class of ministry. He was someone who moved around and founded churches (Ephesians 4:11). Paul was an evangelist of the stripe Christ called for. Peter was a pastor who later entered into evangelism. So evangelical relates to *carrying* or *taking* the gospel to others. One can search fruitlessly through the so-called evangelical congregations in his town without encountering a single evangelist! But, evidently the oxymoron is not a matter of concern. Since virtually nobody in such denominations seized the robe of evangelism, it gradually took on another meaning, having in fact, if not in spirit, a connection to the Bible.

Ask any member of any evangelical sect what that noun means, and he will likely reply that "we teach salvation by faith in the atoning death of Jesus." Ask him what makes him a fundamentalist, and you may have to wait for an answer until he consults with his pastor. When he returns he will say something like, "We emphasize the literally interpreted Bible to be fundamental to Christian teaching and life." He'll be smiling, but he won't have a clue how that actually affects what he believes. Combined, these two descriptors paint the picture of someone who believes in two absolutely astonishing misrepresentations of the Bible! But he is happy because he knows the precise second in which he was saved. Peter didn't. Paul didn't. Matthew certainly didn't. Andrew and John didn't, but this guy does. It was when he recited the sinner's prayer when he took out an hour one Sunday and listened to a sermon, before returning home to watch the football game. Isn't that what saves everybody?

Fundamentalism began as a "movement" in Protestantism of the twentieth century. A "movement" is not something God starts. It's a manmade thing. This particular one was certainly well intended, but it stressed strict, literal interpretation of all Scripture as the guide to a proper Christian life. So what's wrong with that? Well, to start with, that dictates ignoring at least two levels of meaning in the vast majority of Bible passages. Then when two passages appear to conflict, one is obliged to find not concordance or harmony among them, but to remove one of the two from consideration as being "profitable for doctrine, for reproof, for correction, for instruction in righteousness" (2 Timothy 3:16). This caused development of doctrines that were not arrived at in consonance with God! It is clear in Mark 4:34 that through all his teaching of the disciples, Jesus did not speak without using a parable. It is incomprehensible how any Bible teacher could presume that there is some way to literally interpret such teaching, yet that is precisely what fundamentalists are dedicated to. That leads them to problems with their relationship with Israel.

They are Zionists for the reason that they have misinterpreted God's Word in the Bible. Their leaders have been dealing over the past several decades with the politics of American interests in the State of Israel. Fundamentalists have never ceased to lobby their own government on behalf of the militant political parties of Israel. Their fundamental heresy stems from a perception that Jewish priority and privilege for the nation of Israel *in toto* are specified in the Bible to be perpetual. The top leadership—you know who they are—view the New Testament church which Christ came to establish, as only a sort of makeshift arrangement by God (they call it providence). It is intended, they teach, merely to get the Jews through the difficult times of the biblical Great Tribulation. This tribulation, they also teach, is only for the Jews.

God, they feel, needs this sort of respite to get all his affairs organized so he will be ready with resources when he has to assemble his earthly armies to effect a final solution to the Jewish problem. He has to defeat the earthly armies of Gog and Magog (the composition of which have changed with the times) in a battle that will destroy two thirds of the Jews.

Those who may doubt or disagree with what is proffered here have only to avail themselves of some of the older writings of the twentieth century or even better, something newer. As a veracity test, one may simply go to the nearest library and peruse about three issues of any of the several Jewish or so-called Messianic Jewish, missionary-oriented magazines. *Israel My Glory* is one that comes immediately to mind. If a person were to do that, he would see clearly that present-day leaders of the groups who publish these magazines are devoted to the future of Judaic, not Christian, teachings. You see, the fundamentalists put on Jewish spectacles when they read the Bible. The magazines cry out for the continuance of not the Mosaic Law, but Jewish rabbinical tradition. They enthusiastically and repeatedly quote justification for nearly 2,000 years of continuing unbelief by Jews. They insist that the truth resides not in the teachings of Jesus in the New Testament, but in Jewish-inspired unbelief that insists there will be a Jewish "Messianic Kingdom" here on earth after Jesus returns. That will include a literal reconstitution of a literal, earthly Jewish temple located in the literal Jerusalem of Palestine. There will also, in their future vision, be a resumption of the Mosaic Law, complete with animal sacrifices, a priesthood, and holy days as specified in the Old Testament. This is the essence of today's fundamentalism. "Fundamentalistically" thinking, therefore, Jesus will have essentially died for nothing. An interesting perspective on evangelicalism in that light, is that the majority, if not all evangelical, fundamentalist leaders, believe in the gospel of the Jews! Because they slavishly follow the hermeneutic concerning their eschatological views (a manmade invention) they cannot agree with the entire gospel of Christ as presented in the Bible. They become Judaizers within the very church whose name they effect. As a result, many self-styled "Christians" today believe that Old Testament style Judaism will be revived in the last days.

This thumbnail sketch of fundamentalist Judaizers is, of course, incomplete. You also need to know that their propensity for something called "dispensationalism" is what contributes to the making of a fundamentalist. This is a propensity to establish theoretical divisions of history and to assume that the divisions are some sort of operable study mechanism that limits study of the Bible to certain propositions that they develop themselves. This is why they bump up against doctrinal imperatives such as the "Millennial Kingdom," which is a centerpiece of dispensationalist beliefs strictly because they do not allow themselves to glean all the meaning contained in Bible passages.

It has been said that they have erected their own monument to the coming of an earthly kingdom built upon the martyrdom of John the Baptist and Christ. The monument is testament to what they have chosen to believe, despite having to brush aside nearly 2,000 years of God's church as merely an interim measure! They have to accept the Christian gospel as something only partly true, so that their construct for Israel can be inserted where it was never planned for by God. They have adopted a gospel that includes Israel—the entire nation of Israel, which Paul called, "Israel after the flesh" (1 Corinthians 10:18)—as people chosen by God for eternity. In fact, the Bible is clear that God is interested only in the Jew who is one inwardly (Romans

2:29). These people have devised a heaven not for every Gentile, but one for every Jew. This has the effect of denying God's plan that includes a heaven specifically for the implementation of his plan of "grace." Dispensationalists plan a heaven here on earth for the same sort of Jews whom God would not admit to the land of Canaan.

The entire dispensational imperative has become immensely popular in our day. But in reality it has also become destructive to the true gospel of Christ. Christ's gospel is subverted where dispensationalism holds sway. This is doubtless part of why the candlesticks appear to have been removed from many, if not all, of the corporate churches today. The Holy Spirit is simply no longer functioning in the denominations. Witness to this reality is found in their records of service and humanity; the statistics on divorce, teen pregnancy, adultery, and promiscuousness, sexual abuse of minors by clergy, incidence of crimes among professed "Christians," etc. The situation today must be seen in its true light, which simply and realistically is that Satan has taken over the local churches! The Great Tribulation is here!

I.C. Herendeen asked the obvious question for us in his book, *Is Dispensationalism Scriptural?*

JUDAIZING CONGREGATIONS TODAY

THERE IS QUITE AN ACTIVE JUDAIST INFLUENCE AT WORK WITHIN the church today, and certainly it should be considered no less dangerous to God's church than were such influences in Paul's time. In some respects such influences are probably far more dangerous to Christ's church today.

Certainly the church of the living God is not about to come tumbling down. The danger is, as it was in the first century, not so much to the truly committed, but to those who may think they are of the true church but in reality are not yet saved. It also poses a source of irritation since it causes the teachers to have to re-plow ground they may have already seeded. It also is a source of disharmony, which it proved to be in the early churches under Paul, and we have no reason to presume that the same deleterious influences will not result in a similarly unhealthy influence on God's people as it was in the first century. In short, it does not help assure smooth operations in any congregation, being designed specifically to disrupt the status quo.

Then there is a collaborating force outside the church, which is allied loosely with the Judaizers within the church and with some in the corporate churches who may in fact not be part of the true, eternal church. As you know, we mere humans cannot discriminate effectively about who is and who is not really a "follower of Christ." That detail is not given us to know, but we certainly ought to be aware of the influences inside the "church family" because that can affect all of us.

You may already be feeling just how broad a subject is encompassed in attempting to isolate and describe the phenomenon we are trying to deal with here. In order to delimit the subject, we will attempt to shed the light of truth on only two aspects of it. First, anyone who wants to change the church that Christ founded into something resembling Old Testament Judaism. Second, those who do not want to change back to Judaism, but want to follow selected Jewish doctrines not consistent with traditional Christianity. Both are Judaizers according to the Bible.

"Well," some may say, "you have selected for yourself a gigantic population or field to study. Every denomination has attempted or would love to, change the church of God to its own image!" But that's not the big concern here, because most of those operate around an organization that at least loosely subscribes to Christian doctrines. They maintain what must be described as basically a Christian self-image and worldview at least. They really do not want to change anything major about the way the Christian church conducts affairs of the body, with regard to the leading of the head of that church. But precisely like the converts from Judaism to Christianity in the early church, today's supposed converts seem to want to hang onto their Jewishness at the expense of their presumed Christ likeness. One has to experience this firsthand in order to understand the difference. This is not intended to be a condemnation of Messianic Jews in any way, only an honest appraisal of what anyone who wishes to do so can experience for himself. Just as many well-meaning Christians are drawn to experience speaking in tongues or being "slain in the Spirit" and commit to that sort of sect because it is "different" and perhaps more "spiritual" (in their eyes) than traditional Christianity seems to be, so it is with messianic worshippers. The magazines of messianic organizations and churches proclaim not Christ as much as Abraham!

Pick up one of their magazines and see for yourself that their focus is upon Israel and the temple. To sit in one of their Saturday Sabbath worship sessions is to step back into the Old Testament, as men in prayer shawls chant Jewish-oriented inspirations for those assembled there. They blow the shofar. They read almost exclusively the Old Testament and sing Jewish music. And why not? Certainly there is nothing wrong with being a Jew who believes Christ was his Messiah. But the apostle Paul would argue that their men need not be circumcised—but they are. They need not eat unleavened bread—but they do. They need not try to keep the Jewish law—but they say they try! That also is their prerogative. But when Christians are not Jewish become enamored of the "quaintness" and "Old Testamentness" and go to a messianic assembly where they begin to observe the Saturday Sabbath and to keep the feasts because that's what their Jewish-Christian friends do, that's what Paul called a threat to the church! Peter and the other apostles agreed, way back in the first century! It is true that these dear people today are in a sense innocent of wrongdoing, because they are worshipping as they choose. They do not seem to be going into other denominational settings trying to effect change there, as was the first-century problem. The fault, if there is one, is with the gullible people who are not well-enough grounded in Christianity to recognize where the limits ought to be. Quite a few of them visit the "messianic" churches and decide to stay. Then does the trail not lead to the denominations they belonged to or worshipped with earlier? The old saying "what goes around comes around" certainly has application here. Today is no longer the first century! The problem must be recognized as poor teaching in the churches! Such things could be excused in the first century because the church was new. What is their excuse two millenniums later?

There ought to be concern in the churches about the growing fascination with the Saturday Sabbath, but there is not! The fundamentalist, evangelical churches have a focus that makes the situation with the messianics look miniscule. The problem is not simply that they, like the messianics, are Zionists. This focus is not necessarily one of slipping back into Judaism. It is rather a focus on supporting the nation of Israel financially, politically, and militarily, not because we love them, but so we "Christians" can use them to usher in "the Rapture" in our lifetime, and for our peculiar benefit! Now this is a broad and difficult topic to address. It is so entwined in international politics and in the teaching of the fundamentalists, to be almost impossible to separate into its parts. But this book intends to attempt exactly that difficult journey through the valley of deception, misinformation, deceit, self-interest, and death. That, however, is not the main thrust of what this particular book is attempting to achieve. Naturally that reality makes this journey through that valley not a detour, but a scenic drive, necessary to the true objective of the journey. The author certainly does not desire to encompass any broader area of interest than what was originally expressed in the introduction, so please bear in mind that this analysis will bear on the truth of God's revelation of the end times, contained in the Bible.

In order to accomplish that tasking, let us examine somewhat briefly what the teaching and motivation of the Christian fundamentalist denominations actually is. A fundamentalist is not that because he clings to the doctrines of the Reformation or of old-time religion, as would seem to characterize that label. As best it can be characterized today, with the changes wrought in it by modernism and dispensationalism, Christian fundamentalism grew out of a separatist movement in the nineteenth and early twentieth centuries.

It began in conservative denominations, chiefly as a reaction against the modernism that was creeping into the denominations. They got together and agreed upon a set of "fundamental" Christian beliefs that they held dear. These included the inerrancy of the Bible, the virgin birth of Christ, the doctrine of substitutionary atonement, the bodily resurrection of Jesus, and the authenticity of the miracles Jesus performed. Thus they drew their proverbial "line in the sand" as they were revolted by rationalism, liberalism, and what they called, "higher biblical criticism" among an increasing number of their neighbor denominations.

By the early 1900s, theirs had become a separatist movement and characteristically one of dispensationalist theology along, in some cases, with an interest in charismatic pursuits. Since the 1980s, the meaning of their identification has become somewhat blurred by the writings of one Lutheran theologist, Martin E. Marty. The characterizations in Marty's writing were picked up by the liberal media and began to be used in a negative way in an obvious effort to make fundamentalists look bad. Sadly, that was, at least at that time, not terribly hard to do. The American media, ever alert to any opportunity to dilute the reputation of Christianity, despite knowing nothing whatever about it, began to label the Islamic Hezbollah terrorists who held some American hostages in Lebanon, "Islamic fundamentalists."

Since that time the term "fundamentalist" has taken on a pejorative connotation that is undeserved but was doubtless intended. Then, before you could say "Pat Robertson," some of the stalwarts of the movement were being jailed and accused of being in fact, not such solid citizens as had been supposed. Robertson has been in the news repeatedly over the past decade for inflammatory comments, alleged fraudulent activities, and being a generally unsavory sort of fellow, which he might very well be. He has apologized, set the record straight, rephrased, and used his broadcast network to plug the holes in his dike, all of which appear to have been self-inflicted. But, reputations seem seldom to impact acceptance, these days.

Others in that triumvirate group, have just hunkered down and kept on piling up their millions of dollars. One has repeatedly been the target of misconduct allegations. Others cling to the fundamentalist label, while seeming to downplay their evangelical roots and seemingly dodging the dispensationalist handle entirely, through nimble footwork, not altered beliefs. Their ultimate goal, we must not forget, is to bring on the "Rapture" soon enough that they never have to physically die. They are seriously dedicated to that mission.

But make no mistake. These are dispensationalists who also call themselves fundamentalists. What they do not claim to be, happens to be their prime role in life at this point in time. That is, their role as Christian Zionists. The advent of their movement seems to have been facilitated by several nineteenth-century evangelists, including Dwight L. Moody and especially John Nelson Darby, who was known as the "father of dispensationalism." His popularity among the budding fundamentalist movement seems to have hastened the spread, among fundamentalists, of dispensationalism, especially after C.I. Schofield published his "Reference Bible" which was (and is) packed with dispensational theology, which gradually gained dedicated adherents among the fundamentalist community. There seems not to have been any single personality responsible for the birth of fundamentalism, as was the case with dispensationalism.

Fundamentalists see themselves as holding the fort not only against the tide of liberal influence, but also against the Pentecostals, though many fundamentalists are in fact closet "charismatics." They do not see themselves as evangelicals, whom they criticize for a lack of concern for doctrinal purity, and for being involved with other Christians who have differing doctrinal views. Of course, some fundamentalists are similarly accused.

For instance, evangelist Billy Graham began as a fundamentalist but was repudiated by many fundamentalists for cooperating with other Christians. So, his movement may be said to be one that arose from within fundamentalism, but outgrew it. He has been labeled "one of those Neo-Evangelicals." Although fundamentalism has certainly changed, or "developed," in different directions, there still exists a core who claim to be true fundamentalists, and there are some who fit into other pigeon holes better. Some evangelicals have adopted definitely fundamentalist doctrines. Many of the non-TV evangelists of today, who are nonetheless among the "giants" of their denominations, do not identify with what is known as the "fundamentalist movement." Today, what makes a fundamentalist different from an evangelical has become somewhat obscured, but remains an issue of doctrine.

SHALL WE BELIEVE THE NEW TESTAMENT?

SOME WHO GO ABOUT MAKING LARGE NOISE ABOUT BEING Christians probably never stop to consider that they may not be that at all but may be completely mistaken without even knowing it. This is particularly true when it comes to being evangelical.

That is because increasingly what it is that an evangelical Christian is—is open to ever changing definition. The state of "being" an evangelical was recently described in a national publication by an evangelical pastor as simply a person who "knows he is saved"! This has become a definition completely independent of any biblical support whatever, or biblical connection, as a matter of fact.

When something is told and retold by someone a person has been conditioned to believe is an authority, such as, let's just say, our pastor, that something becomes a part of our belief system.

That process is known variously, depending upon the observer and the circumstances, as instruction, propaganda, brainwashing, education, preaching, to name just a few of its potential characterizations. To evangelicals it has become, despite there being no instance in the Bible where there exists any suggestion whatever, that simply reciting a particular prayer can save a person. That is what most evangelicals believe, because that's what they have repeatedly heard from the pulpit. Merely being raised out of water after being immersed for "baptism" or merely confessing in the presence of others that one is a sinner guarantees salvation in other evangelical assemblies. In still others, the special work to be preformed amounts to a reflection of old-world Catholicism, in being prayed over at the front of the crowd. One or another of these surefire paths to immediate salvation is taught in a majority of evangelical denominations, despite none of them being included in the Bible's discussions of soul regeneration, commonly known as "salvation." But in all of them, the concept of a "free will" involved in being "born again" is mandatory, despite the Scriptures declaring repeatedly that men cannot become saved through any effort or will of their own at all.

Can we be children of that promise given to Abraham if we do not know, "If ye be Christ's then are ye Abraham's seed and heirs according to the promise," as the Bible clearly advises in Galatians 3:29? This wonderful statement of the fruit of the promise brings the Old Covenant to a close. It abolishes the law, recognizes that the temple is no more, that circumcision in the flesh has passed into history, along with the nation of Israel as a people special to God. Israel is, in reality, characterized in the Bible as a nation whose exclusive rights and privileges were squandered away and finally denied by God. This closing of the door on Israel, with God's acceptance of the heirs with Christ, gives his disciples what is necessary to their understanding of the law, the prophetic writings, and the prophets themselves.

If one is truly a disciple of the Son of righteousness, truly a follower of the one who came to end the curse of the law, truly a child of grace, then this verse in the Bible becomes the death knell of dispensational heresy. Yet that heresy has piled rubble into the sanctuaries of most of the Protestant houses of worship for a century! It will be recognized by the true believers as craftily dismantled legalism that aims to impose once again, in an age soon to come, all of the temporal qualities, the restrictions, the terrible costly mistakes that the Lord Jesus Christ came to once and for all time abolish. The true believer will know that there can be no washing away of grace in a "golden age" millennium of reimposed Jewish privilege, in a kingdom set aside for an entire nation which has never repented, never received the circumcision of the heart, never welcomed their Messiah. The true believer knows that Jesus has confirmed for him that there will never be a gospel of works to replace the grace of God. Yet the leaders of Protestantism do not know!

We earnestly pray that all of our readers will reflect that every cult, every false gospel that has sprung from the body of Christ in the past century and a half, has been, and is, a purveyor of the false doctrine of dispensationalism. It follows a doctrine that concludes that the fulfillment of Christ's work must lead to a revival of Jewish, of rabbinical traditions, dependent upon a gospel of works, a methodology of performance-based salvation, such as God has never, ever proposed. It is our prayer as well that the reader will reflect that one can have little hope of the blessings of heaven in his life or on his death if he continues to insult God's heaven through the impiety and folly of popularized but unbiblical religion.

It is my contention, arrived at deliberately and established with such force that it could be avoided only by ignorance of the Bible, coupled with a blindness that prefers obfuscation to truth, that the position herein advocated is precisely that contained unmistakably in the Holy Writ.

May we be allowed to inquire of our fundamentalist-dispensationalist friends what it was that the Lord God of Israel hid from the "wise and prudent" Jews of his day through parables, then revealed only to "babes" in Matthew 11:25? Could it have been that "the things" pertaining to his kingdom which he had come to establish on the ruins of the empire of sin and death, established by Satan and subscribed to by the Jews, could only be spiritual? This, when the Jews, even many who claim to follow God, expected that he would "offer" them a temporal kingdom. This was to be concealed, even is today, from all except those with eyes to see and ears to hear. Isn't that exactly what the Bible is telling us and that the fundamentalists are for some reason of their own , not comprehending?

Chapter four of the book that is the Epistle written to the churches in Galatia contains a final argument—that of the Apostle Paul—that proves two points for our edification. First, Paul shows us that God has previously proven conclusively that the New Testament church composed only of true believers is the legitimate and *only* successor of the Israelitish "church" of the Old Testament. This is shown by the work of "adoption," completed solely by Christ and performed in the hearts of all true believers.

Second, the apostle reinforces that concept of his church by an allegory (parable) built into and upon the biblical history of Abraham. It shows that the natural law is not Israel at all. It is Ishmael! He shows also how the church of the Gentile and Jewish believers is the true, the only, and the exclusive Israel of God. This being the reality of the promise, the prophesies of the Old Testament, given there to Israel, are to be understood spiritually, especially when they speak of literal and material restoration of "Israel" and Judah. This then becomes entirely the key to unlocking—to recognizing—the true meaning of prophetic interpretation.

In Galatians chapter four, Paul speaks of the Old Testament being the time of the minority—of the childhood—of the sons of God, the "heir" for whom it was necessary to provide tutors and governors. But only until the time when Christ was sent to redeem them in order that they "might receive the adoption of sons." Paul is saying that the people of God - the true church - had not yet "come of age." They were therefore treated much like a child in a rich man's household in which the child, one day when he is grown, will become heir to privilege, to an estate. But earlier, the child is treated little different from a servant, living under rules, regulations, tutors, and governors who restrict his liberty to enjoy fully the privileges which await him at some later time—"the time appointed of the father."

But in the meantime, Paul says of the Galations when they were unsaved: "When ye knew not God, ye did service unto them which by nature are no gods" (Galations 4:8). To what was Paul referring? He tells us as he continues in verse ten, referring to *the law,* "Ye observe days, and months, and times, and years." In verse nine he calls these "weak and beggarly elements." They are the "tutors and governors" that restrict the freedoms of the heir—the Mosaic Law of the Old Testament.

Paul makes it abundantly clear that he is speaking of the church in its Old Testament minority: "Even so we, when we were children, were in bondage under the elements [rudiments] of the world" (Galatians 4:3). The childhood form of the church was Hebrew. The "bondage" was subjection to the "rudiments" of visible temple, sacrifices, circumcision, and all the other legalities of the state of being "in the flesh" prior to the first coming of Christ.

Anyone who reads this knows what it means and knows that God cannot possibly intend to have his church go back again into the world of "rudiments" after being in the world of the light!

That is true for many reasons, not the least of which would be God having no desire expressed anywhere in the Bible to undo the "adoption of sons," which was entirely contingent upon Christ coming in the flesh. The preparation period was completed at that time. The true church passed from the law into the full glory of the gospel of full liberty in faith. All of the purposes, all of the promises have been fulfilled. They are complete. To suppose that God would then return to what was, is to deny Christ and his Gospel entirely! That's easy to imagine, but it's not so easy to imagine God falling for dispensationalism the way men have!

The dispensationalists evidently never supposed that God could surely add one and one and realize he cannot count either one a second time. These people want you to believe there can be a "time" after "the last time"—a kingdom to come after the "Kingdom of God" has run its full course, another age after the gospel age. Let's put all this another way. There truly is a difference between the spiritual experiences of the people who lived in the Old Testament, from those who live in the New Testament. The difference is not defined in the nature of their faiths or the quality of their salvation. The difference is in the spiritual status and privilege each could enjoy. They actually became saved in the same way, but most Old Testament people couldn't accept God freely. Christ provided full restitution of the soul in direct communion with God, through grace alone. The believer now receives the status of heir and has no obligation of service to outward ceremonies or uncomfortable rules which control his life. That's a huge difference!

We are very glad for one teaching aid that Paul provided to us in Galatians 4. That is his reminder of the Bible story of Sarah and Hagar, given in Galatians 4:21–31. He even agrees with good, modern exegesis and calls it an allegory in verse twenty-four. With this Bible lesson, we end all argument concerning prophetic interpretation. That is, we end it for those who trust the Bible for their instruction, after the manner of 2 Timothy 2:15 and 3:16. It is sad to have to report that fundamentalists, evangelicals, and dispensationalists mostly do not reflect such trust.

As the story goes, Abraham had two sons; the first was Ishmael, with the bondwoman, Hagar the Egyptian, with whom Abraham had no business getting comfortable. The second son, Isaac, was from his true wife, Sarah. Quite naturally, God rejected the first son as not being a true heir. The son of the true wife of Abraham's bosom was the "true seed" through whom God would deliver his promise to Abraham. But then, in verse twenty-four, we are startled to be told by God that Hagar, the bondwoman, is identified with the Israel of the Old Testament—the physical Israel—in verse twenty-five, "The Jerusalem that is." God also speaks here of two covenants, the first of bondage. We are often told from the pulpits that Ishmael is identified with the Islamic world. This must be a dispensationalist maneuver to deny the truth of the Scripture and impose their own gospel. Read it!

God is here telling us that the earthly Israel—the people of the original kingdom of Israel—are to be regarded as Ishmael! This is the most startling reversal in all of Bible prophecy, but that is so only because we have not "studied to show ourselves approved unto God, a workman that needeth not to be ashamed, rightly dividing the word of truth" (2 Timothy 2:15). Or perhaps we have believed the teachings of the evangelical churches, who pass over this verse without mention. You see, Israel remains today still in bondage to the law and not free. The true church—the church God created for himself, the church composed of both Jew and Gentile, without distinctions based on race, degree, or privilege—is the true Israel to whom the promises made to Abraham will always apply. Can you see in reading these passages that Hagar and Ishmael stand allegorically for the Jerusalem "which now is"—the earthly Jerusalem of Paul's time? But in the allegory, Paul says in verse twenty-six that Isaac (and Sarah) represent that which is free, the true gospel church, the "Jerusalem which is from above." The promise to Abraham was not for a free earthly nation of Israel, but is the promise of the gospel, a promise from which every "natural" Jew who ever lived is clearly excluded unless he walks the same road to salvation trod by every Gentile who was ever saved. More importantly, the road Jesus walked must also be his path. We invite the skeptic to regard the reinforcement to his allegory provided by Paul, in the words of the prophet Isaiah:

Rejoice thou barren that barest not [this is Sarah]; break forth and cry thou that travailest not for the desolate [the New Covenant—this may be a puzzle at first] hath many more children than she that hath an husband [the Old Covenant]."

Isaiah 54:1

Paul expresses the relationship rather tersely in verse twenty-eight: "Now we, brethren, as Isaac was, are the children of promise." As an apostle of the New Testament church, Paul is here speaking only of Christians—those who make up the true church.

In verse twenty-nine, Paul alludes to the envy of the Jews that was, and still is, expressed in persecution. Their privileges have passed to the new church, as Ishmael's privileges passed to Isaac. He concludes his argument (verse thirty) by quoting against the Jew precisely the words originally uttered against Hagar and her son, Ishmael: "Nevertheless, what saith the Scripture? Cast out the bondwoman with her son [the Old Testament and earthly Israel]: for the son of the bondwoman Ishmael shall not be heir with the children of the free woman [the New Testament church]" (Isaiah 54:1).

This is a dreadful judgment, but the Word of God is entirely unmistakable. Paul neither here, nor anywhere else in the Bible gives any hint of a "restoration." Only fundamentalists promise that, and it's doubtful they have the power to bring that to their patented conclusion. Had he wanted it to occur, would this not have been precisely the appropriate place for God, through Paul, to introduce the concept of a total restoration and abolition of Christ's earthly as well as his heavenly work? We honestly believe because of what we are told in the Scriptures, which seem to have been validated by God, that Jewish position and privilege are ended for all time. The Covenant has passed to the New Testament church, and only individual, believing Jews whom God has accepted have a place in that church.

Now, as we come to a close with this analysis of the problem of the churches in Galatia, the most purely Gentile of all the first-century churches, we reflect that Paul has let the Galatians know they have clearly been included in the Covenant. They shall enjoy the glory, the birthright, the privilege, and the redemption hope, of those who serve Jesus. His last words to the Galatians (Chapter four, verse thirty-one) were these: "So then brethren, we are not children of the bondwoman, but of the free."

Friends, the consequences of what we just finished reading here are far-reaching. Virtually all of the words of the prophets are addressed to "Israel and Judah" when prophecy of the New Covenant is foretold. They were, we have just seen, speaking of and to the New Covenant church, even though their words may be couched in terms of the "land of Israel." The topographical and geographical details drawn from earthly references, earthly territory of the twelve tribes, were "figures" of what was actually meant and designed to portray truths of the gospel to the few whose ears have been opened to hear God's Word. We are sorry to suppose, and greatly fear, that very few, if any, of our modern prophets and teachers in the corporations we know as churches are equipped by God to hear these words. How many of them do you suppose could hear God say, "Blessed are your eyes for they see, and your ears for they hear" (Matthew 13:16)?

So, to recap, we must say that the reason the Jews and their sycophants who think they are a part of God's church, reject Jesus their Christ today is the same as that for which the Jews did the identical thing yesterday. Of course today the Jews have the support of a great mass of their parasitic flatterers in the corporate church populations, which they did not have yesterday. Dispensationalism is new. Fundamentalism is new. Evangelicalism in multiple forms is new. Adventism, Mormonism, Kingdom Hallism, and other kingdom followers are relatively new to prominence, but all believe the kingdom of the Jews will supplant Christ's work! Their shared view started out to be that Christ was rejected for the same reason he is rejected today. That being because he did not bring the Jews an earthly kingdom as they expected. But the one prophetical theory that now prevails among all the "isms" mentioned above, and that binds them to the nation, or state, of Israel or whatever grouping the Jews choose to assume, insists that Christ in fact did "offer" such a kingdom to the Jews. Then, their theory posits, they rejected his offer, so the gospel was brought forth as a sort of substitute to that kingdom! Then, in the last days, they figure, God will relent and will give the Jews exactly the kingdom they crucified him for rejecting at his first coming. That's a wonderfully loving and forgiving attitude for God to have. It's just too bad it is not written into actual prophecy that way. Dispensationalists actually believe that what their heroes, the Jews, teach is valid. They expect Christ to gratuitously confer on Israel the very kingdom they crucified him for not offering in the first place! If one actually trusts Christ and what Christ breathed into the Bible, is there any imaginable way he could believe such a preposterous story? We must marvel at the hopeless dilemma our friends' theories involve them in. We ought also to marvel that the success of such theories, while obviously advanced by the power of darkness, have actually taken over the churches and have nearly destroyed meaningful scriptural understanding along with accurate exposition.

You see, there is no suggestion in the Bible that our Lord ever even considered, much less offered, any other "kingdom" but the one spoken of in his gospel. In fact, when we actually come to grips with God's salvation plan, not just with what we wish it to be, it is clear that Jesus never really "offered" anything to anybody he had not already prepared well in advance to be *able* to accept! Everything that Jesus put into a form that might have resembled an offer came with a caveat of repentance. This included the modified proposal of Jesus and John Baptist's common text, "Repent, for the kingdom of heaven is at hand." On the mount the only ones to receive that "offer" were "the poor in spirit," the "mourner for sin," "the meek," "brokenhearted," and those who "hungered and thirsted" for true righteousness. In every case, these were spiritual needs that he came to address.

It must be a terrific disappointment both to God and the dispensationalists that such dispositions are entirely wanting in the Palestinian Jewish population. In fact, it was such an embarrassment that the dispensationalists had to change their story a bit. They began to teach that the Jews had to go back to Palestine in unbelief, despite the earlier doctrine that this was precisely why they were cast out of there in the first place. So now they teach that "in a day" Christ will convert every last Jew in Palestine. Now understand—this will happen despite the Jews not being convinced that there will be an earthly kingdom of Christ. The reason they are not convinced has something to do, evidently, with their earlier experience with Christ—you know—having to crucify him since he wouldn't do what they wanted him to do the first time. Is that idea making some sense to you?

Oddly, despite the enthusiasm for rabbinical theory among those who espouse these dismembered theoreticals, these people exceed the rabbis in excitement over this supposed future. They actually have been known to advise the Jews that their present occupation of Palestine, despite its being in conflict with the Christian gospel and the prophecy of its author, is a fulfillment of prophecy. This is a part, no doubt, of that unwritten prophecy that says the ungodly zeal of the Jewish establishment against Christ and biblical truth is to be surely rewarded in the near future. What reward would that be? Why, they say that God will reward Jews with an instant faith. Now, understand, this is despite the evangelical opposition to those parts of the Bible which say that faith must be given to men by God. That means one is left to suppose that, although Christians get their faith without any help from God (despite the claims of Scripture to the contrary), Jews have to get theirs through an act of God. At any rate, this extraordinary largess on the part of God will be the fulfillment of the promises originally made to Abraham.

This, the reader should recognize, comes despite the biblical claim that those promises were already fulfilled. This can be seen easily in the book of Galatians. The reader should read carefully, from the King James Bible, Galatians 3:7–9 then 3:16, followed by 3:26–29. There are others as well, but what God promised Abraham is distilled conveniently and very readably in these verses.

We are left to believe either the dispensation theorists, or the Bible. Can upwards of 80% of the corporate church memberships possibly hang their hats on doctrine that is in direct contravention of the Bible? Apparently they do!

In Galatians, Paul has already shown clearly who Abraham's seed are. That's to whom the promises will be paid. Paul says not a syllable about any restoration of Jews to Palestine. Like Jesus, the apostle builds all of the intent of our Lord, with the church as the lawful extension of Old Testament Israel. That makes the church the heir—the inheritor—of the Abrahamic Covenant, along with all the other riches Christ offers. There are no Jews listening in when Jesus says, "I go to prepare a place for you," and talks about the many homes for his church in heaven. These are not efficiency apartments, but "mansions" he is preparing. Likewise, Peter seems not to be aware of this great gift to the Jews when he speaks of Christ returning "as a thief in the night." Had Peter known, he doubtless would not have finished 2 Peter 3:10 with language of "heavens passing away" and "the [all] elements melting with fervent heat," and surely would not have mentioned that "the earth also and the works that are therein shall be burned up." But Peter needn't have worried, since the dispensational gospel discounts this entire passage and a number of others that do not serve their life goals. You'd think that if Jesus was going to completely switch signals, he'd have let the fellows who were responsible to get his church going, in on it.

But to a man, they knew of no other "second coming" apart from the one that cancels out the earth and the heavens in one

big bonfire. Where do you suppose these several earthly kingdoms will be set up—the one for Jews, the one for Jehovah
Witnesses, that of the Christadelphians, the Adventists, and
Armstrongites—these folks are all convinced that their "special"
kingdoms will be right here on this planet!

I am sore afraid for them, that the Apostle Paul would have
to conclude, as do we today who believe the Bible, that those
folks have been sadly misinformed on what the Bible says about
these matters. Although there is a different topic being discussed in Romans 1:20 where the Bible tells us that "they are
without excuse," it is clear from the sentence that follows, that
God means that men who know God and do not glorify him
will one day stand guilty as accused, before his Son.

LIGHT FROM GALATIA

THERE ARE A MYRIAD OF VARIED AND DIFFERING BELIEFS ABOUT virtually every doctrine we associate with Christianity. These are differences between professing Christians—between groups of people all of whom think they are saved.

Much of this seems to be due to lots of folks not carefully reading the Bible. That means, if this observation is accurate, there are many, including leaders in the corporate churches, who are too complacent to study. Perhaps they feel as if they already know it all. There may also be many who really don't believe God really requires that his followers must continue to study. (This knowledge comes from five years of adult Bible teaching.) Then there are undoubtedly those who simply can't be bothered to actually seek the meanings God put for them into the Bible. Among this last category is a group that includes the "strap hangers" in the congregations, who are there to look like Christians. This likely includes many of the mega wealthy, so-called "Christians" who abound these days.

Those who attend churches, for whatever reason they do that, have mirrored the community at large, since about the middle of the century recently closed. So they constitute a fairly productive group in which to study "types" and dispositions. We can say for instance, without significant concern of being mistaken, that Christians represent almost ideally the proof of some very common sociological observations concerning human nature "ad genera." Wealth, as an example, is seen to wrap itself in arrogance, among professing evangelicals. We see that regularly, in the many wealthy TV evangelists who abound today. Once they get to the top of the offering plate, such men gain power, which we have watched corrupt some of them over the past two decades. It was not surprising to see one of them in a political campaign for president! Watching the arrogance and power manipulation in that group of men and women prompts one to abandon the idea that a Christian can hold a very high public office in today's environment without abusing it.

In that environment, the American Christian community in recent years, and in overwhelming numbers, has taken on a surprisingly similar character to the Galatians of the New Testament Bible. They in fact are being misled down the same wrong path by the identical influences that pulled the Galatians churches in the first century, away from the teachings of Lord Jesus Christ. The influence of the Judaizers is alive and well today, just as it was when Paul wrote his letter to the Churches of Galatia, and Christians still need to beware of it. That Epistle from the great apostle to the Gentiles, Paul of Tarsus, to the churches in the region of Galatia, seems to be the best short course in the Bible on just how men are saved. But it does more than that. If read diligently, and with a true desire to be informed, the book of Galatians can go a long way toward settling the controversy over how the end times will play out, according to God's plan. But there are those who think God requires some prodding.

A modern controversy was given life by a majority of church teachers refusing to consider the entire Bible, when they constructed the framework for their own end-times doctrines. We say "their own" because they have largely ignored the teachings of what we call the New Testament when it comes to eschatology, the study of the doctrines of the "last days." Then when that failing is coupled with the arrogance and lust for power that seem to be relatively new among Protestants, you have the situation existing in the churches today.

While the vast majority of confessing Christians are in fact not dispensational-believing fundamentalist Zionists, they have been captured by the high appeal and artificial glamour of the fundamentalist end-times vision, which is not found in the pages of the Bible. Basically, their idea is supported in dollars spent on books and movies, by the evangelicals who have bought into the end-times charade marketed by profit-seeking fundamentalists. They are convinced they can gain ground on their political goals by having lots of Americans believe what they believe, concerning something called the "Rapture."

That is the influence of the Judaizers who remain alive and well in the guise of fundamentalist Christians, and "Messianic" Jews. Entire congregations are allowing themselves to be led down an incorrect path by Zionist beliefs shared, not with Christian heritage, but that of Old Testament Jews, in exclusion of the teachings found in the New Testament.

Recognizing the popularity of such misleadings today, one would scarcely expect many to believe what was just written here. We therefore, leave it to God and the Bible, to explain what needs to be examined by everyone who wants to go to heaven. Will you join me in allowing the Bible, and nothing but the Bible (*sola scriptura*), to show you what we firmly believe God wants you to know? I will simply try to assist in guiding your study, as together we involve ourselves further in the Apostle Paul's letter to the Galatians. It doesn't even require reading the entire book. We will examine only parts of the short third chapter of the Epistle to the Galatians, recognizing of course, that in the original manuscript, there were no chapters, no numbered verses. The situation Paul is presented with, is that the Galatians who first became saved, recognized that they got that way by the action of the Holy Spirit, and by hearing the gospel of Jesus Christ preached, just as believers today are saved. Paul knows that, because he was the one who preached to them and established their churches on his first missionary journey. He made later visits, reinforcing the gospel he had first taught them. Somehow, Paul learned that they had since departed from the truth and had been tricked into falling for a lie! The lie was that all believers must be circumcised. Where can this come from? Paul does not suspect Hindus or Buddhists have been meddling in Galatian beliefs. The scalpel seemed to very likely point at men whose religion included "cutting" rituals. Paul knew who that would be. Only the Jews taught a doctrine of salvation through specified works. The same problem exists in many congregations today. Some insist on a requirement for water baptism. Others have different rituals such as reciting a certain prayer, or joining into a membership, or asking the Lord to come into one's heart. These are all works that someone must perform, so their doctrines (their gospels), include a requirement for performance in order to be saved. But the Bible contains no such requirement. None at all! As we work through this one chapter of Galatians, you will see that, and I hope, begin to wonder why nobody ever showed it to you before.

In addition, you will see that the "promise" has, ever since God first created man, been one of salvation by grace. Many of us were taught that the Old Testament claimed a salvation plan different from the New Testament. You will see today that this is simply not the way the Bible explains salvation! You will see that there is one and only one, salvation plan that God has ever been concerned with in the entire Bible. You are going to be able to prove to yourself, using only the Bible, why the law was given, and why performing *any* works associated with salvation puts one back under the law, where he cannot be saved. You will learn (and this may affect everything you have been taught about the end times) that not the Jews, but Jesus Christ, is the seed of Abraham.

So your next step is into chapter three of Galatians. The entire book is wonderfully instructive, God-breathed reading. But chapter three alone should be sufficient to give you a strong desire to read all the rest of the book of Galatians. Here is verse one: "O foolish Galatians, who hath bewitched you, that ye should not obey the truth, before whose eyes Jesus Christ hath been evidently set forth, crucified among you?" The English word *evidently* used here was a poor translation, which makes understanding a bit more difficult than it needed to be. The Greek word used here in the original autograph, has a meaning closest to the English "before written." That makes the line beginning after "Jesus Christ" mean "has been set forth in what was previously written." We find out a little later that Paul is referring to his own teaching to them, from the Old Testament. That was of course, the only Bible available to them at that time. But we will see that was enough for them to learn the gospel of Christ! "Before whose eyes" tells us they "saw," or were able to visualize, from Paul's earlier teachings, Christ on the cross, crucified in their presence.

As an aside to what we are reading, why do so many doctrines exist today that strive to teach some requirement for us to perform, in order to receive the gift of grace? We humans seem to share some kind of problem with the idea of an unmerited gift, given despite our not deserving it! Would it be a gift, or would it be a payment to debt and not a gift at all, if we had to work for it? The Bible suggests that pride is behind all our sins and tells us that pride itself is sin. Perhaps it is pride that makes us want to be recognized for something we do. Have you ever pondered Galatians 2:20? There we read that if we are saved, we have been crucified with Christ. There would be nothing left of the old us! The sort of person we are after that crucifixion, we owe (all of it) to Christ. We give him all the credit! Must we then not view every doctrine to which we subscribe, in that light? If Christ has done it all, then where is our ability to acknowledge to ourselves what we claim to believe? It's possible that pride stands in our way!

But let's go back to chapter three, and have a look at verse two, bearing in mind that this comes though the same process in which verse one was received. It's a continuation of Paul's question: "This only would I learn of you, Received ye the Spirit by the works of the law, or by the hearing of faith?"

In some denominations, the faithful would, if they were truthful, have to answer by saying, "by the works of the law." Those who had first to be baptized, or had to ask Jesus to save them, or had to recite the sinner's prayer, have no choice in their answer! Of course Paul's was a rhetorical question, but yours to yourself should perhaps not be. The Bible is going to tell us that no one *ever* receives the Holy Spirit for doing works, and that works are of the law. Performance is of the law, whether we have been taught that or not! What about this "hearing of the faith"? Does Romans ten, verse nine not say, "If thou shalt confess with thy mouth the Lord Jesus, and shalt believe in thine heart that God hath raised Him from the dead, thou shalt be saved"? Don't we Christians consider this God's faithful promise? And it is faithful. It was the same in the Old Testament. Here is what God promised in Jeremiah 29:13. Note how similar this is to New Testament doctrines, "Ye shall seek me, and find me, when ye shall search for me with all your heart."

But what then are we to do with Romans 3:10–11, where God declares plainly that, of ourselves, not one of us will ever seek him? "There is none righteous, no, not one; there is none who understandeth, there is none that seeketh after God." That's a flattening statement! He tells us in other Scriptures, that we are blinded by sin. We do not possess the spiritual ears necessary to hear God's invitation, and we can therefore in no way respond to it! (Romans 11:8).

But God did decide to save a remnant of true believers. He chose just some, before the foundation of the world, and the hearts of those few, he inclines toward salvation. He gives them ears to hear. So, the only reason some few will believe in Christ, is that God has drawn them to himself. You may read about this in the Bible book of Ephesians. See Chapter one, verses three through six, nine through eleven, and chapter two, verses one through three, and eight through ten. As a matter of interest, God has written of this foreknowledge of men, even in the Old Testament, and still most of those who call themselves by his name, deny such truths! God told Jeremiah in chapter one, verse five of the Old Testament book that bears his name, "Before I formed thee in the belly I knew thee; and before thou camest forth out of the womb I sanctified thee."

The fact that most denominations fail to teach these and other passages of truth, allows them to pervert the gospel with requirements that God does not specify, in order to be saved! Men will come to very different conclusions if they are fed with all of the pertinent Scriptures. But if we are spiritually dead, and none will seek God, how can we make confession of our sins, or even know we should? We can once again, learn of Christ's salvation plan from the *Old Testament,* this time in the book of Ezekiel, where we find the prophet saying, "For I will take you from among the heathen. [...] Then will I sprinkle clean water upon you, and ye shall be clean [...] a new heart also, will I give you: and a new spirit will I put within you" (Ezekiel 36:24–26).

It is God who cleanses the sinner, who gives him a new spirit—the Holy Spirit—and an entirely new, not-reconditioned heart (soul). The evidence has two parts, first that God says he does it, and second, the sinner suddenly begins to confess the Lord Jesus Christ, because he has just realized that, in his heart he now believes that Christ is indeed who he said he is. Before long he will begin to recognize that God has also raised him from the dead. To "confess" Christ, means that the saved sinner has recognized that God has chosen him.

Having given this new heart, how do you suppose God gives us the faith we need, in order to trust him? Did you notice back in verse two, Paul mentions not the hearing "in" faith or "through" faith? No, the hearing is the hearing *of faith,* and it's talking about the faith of Jesus, in going to the cross to die for those he came to save. Romans 10:17 tells us, "So then faith cometh by hearing, and hearing by the Word of God." Hearing the word, means hearing the Gospel preached. That's the hearing to which verse two refers. But we said that before God drew us we were spiritually dead, so we would not seek him. We also couldn't hear him until he personally opened our ears to his word and to his call. In the salvation plan laid out for us in the Bible, we can obtain saving grace, only by hearing the Word of God, the Gospel. That depends on us having received new, spiritual ears. An example from the Bible is found in Romans 10:18, where God is talking about the nation of Israel: "But I say, have they not heard? [...] verily, their sound went into all the earth, and their words unto the ends of the world." God is saying that the Israelites did hear with their physical ears. Their problem was, they never came to believe, because as God says in Romans 11:18, "God hath given them the spirit of slumber, eyes that they should not see, and ears that they should not hear."

So it is clear that, trusting in God, believing in Christ Jesus, is entirely a function of God's personal actions on behalf of those he chose to save, "before the foundation of the world" (Ephesians 2: 4–10). Next, Paul asks a telling question of the Galatians in chapter three, verse three, and his words are not terribly polite: "Are ye so foolish? Having begun in the Spirit, are ye now made perfect by the flesh?" They were initially saved by the grace of God, through the Holy Spirit, just as it occurs today. He asks, "Now do you think living by the flesh (the law) will perfect you? Again, it's a rhetorical question, and again, the answer is no. Yet, my friend, there are many churches today, where they teach foolishness such as when a person was saved all his past sins were covered by the blood of Christ, but to remain saved, the person must enter into "good works"! O foolish Galatians! Such teachings thrive because of man's pride. Man wants somehow to be able to take some credit, in some way, for the completed work of God. Isaiah said in chapter fifty-three, verse six, referring to Jesus, "All we like sheep have gone astray; we have turned every one to his own way; and the Lord hath laid on him the iniquity of us all." Hebrews 12:2 declares that "Jesus is the author and finisher of our faith." This means that Christ Jesus is wholly responsible for the beginning of our program of salvation, and he also will complete it, without any help from anybody, including the person being saved! He is, after all, God, and that's what he does. In the interest of clarity, we shall read verses four and five of Galatians three connected together, since that's the way they appeared in the original Greek manuscript of our Bible:

> Have ye suffered so many things in vain? if it be yet in vain. He therefore that ministereth to you the Spirit, and worketh miracles among you, doeth he it by the works of the law, or by the hearing of faith?
>
> Galatians 3: 4–5

Note that Paul considered suffering to be pertinent to a discussion of salvation by grace. In John 16: 33, Jesus gives those who are saved the warning that, "In the world ye shall have tribulation." But he reassures them with the words, "but be of good cheer; I have overcome the world."

You and I couldn't have overcome the world in order save ourselves, but Christ could and Christ did! But we also know that the Great Tribulation is upon the churches, and that is already bringing suffering of a sort we did not really anticipate. Fortunately, the saved have been reassured by Christ that, if they endure, in the end they will have victory. Persecution will be a part of the suffering in the tribulation, that is even now upon the churches. Suffering is not new to believers. Tens of thousands of Christians were martyred because of their faith and are being martyred today, in places like Sudan. Persecution inside the churches often takes the form of ridicule—the ridicule of actually faithful people by the unfaithful in the churches who take the Bible lightly, who interpret it liberally, and obey it only marginally. Paul may have meant that the Galatians will suffer greatly on judgment day, if they continue in a grace-plus-works gospel. Certainly, it is also possible, that not until that day, will many learn that they were in fact not saved at all!

The Thessalonian church knew something about suffering, and Paul spoke of that:

> ...For ye also have suffered like things of your own countrymen, even as they have of the Jews: Who both killed the Lord Jesus, and their own prophets, and have persecuted us; and they please not God, and are contrary to all men: Forbidding us to speak to the gentiles that they might be saved, to fill up their sins always: for the wrath is come upon them to the uttermost.
>
> 1 Thessalonians 2:14–16

As Paul himself suffered for Christ at the hands of his own countrymen, so did the Thessalonians. We too can expect some of the same as we follow Christ. When those who were lost in sin, and trapped in the realm of Satan, respond to the gospel, they become enemies of Satan. He will use the unsaved to persecute the saved. This is the reason for Christ's warning in John 16:33, above—to emphasize his point that, believers are saved entirely and only, by the grace of God, and because of the faith of Jesus. The apostle rephrases in the end of verse five, the question he asked in verse three, but he here declares it is God who "ministers" or gives, the Holy Spirit to those he chooses to save. The question then becomes, "Does God give us the Holy Spirit because we have done good works, like being baptized in water, or because we reached out to Jesus?" Or is it by hearing the faith of Jesus spoken of from the Bible? It is the latter, and he facilitates that, by giving us spiritual ears, that we may hear and understand the Gospel. He also freely gives the gift of Christ's faith, which accounts for the responding of the new believer, to the Gospel message, and he gives the Holy Spirit to ensure salvation. It is all by gift, all by grace, and totally unmerited.

Some will be bothered by what seems to be a conflict with the words of Revelation 3:20. But be assured, the Bible does not contradict itself. It is up to us to determine how to understand the interrelationships that seem to our minds, to be conflicting. Here's that passage: "Behold, I stand at the door and knock; if any man hear my voice, and open the door, I will come in to him, and will sup with him, and he with me." On initial reading, it does appear that unless we open the door, we will be denied salvation. The free-will crowd says, "Oh, God won't force his way into anyone's heart. He waits for us to decide and open the door." That idea, however, does not come from the Bible! It contradicts completely what the Bible is teaching in these passages. This entire verse is keyed to the hearing of God's voice. But we have already learned that no one can hear God's voice unless God has already chosen him for salvation! We will not, we cannot, respond to hearing, unless that hearing has been turned on, to and by Christ. So it is, that Christ does not waste his own time. When he comes to knock on the closed door of a sinner's heart, Christ will give the sinner spiritual ears to hear the knock, and to respond to Christ's call. Then will he come (now pay close attention to this) *into* that person. The translators did not handle this verse quite properly. Our Bible says "in to," but if we survey this passage in the Greek, we find it actually says "into." Is that not precisely where God makes his habitation, once he has extracted a soul from hell? When the knock comes, we can be assured, because the Word of God says it is so, that the receiver of grace was already earmarked and had no personal influence whatever in the matter. It is then, that our Lord will enter into him and "sup" with him. The verb *sup* refers, of course, to a meal. That meal is the wedding supper, or marriage feast, of the Lamb of God! This, dear reader, should be recognized as the full-fledged miracle that it is!

It's probably appropriate here, to diverge just slightly but purposefully, just long enough to consider the case of miracles. There's just something about miracles. Many congregations these days place a lot of emphasis on miracles. They call them, as the Bible does occasionally, "signs and wonders." The New Testament Bible word for miracle is not one, but three! Three separate words are found translated into one. Makes one think of the Trinity, hmm? The first word is typically translated into either *sign* or *miracle*. This places the word into the category of a verb—an action word. The Greek *semeion* we find used, when God chooses to set aside some of his created processes—what we call "natural laws"—to achieve his purpose. Matthew used this word when he told of Jesus "multiplying" the loaves and fishes to feed a herd of folks who hadn't packed a lunch. He also used the word when he wrote of walking on water. We find *semeion* used also by John. The favored disciple used the word in John 2:11, referring to the vinting of wine from water, in the very first of "semeions" performed by Jesus. Why was such an action employed? The Word of God on that subject is, that "This beginning of miracles did Jesus in Cana of Galilee, and manifested forth his glory; and his disciples believed on him." The second of these three Greek words that we find translated into a form of *miracle* is *teras*. We find it translated always in the Bible, to the English word *wonder*. Recall that not only Jesus, but for a time after his ascension, the apostles also, performed "signs and wonders." For the apostles, these were all what we might categorize as,"human" miracles. They were concerned with physical healing, and bringing the dead back to life. There may have been lots of such signs and wonders performed by the apostles, but only a few are mentioned in the Bible. After the Bible was finished, there was a hiatus on these demonstrations of God's power through men. They had to do with revealing God to the condemned. After that period, the Bible was given as the only source of God's revelation (Revelation 22:18–19). "It is finished" our Lord cried from the cross.

There is another reason as well for God not employing signs

and wonders when he is not visually present. They didn't produce faith! They were not meant to do that. Recall with me that in Matthew 12:39, when some of the scribes and Pharisees asked him to produce a sign, Jesus snapped back at them, "An evil and adulterous generation seeketh after a *semeion*." The Apostle Paul explains the attitude Jesus displayed, showing that Jesus wants men to, "Walk by faith, not by sight" (2 Corinthians 5:7).

One clear purpose of such displays by Jesus and the Apostles, was verification of credentials. That was in a day when people were most impressed by signs and wonders. It was a lot like today! We like to think we are very sophisticated, yet any unusual occurrence, and especially an out-of-the-ordinary action by someone, draws an inordinate amount of attention in our society. That may be why Satan is said in the Bible, to employ attention-getting activities as time approaches its end. Jesus warns in Matthew 24:24, that in the last days, "... there shall arise false Christs, and false prophets, and shall shew great [semeions] and [teras]; insomuch that, if it were possible, they shall deceive the very elect." If the "very elect" were to pay attention to the Word, they might recognize that in every instance relating to biblical descriptions of end-times miracles, such activities are attributed by the Word of God, to Satan! Read the last sentence again!

Now, before we return to the main message, we said we would examine three Greek words. We need to examine just one additional word translated into the English as *mighty works* or sometimes as *miracles*. Interestingly, the same Greek word, *dunamis,* is found even more frequently, where in English we read *power*. Then, there is yet another curious aspect to this word *dunamis*. The power it speaks of, is closely associated with works of salvation. An example is found in the book of Acts, where Jesus, speaking to his apostles, immediately prior to his ascension back to heaven, says, "But ye shall receive power (dunamis), after that the Holy Ghost is come upon you; and ye shall be witnesses unto me both in Jerusalem, and in all Judea, and in Samaria, and unto the uttermost part of the earth" (Acts 1:8). More to our point here, *dunamis* is the word found in the last verse we read, chapter three, verse five, of the book of Galatians. Look back at that verse, and where you read the word *miracles,* know that the same word often means "power" and that, power is typically connected to salvation. So, let's look at verse five again, and substitute power to see if salvation is in any way, suggested there for "miracles":

> "He [God] therefore that ministereth to you the Spirit and worketh miracles [power] among you, [gives you the power of salvation] doeth he it, [gives you that power] by the works of the law, or by the hearing of faith?
>
> Galatians 3:5

This certainly does seem to make verse five a lot more understandable. Again, we see throughout the Bible, that God is concerned mainly with the concept and ideas, of salvation. The saving grace available from God, *is* the message of the Bible! But there is another reason why this is an important point in Paul's teaching.

POWER AND THE
CORNERSTONE

THE TEACHING OF THE APOSTLE TO THE GENTILES WAS CRITI-
cally important in the Lord's battle against ignorance and
heresy, in his newly established church. It is also, or certainly
should be, a cornerstone in understanding today's church, and
what God is attempting to teach his followers about his world
and its future. But many- most in fact- are stoutly resisting his
teaching.

What is being revealed here in the Epistle to the Galatians, could not be more important to understanding why the
construct for the end times, of the dispensationalist teachers,
and the so-called fundamentalist churches, is entirely bogus!
The fundamentalists who follow C.I. Schofield's version and
vision of the Bible, are also influenced by the Judaist Zionists,
in arriving at what for them, passes as Bible truth. Paul shows
the Galatians the error of those known in his day as "Judaizers."

We hope to demonstrate with successive scriptural proofs, that not the dispensationalists, not the fundamentalists, not many of the evangelicals today who follow the doctrines of these two groups, but the Apostle Paul, had the correct interpretation of the Bible!

This chapter will reconstruct for you, several separate and actually related, but distinctly different viewpoints, from which God's message of salvation can be clearly seen. This is important to recognizing the errors in end-time theology, which grow out of incorrectly interpreting God's redemption plan for mankind.

What you will see, by the time we finish this examination, is the glaring difference between what is taught in the majority of corporate churches today, in most popular books, movies, and lessons relating to the end of time, and as it is described by the one who will make it all happen. The reader may be quite surprised at what will be encountered here.

We discussed verse five of Galatians chapter three, in the previous chapter, but we will be retracing that verse, since it actually represents an introduction to the four vantage points from which we will be examining Paul's words. Leading up to our understanding of verse five, Paul discussed power, as well as signs and wonders, as they related to salvation. Then we read how our Lord declared that such displays at the end times, and in the Great Tribulation, would not come from God, but from Satan, who will take over the churches. Not the true church, of course, since it is composed entirely of God's elect. The corporate agencies that meet weekly to mix both believers and unbelievers, are the domain of Satan, during the Great Tribulation. We traced the connection of miracles, of signs, and of wonders, to power—the power of God, and in the end times, power given by God, to Satan. It is he, who will be the only source of miracles during the last days. If it were otherwise, how would anyone know who is doing them? This is the distinction that allows true believers to be assured in our day, that the phenomenon of tongues, for instance, cannot be of God. Revelation 22:18–19, makes that clear. The only miracle God is performing today is that of birth. This includes being born into the world, and being born into the kingdom of God. Dreams, messages, visions, falling over backward, etc., cannot be from God, according to the Bible! We would ask you here, to go back a couple of pages, and look once more at the quote from Matthew 24:24. You will be looking at the words of Jesus!

The Bible foretells that the churches will become apostate. Certainly the Bible does not teach that the entire church will rebel. But because some in the corporate churches are not saved, there will be falling away, as there was in national Israel, and there will be some unfaithfulness. Jude speaks in one way about this reality, telling us there will be "mockers in the last time, who should walk after their own ungodly lusts" (Jude 17–18). Second Peter 3:3 repeats this almost identically. For those who say this is meant for those outside the church, why would it then even appear here, since everybody knows what is certain? For the skeptics, 2 Peter 2 shows clearly who is being spoken of: "There shall be false teachers among you, who privily shall bring in damnable heresies, even denying the Lord that brought them [...] and many shall follow their destructive ways."

It is clear that in the "last days," heresies will divide the church. This is already happening all around us. The popularity of fundamentalist teaching, offers abundant proof of that reality. The Zionist cause is being advanced as this is being written. If you are not entirely conversant with the false prophesy these comments are directed to, you will be familiar with their content before you finish reading this book. Now, having covered the aspect of power, as a way of opening up scriptural truth, it is time to move on to verse six of Galatians, chapter three. When reading what follows, remember that although we have a lot of discussion here after verse five, in reality, verse six follows directly after verse five and embellishes upon it:

"Even as Abraham believed God, and it was counted to him for righteousness."

Abraham keeps popping up in the epistles as perhaps the best example of how someone gets saved, be he an Old or New Testament character. That's because the process was exactly the same in both time periods. Some denominations teach that there were two or more salvation plans in God's bag of tricks through the ages. That is taught because they do not read the Bible carefully enough to gain an understanding of what it contains. That phenomenon is quite easy to understand, and to explain. You see, it's just a fact of the modern church, that many teachers and scholars, approach the Bible as a means to prove whatever it is they have preconceived into their doctrines. They fail to apply the doctrines built into the pages of that wonderful book, because they have their own gospels to teach. Yes! It really is as simple as that.

But right here, we who truly desire to learn from the Bible, instead of trying to insert something into the Bible, have to proceed slowly and carefully. Abram obeyed God, both in leaving his homeland and people, and in preparing to sacrifice his son, Isaac. It was the second testing of Abram that draws the most attention. Abram was not rewarded for doing what God asked. That part of his response was a "work." God was not in debt to Abram for work performed. Hebrews 11:17–19, may shed some light on this idea for you. There we read: "By faith Abraham, when he was tried, offered up Isaac, and he that had received the promises, offered up his only begotten son." This part of the verse speaks to the reality that here are two entities, two persons, who are being spoken of. One, is obviously Abraham. But who is "he that received the promises"? God is definitely in view. We know that, from the language of the "only begotten son." But God received no promises. Isaac was the child of a promise, and the only begotten son of Abraham, so he must actually be, the second person here. So, we are seeing Abraham as a "type," or representation, of God the father. He is the "father of many nations." In finishing the sentence, we see that relationship clearly, "of whom it was said, that in Isaac shall thy seed be called: accounting that God was able to raise him up,[if necessary,] even from the dead."

So Abraham believed God sufficiently that, he was certain God would, in the worst case, raise his son from the dead. God had after all, promised that Isaac would receive the promise and would bless many nations. But you and I have to be careful, not to suppose that this verse, is in any way, suggesting that Abraham's trust in God, something Abraham did, resulted in God regarding Abraham as righteous and rewarding him for his trust. This would be an internal contradiction in the Bible, and we know that the Word of God does not contradict itself. We can go to Romans chapter four, to find guidance. In verse three of that chapter, we read: "For what saith the Scripture? Abraham believed God, and it was counted unto him for righteousness." Here we have the very same rationale as that expressed in Galatians 3:6! Then, if we read the next verse in Romans four, we find the author (God) saying, "Now to him that worketh is the reward not reckoned of grace, but of debt." Had Abraham done some sort of work to become saved, his personal salvation would have been a reward rather that a gift by grace. It would have turned into God paying a debt of salvation. That would not have been consistent with the Gospel! If we continue reading into verse five, we see, "But to him that worketh not, but believeth on him that justifies the ungodly, his faith is counted for righteousness."

So then, one may ask how we rectify this with what we learned in 1 John 3:23, where we find mankind commanded to believe on Jesus Christ? That's part of the law isn't it? It sure is; and if someone obeyed the law to become saved, that would be a work, and that someone would not be saved by God's grace. But, let's just remember, there is no salvation under the law, only under grace, so it's a moot point. Yet sadly, we find ourselves surrounded by whole congregations full of people trying to get themselves saved by works! By being baptized in water, by asking God into their hearts, by reciting a certain prayer, by learning to speak in meaningless gibberish, and other actions, none of which God cares a whit about! None of which he has asked for, from his elect. It can be confusing if the churches do not teach the whole Gospel. What we have said above, reinforces what is found in Romans 3:20: "Therefore by the deeds of the law there shall no flesh be justified in his sight; for by the law is knowledge of sin."

Do you feel the reinforcement you are receiving from each of these successive passages all saying essentially the same thing? That's my hope for you. Now I want to direct you to the next three verses of Romans.

> But now the righteousness of God without the law is manifested, being witnessed by the law and the Prophets. Even the righteousness of God which is by faith of Jesus Christ unto all and upon all them that believe; for there is no difference; for all have sinned, and come short of the glory of God.
>
> Romans 3:21–23

It is the righteousness of our God that saves, and that righteousness flows out of, or because of, the faith, not of us, but of Jesus the Christ! Ephesians two, verses eight and nine, support this, as one would expect. We read there, that it is grace that saves, and it is through faith that the grace comes. But it is not speaking of the faith of the believer. That comes after salvation as a second gift. The first faith, it says, is the gift of God. And we are then assured that the gift does not come from works, lest any man should boast! If we are truly saved, we have nothing to boast about. It was completely the gift of God, who did all the work to save us.

If any teacher ever takes the time to actually add up the work that God had to do to get us saved, he would realize there is nothing anyone could possibly do, that would have any bearing on getting someone saved! Sadly, not one teacher in one thousand, is willing to do that sort of calculation. It is impossible to comprehend why! It may be supposed, that to do so would interfere with the preconceived doctrines they want to slip into the Bible. It has been oft said, that men can prove anything using the Bible. To that saying, should be appended the parenthetical words "to themselves."

The above references show why Romans 1:17 says, "For therein is the righteousness of God revealed from faith to faith; as it is written. The just shall live by faith." Another way to say this might be, God's righteousness is revealed by the faith of the Lord Jesus Christ, demonstrated in his going to the cross, and given as a gift to those he has saved. The point of all this then, is for us to recognize, that when we read of Abraham "believing" God, we are to recall that Abraham's faith, was a result of the faithfulness of Jesus, in providing justification, and the faithfulness of God to provide the salvation he promises. The faith Abraham received, was the evidence that indeed he had become a child of God. So, this understanding leads into verse seven, of Paul's epistle: "Know ye therefore that they which are of faith, the same are the children of Abraham."

Most true believers already know that individually each is considered to be a child of God, and that collectively they are the children of God. From this point forward, we are dealing in an area that, when we have finished, will put us into a position very different from teaching by fundamentalists. To be saved, puts Christians collectively, into the category of being God's chosen people, or at least among the chosen people. Fundamentalists and Jews teach, that only the nation of Israel is still "God's chosen people." Hold this in your memory bank, as we progress through this study, because the truth will come out in the wash!

Verse seven (above), puts any who have been separated out by the same faith, that selected Abraham, into the category of being "children of Abraham." Now, according to the Bible, the children of Abraham—his "seed"—are inheritors of what God promised to Abraham and to his seed. Since Abraham has always been considered the father of Israel, the Jewish people, wherever they lived, always considered themselves the seed that was promised to Abraham, and therefore, the inheritors of the promise. But, there is a conflict in apprehending who is what!

If as we claim, we in fact, consider the Bible to be inerrant and the word of Almighty God, can this failure of apprehending be the fault of the Bible? Must our answer, of course, be no? Yes, it must be no! Then the fault in apprehending, must be that of the observer, along with any teacher whom we have relied upon, if our conclusions have been other than what we just exposed as truth in the Bible. Let me assure you, that any disparity in beliefs, can be attributed to teachers who take their knowledge from the Old Testament, without updating their knowledge of the Bible story, with the New Testament. This is precisely the problem with end-time theory, as espoused in the fundamentalist churches. In essence, their eschatology is crippled by their desire to experience a different scenario, from the one God placed into the Bible. We will expand on that as we go along.

Let's turn our scan just slightly, to view our scene through the eyes of God, as concerns whether or not God would agree with the Jews, that only they are the children of Abraham. We refer you to the words of Jesus, contained in the book of John. There, in chapter eight, verse thirty-nine, wherein Jesus responds to the assertion of some Pharisees, that Abraham is their father. Jesus said to them, "If ye were Abraham's children, ye would do the works of Abraham." Who is Jesus to judge? Only God; that's who! Here, he is saying that, despite being blood descendents, in God's eyes they are not Abraham's children at all! Had they been, they would have followed the example of Jesus and trusted in God, instead of trying to kill him! Jesus follows that, in verse forty-four, with a declaration that they are sons of the devil. If we accept Bible truth, the Pharisees must be seen, as representing the spiritual condition of all the nation of Israel, apart from the very few who trusted in God for salvation. This reflects the problem that so-called Messianic Jews have today. They believe they are saved from the wrath of God, but still they consider themselves of the nation of Israel. Obviously, God will sort them out, but it may be very disappointing to some of their number!

Now, we have come to what will be a very important and descriptive passage for the reader. Here, Paul tells the Galatians, "And the Scripture, foreseeing that God would justify the heathen through faith, preached before the gospel unto Abraham, saying, in thee shall all nations be blessed." (Galatians 3:8) If any Jew or fundamentalist ever tripped over this statement, it would be a bombshell for him! Fortunately, none has ever read it, from what can be determined from their doctrines. What does it seem to be saying to you? Is it not telling the reader, that it was always God's plan to offer grace to the Gentiles? Of course, that's exactly what it is saying. Naturally, the Scripture foresaw God's plan. Not only that, it was somehow given to Abraham long before the Scripture was ever written down! The words *all nations* certainly do not limit the selection to Israel! Telling Abraham what is contained in the last phrase of this verse, amounts to delivering the Gospel to him! Then we know that God repeated that promise numerous times on subsequent occasions, both to Abraham and to Isaac, and Jacob as well. We find instances of this (for example) in Genesis 26:3–4 and Genesis 28:13–14. God also told both Abraham's son and grandson that, "in thy seed shall all the families of the earth be blessed." The phrase "all the families of the earth" likewise, did not limit the blessing to only the families of Israel.

But significant to note, is that with both of Abraham's descendents, a part of God's promise became a grant of land. That was actually a part of the original promise to Abraham, back in Genesis 13. That was when God told Abraham to look in all directions, and everything he could see would be his.

Another time, God promised Abraham "the land of Canaan." A significant part of that promise, was that it was to be an "everlasting possession." Why significant? This is a point made today, by Jews and adopted by fundamentalists—the point that Isaac and Jacob never, in their lifetimes, received the land that was promised. Their descendents did, however. That occurred in 1948, and the Jews insist that the secular State of Israel is that "seed" of whom the Bible speaks the words of inheritance. But God did say to Isaac and to Jacob, that he would give the land to them and their seed. So, did God break that promise? If not (as I maintain), how not? Can you figure out how God could do that?

If the possession was to be everlasting, could any of the recipients of the promise possess it that long? The Bible does not always solve such riddles for us, until some later analysis has been done. We know that the Bible does not lie, and God's Word is always good. So, how would it affect the promise, if the land was only symbolic of something else? Well, what if Abraham, Isaac, and Jacob's descendents, accounted for the "everlasting" part? But we still have the problem of their not having received the land. All right, what if the land symbolized a place they would go for eternity? But what about their descendents not being saved? Most of them were still under the law! Or, could the promise have been fulfilled, when Joshua led the Israelites into the "promised" land? But if it was, how do we handle the information that we—the Gentiles—according to verse seven that we just looked at, are the children of Abraham, that all who have faith, i.e., have been saved, become those children? What if God has to raise up the children of the promise at some future time to give them the land?

If that were the case, when would that be likely to happen? There may be a clue to that, in John chapter six. Four times there, Jesus says he will raise up those who have been saved—all of them, on the *last day*." Then Martha, speaking under the influence of the Holy Spirit, in John 11:24, about her brother

Lazarus, says she knows that he will "rise again in the resurrection at 'the *last day*.'" The last day is that day in which Peter said, in 2 Peter 3:10, that "the heavens shall pass away with a great noise, and the elements shall melt with fervent heat, the earth also and the works that are therein shall be burned up." Then in verse thirteen of 2 Peter, we are told, "Nevertheless, we, according to his promise, look for new heavens and a new earth, wherein dwelleth righteousness."

It would seem that we now have sufficient information to conclude that the children of the promise, are the righteous—the saved. This includes Abraham, Isaac, and Jacob, and all will be raised up on the last day, and given their inheritance. That inheritance will not be land on this earth, since we know from studying the books of Matthew and of Revelation that the earth and the universe will be destroyed on that same day. We are talking here, about the last day of the earth's existence, the last day of time as we know it, the day eternity begins. So the land of the promise, appears to be the new creation, and that fits, since it will be eternal! That's when their everlasting possession and ours, will begin. We see this solution grow more prophetic when we read Hebrews chapter eleven and its last several verses. There, God speaks of a group of Old Testament men of faith, believers, children of the promise. It closes with these words, "And these all, having obtained a good report through faith, received not the promise: God having provided some better things for us, that they, without us, should not be made perfect."

This makes Old and New Testament believers equal before God. All who are saved have been or will be, saved by the same gospel of grace. All have been given a good report through faith—the faithfulness of God. For all, the consummation will be on the last day, when all will be called into heaven with Christ.

Many teach that salvation by grace occurs in only one "dispensation"—that of the church age, in New Testament times. This is a doctrine originated by Zionist Jews, shared by Messianic Jews, fundamentalist Zionists, dispensationalists, and many evangelicals. They represent a large segment of today's churches. They say that the New Testament period was simply an interlude when God, disappointed in his rejection by the Jews, decided to save some Gentiles. Before the cross, they claim, God had a very different salvation plan for the Jews. Then, they go on to state that, after the end of the current "dispensation," God will make Israel another offer, the offer of a new dispensation, in which Israel will again, be made a great kingdom. Unfortunately for these dear people who think they have it figured out, God may be saying he never knew them!

They continue to seem not to recognize, that God is in charge. These folks also share the common belief that God promised to give a specific plot of ground on this earth to the Israelites, and that he will make good on that promise. Many theologians argue that God is still obligated to fulfill that promise, and that somehow or other he will. Well, in light of what we have already proved to our satisfaction, using nothing but Bible passages, let's examine this claim. Do we think God remains obligated to this promise, first given in Genesis 15, verses eighteen through twenty-one? Unlike his other promise, God did not include Abraham, but only his descendents in this one. He also does not mention everlasting possession. But then, there was another promise as well. This one was from Moses, speaking for God and warning the nation of Israel not to be disobedient to God. In the next chapter we will examine that promise, using the Bible.

A PROMISE OF MOSES

I**N THE BIBLE BOOK OF DEUTERONOMY, MOSES TOLD THE NATION** of Israel:

> And it shall come to pass, that as the Lord rejoiced over you to do you good, and to multiply you; so the Lord will rejoice over you to destroy you and to bring you to nought; and ye shall be plucked from off the land whither thou goest to possess it.
>
> Deuteronomy 28:63

According to theologians looking ahead to a golden age for Israel, the twelve tribes never received all the land included in the promise. But God seems to have some differences with that opinion. God placed the following information into the book of Joshua for all to see, including the Jews and the fundamentalists. But neither wants to admit that it exists. It's likely neither has been given eyes to see! Here is what Joshua had to say. See what you think it discloses:

And the Lord gave unto Israel all the land which he sware to give unto their fathers; and they possessed it, and dwelt therein. And the Lord gave them rest round about, according to all that he sware unto their fathers: and there stood not a man of all their enemies before them; the Lord delivered all their enemies into their hand. There failed not ought of any good thing which the Lord had spoken unto the house of Israel; all came to pass.

Joshua 21:43–45

Or, we can examine the words of God written by the prophet Nehemiah, as can anyone who wants to seek the truth of the Bible:

Thou art the Lord the God, who didst choose Abram [...] and foundest his heart faithful before thee, and madest a covenant with him to give the land of the Canaanites, the Hittites [...] to his seed, and hast performed thy words; for thou art righteous.

Nehemiah 9:7–8

Can anyone read these quotes from God's Word, and still doubt that the promises were completely fulfilled in God's opinion? You have to wonder, what part of "hast performed" they fail to understand. Does any other opinion matter to this study? God is here, flatly declaring, that he *owes* Israel exactly nothing! He says clearly, that not only has he performed as specified, but that he did so because he is a righteous God. We can see easily that the reason Israel never completely possessed the land is because they never completely followed God's commands!

This last, was a prerequisite! Now, would you say that anyone, it matters not who he is, that says God owes national Israel some land, is absolutely contradicting what the Bible says? Someone ought to tell the fundamentalists!

But one must suppose that, if they are willing to contradict God, they are not going to bend to any persuasion from a book written by a mere man. Their position on eschatological matters is a political one, clearly having little to do with

Scriptural considerations. That position is explained elsewhere in this book. We come now, to verse nine of Nehemiah, which summarizes what was contained in the preceding three verses: "So then they which be of faith are blessed with faithful Abraham." Now, right off the bat we need here to recognize and internalize, the reality that Paul is using this language to impart something to the Galatians, and therefore to us. Being "of faith" refers to someone who has been saved. The "faithful" being used here, to describe Abraham, is actually in the Greek more properly translated, "believing," but "faithful" should elicit the correct interpretation in us also. This too, refers to someone who has been saved. *Blessed* is the Greek word meaning to be "well spoken of." A great many pastors apply the meaning "happy" everywhere they find the word *blessed* in Scripture. That is a sign of sloppy, inadequate study. The important element is the "who." Who is it, that does the blessing—the speaking well of. It's the same one who does the saving! The message of Paul is, that anyone who is saved, Greek or Jew, is as tight with God, as was Abraham. They are among those spoken of as Abraham's "seed." Whether or not a person is a blood descendent of the prophet, if like Abraham, he has been given by God, the faith to believe God, and has been saved out of the faith of, and through, the blood of Christ, he is considered by God, to be among the children of Abraham! Why would that be? Because that qualifies him to receive the promise! The Old and New Testaments offer the very same gospel of salvation. This is an undeniably significant doctrine of the Christian faith, built upon the words of Romans, chapter four that we surveyed earlier.

But why, some will wonder, is this so very significant? For the reason that it totally invalidates the erroneous gospel, in high fashion among the Messianic Jews who think of themselves as Jews who are also Christians, along with the fundamentalist Christians who dominate the so-called Christian book, movie, and video markets. When you contemplate the big names in so-called "Christianity" today, the very wealthy come first to mind. These are the men who champion a gospel that has no relationship to the Bible, apart from being absent from between its covers.

The Galatians were being assailed by Judaizers, come from Jerusalem to stir up the church and try to bring in heresies, much as is being done in many churches today. (Paul is going to emphasize that whoever tries to keep the law is damned.) Paul didn't have the book of Romans to back up his teaching. He was constrained to using only the Old Testament, because that was all that existed then. Had the book of Romans been available, Paul would doubtless have shown the Galatians, that Romans 4:12 shows clearly, that Abraham was the father of the circumcision (the Jews).

But that he was also the father of all who believe, circumcised or not! He is, in short, the father of all believers. National Israel, this is saying, is certainly no exception. Abraham is not the father of all Jews just because they are Jews and circumcised. He is the father of all Jews who believe in Christ Jesus. Abram, we must remember, was accounted righteous by God *before* he was ever *circumcised* with a stone knife! The prophet did not promise anything at all to all of the Israelites!

It is no stretch of imagination at all to understand why Abraham's spiritual family had to extend beyond national Israel. First, almost none of the Israelites ever believed, and second, God told him he would be the father of not one nation, but of "many nations."

We also need to understand "the curse." With verse ten, Paul begins to discuss the problem he sees from the standpoint of trying to work for salvation. He starts in Galatians 3:10 by saying, under the inspiration of the Holy Spirit, that if someone tries to do the works of the law in order to gain salvation, whether he knows it or not, he is under God's curse. He turns to Deuteronomy 27:26 in the Old Testament as his basis for this observation, and it becomes not only the pattern for his words, but also a serious warning to his listeners: "Cursed be he that confirmeth not all the words of this law to do them." Paul is saying, "If you're going to do the law, you have to do all of it—every last bit of it." We find a reiteration of Paul's warning also in the New Testament book of James. "For whosoever shall keep the whole law, and yet offend in one point, he is guilty of all" (James 2:10). This certainly ought to clarify the point for anyone who needs it! What Paul is showing the Galatians, whom he really does love or he probably would not have spent so much energy on them, is that every human being that God creates (since Adam and Eve) comes into the world equipped with natural sinfulness. Even King David recognized the sinful condition of mankind. He wrote in Psalm 51 verse five, a thousand years or so before Paul was born, "Behold I was shapen in iniquity, and in sin did my mother conceive me." In Psalm 58 David also wrote, "The wicked are estranged from the womb: they go astray as soon as they be born, speaking lies" (verse three).

That strikes most of us as kind of harsh, but these are words approved by God to go into his Bible! Even before baby men and baby women see the light of day, this says they are in rebellion against God! We humans were cursed before we were born.

Paul's next argument is intended to show that, nobody can get justified by, or because of, the law. This is a change of pace designed to build upon what he has already said. Another way to look at this next argument in verse eleven of Galatians three, is to think of it as going like this: "You can't get saved by the law. You can't even get justified by the law for crying out loud!" Now, let's hear Paul, "But that no man is justified by the law in the sight of God, it is evident: for, the just shall live by faith." Think of *faith* in this verse as meaning conviction or reliance upon Christ for salvation. The author likes this Greek meaning, because it seems to contain a wonderful counterpoint to speaking of the law. If one accepts the meaning above, this passage says, "Man cannot be justified by the law, since his salvation will come through trusting Jesus, and then too, God said it is not going to happen any other way!"

Even more important to our understanding, perhaps, is that Paul was always scriptural in his teaching. In this verse he borrowed again from the Old Testament, this time from the book of Habakkuk. That's not a book most of us quote a lot from, but it is the Word of God. As the Galatian churches had heresy problems, and just as the churches today are mired in it, apostasy overtook the Southern Kingdom (Judah) when Habakkuk was a prophet. This disturbed Habakkuk, and he pleaded with God to let him know why God allowed such wrong teaching in the synagogues. God did reply, and he told Habakkuk to be patient, that change was coming. That change was to be in the form of the Chaldeans (Babylon), who would judge Judah and destroy it. This put Habakkuk into despair until God told him that the Chaldeans also would get their just desserts in good time, and that God would save "his people." God told Habakkuk to write the following verses:

> And the Lord answered me, and said, Write the vision, and make it plain upon tables, that he may run that readeth it. For the vision is yet for an appointed time, but at the end it shall speak, and not lie: though it tarry, wait for it: because it will surely come, it will not tarry. Behold, his soul which is puffed up is not upright in him: but the just shall live by his faith.
>
> Habakkuk 2:2–4

This passage eludes translation to some degree. The "puffed up" soul is rendered "lifted up" in the King James Bible, lending itself to the idea of a haughty or proud aspect. But regardless of what resolution is assigned to that phrase, the final phrase is clearly determined. The Hebrew word *tsaddiq,* here translated *just,* signifies right, righteous, or rigid, in a spiritual sense. So, we can accept that the writer was referring to someone who is "just" in the same sense that the word is used in Hosea and Ezekiel, speaking of men of God. This is a man whom God has chosen, a saved man, and here in the Old Testament it is recognized that he is such, due to his faith in God, not to his keeping of the law. The import of this passage is that it clearly demonstrates that God has never advanced more than this single, defined redemption plan from the very beginning. God will save only those who will live by faith. His next turn in this discourse brings Paul into the same argument, but from an opposite direction. He has established in the minds of his listeners in verse ten that if a man tries to keep the law, he is under the curse of the law, because there is no way he can keep it all. He will surely disobey some part of it eventually. Then he goes back into the Old Testament to show that the law will justify no one, because the law itself says in the book of Habakkuk that it cannot, that man is justified by faith. Paul will next show that because it is not founded on or responsive to faith, the law cannot possibly justify anybody because it simply is not of faith. He says this succinctly in Galatians 3, verse twelve: "And the law is not of faith: but the man that doeth them shall live in them."

Paul takes this idea from the Old Testament also, showing that there is plenty of evidence there to make any case that needs to be made, concerning God's salvation plan. This direction of assault on heresy comes from Leviticus 18:5, which says, "Ye shall therefore keep my statutes and my judgments; which if a man do, he shall live in them."

Many take verses such as this to mean that God is encouraging the Jews to keep the law, and he was! But he does not say this is the road to salvation. What he is saying is, "If you keep my law, you will have to live by the law." But in no way did God mean therein is the path to heaven. This is still misunderstood by a great many theologians, especially those who somehow have come away with the idea that for a society to attempt to keep the law, guarantees the entire society redemption from the curse of the law! This is essentially the teaching of modern fundamentalists. The bottom line of this group of verses is that Paul is trying to show the Galatians that since the Mosaic law does not operate on a foundation of faith, and since it is clear that those who are seen as righteous by God, live by faith, anyone who chooses to live by the law will remain under the curse of the law, unsaved, because no one can keep all of the law.

Paul goes once again into the Old Testament Bible, this time to show why it is, in contrast to the folly of following the law, a man can have an expectation of eternal life, solely and completely by faith.

> And if a man have committed a sin worthy of death, and he be put to death, and thou hang him on a tree, His body shall not remain all night upon the tree, But thou shalt in any wise bury him that day; (for he that is hanged is accursed of God;) that thy land be not defiled, which the Lord thy God giveth thee for an inheritance.
>
> Deuteronomy 21: 22–23

Here is Paul's message in verse thirteen to the Galatians. Notice that this brings together in an inseparable bond, the interdependence of the two covenants. Notice also, how Paul goes right to the point: "Christ hath redeemed us from the curse of the law, being made a curse for us: for it is written, cursed is every one that hangeth on a tree." Christ, in other words, has redeemed those he came to save from the curse of everlasting damnation, which comes to all who are not of him. Notice also, that in the passage from Deuteronomy, to leave someone on a tree overnight cursed not the man who was hung. He was already cursed. This was a representation of the second death. Leaving someone hanging cursed the entire land! The entire area of that tribe's possession! This is why the Pharisees were in such a hurry to get Jesus down from the cross. It would have been doubly bad, evidently, if the next day was a Sabbath. The penalty that our Lord Jesus paid for us, was the penalty of hanging from a tree—the second death—which is the wrath of God. That is in part why no one can do anything to get himself saved. Only God himself could arrange to have that penalty paid, and he did. To presume that something I could do would grease the skids for me would be heresy and an insult to Christ. Let's move on, as Paul did, to verse fourteen in Galatians, chapter three.

Now, just before we read verse fourteen, let's go back to verse thirteen, which leads into fourteen. The first phrase, "Christ hath redeemed us from the curse of the law" is what verse fourteen follows. Standing alone, this next verse stands rather awkwardly: "That the blessing of Abraham might come on the Gentiles through Jesus Christ; that we might receive the promise of the Spirit through faith."

What an incredible gift this was! Is it not shameful (the better word is *elusive*) that mainstream Christian leaders in the fundamentalist and dispensational ranks fail to accept this part of Christ's sacrifice as truth (we must suppose)? What they cannot for some reason comprehend, or perhaps do not desire to recognize, is the enormity of what our Lord gave. Those who trusted in him received a portion of his great faith—enough to believe he was who he claimed to be. Then they received the first promise, their own budding faith that would grow eventually into perfection—the same faith that Abraham received. They also escaped another promise—the promise of eternal damnation, suffering the wrath of God for all eternity. Then they received the blessing—the same blessing that Abraham, Isaac, and Jacob received (this is the part the fundamentalists deny). This is the promise of a place to spend eternity with Jesus as joint heirs to his kingdom. Abraham received what was promised through faith. Christ died so that some of the Gentiles might share in the promise to Abraham. That is the blessing Paul was so adamant to get across to the faltering Galatians. Paul didn't have Revelations 13:8 to refer to, but we have. What more proof of God's intent is necessary than this verse from the last book of the Bible, which we believe shows that, from the beginning, God intended to make the promise of Abraham available to the Gentiles. This verse calls Christ, "The lamb slain from the foundation of the world."

In essence, the second half of verse fourteen, is a restatement of what is contained in the first half. The first half was fulfilled the night before Jesus went to the cross. Remember it? Our Lord made this promise to his eleven remaining apostles: "I will pray the Father, and he shall give you another Comforter, that he may abide with you for ever; even the Spirit of Truth" (John 14:16–17). Peter repeated this on Pentecost. The "promise of the Spirit through faith" in the second half of the idea begun in verse sixteen is presented in verse seventeen. It is essentially the earnest, the down payment, for our redemption! Being "sealed" with the Holy Spirit is the down payment, the guarantee, that the saved will indeed receive their inheritance.

In following through this, have you stopped at all to wonder how anyone who actually studied the Bible could possibly not understand grace enough, to recognize the fallacies in the arguments of the Judaizers about the requirement for circumcision? How about the requirement for anything, beyond grace leading to faith? Of course, in that day, the New Testament was not available. But neither was it to Paul! And it is available to modern fundamentalists who insist that, at the last day, God will redeem all the Jews, because they are his chosen people. That eludes comprehension, and we should pray for all of them.

Paul now begins yet another new approach to explaining the gospel of grace. Verse fifteen of Galatians, Chapter three; "Brethren, I speak after the manner of men; though it be but a man's covenant, yet if it be confirmed, no man dis-annulleth, or addeth thereto."

Paul here likens God's promise to Abraham, to the sort of testament men draw up to divide their estates. Once a will has been validated, it cannot be changed, except by the author. After he dies, it remains as written, and its instructions have the force of law. The implication here, is that God's covenant, is likewise binding. He continues into verse sixteen, maintaining the analogy to a last will and testament, saying, "Now to Abraham and his seed were the promises made. He saith not, And to seeds, as of many; but as of one, And to thy seed, which is Christ."

What a shock that must have been to the Judaizers in Paul's audience (and to modern fundamentalists). Paul declares that the seed spoken of is the Lord Jesus Christ, and not at all the blood descendents of Abraham. Now, to deny this revelation, is to discount the truth of the Bible! That is what many today have done, while they still insist, they are true to the Word of God.

Notice that Abraham himself, was the first beneficiary of the promise. But why would Christ, who didn't need to be saved, be named as a beneficiary also? Christ is God. He does the saving. He was sinless. But we must not forget that he came as a man. He died as a man and needed to be, figuratively at least, taken out of hell, in order to pay for the sins of "many." There are, as a matter of fact, some other biblical references to this necessity. Will you look at Psalm 69? We can know this is a Messianic Psalm, because the first half of its verse nine, is quoted in the book of John. We find, "For the zeal of thine house hath eaten me up" in chapter two, verse seventeen of John. It is in connection with Christ chasing the merchants out of the temple. Then the second half of Psalm 69:9, when you read carefully, shows us that it is speaking of Jesus when it says, "and the reproaches of them that reproached thee are fallen upon me." Doesn't that suggest Jesus becoming sin for you? Our reproaches all fell upon our Savior, and he forgives us for them. Interestingly, Jesus was a beneficiary, but he was also testator of the will, which meant he had to die in order to make it produce what it promised. But he paid all the debt under the will, and the curse as well. But, he also had received God's promise of salvation from hell. He was resurrected, and he inherited the title to the new heaven and the new earth. According to the promise, all who are in Christ, and he in them, are joint heirs with Christ.

Dear reader, before you sleep tonight, will you read the song of Zacharias, the father of John the Baptist? It's in Luke chapter one. It's not very long, maybe seventy-five words in verses sixty-eight to seventy-three. But it fits nicely here in our thought pattern concerning the covenant. Knowing that it would be his son, the son of a priest, who would introduce the Messiah to his people, Zacharias praised God. His thanks were for the one who was coming to perform, "the oath which he sware to our father Abraham." Zacharias, an Old Testament prophet and priest, knew that Jesus "would perform" what was necessary, to fulfillment of the promise! He understood God's salvation plan. But how could just a very few catch on, and so many others miss his message? Well, isn't that exactly what is happening today?

Now, as we approach verse seventeen, please look back behind your eyelids for a moment at verse fifteen, in which Paul argued that even the terms of a human last will and testament cannot be altered once validated. He is now going to tell the Galatians that God's testament is a much bigger deal! "And this I say, that the covenant, that was confirmed before of God in Christ, the law, which was four hundred and thirty years after, cannot disannul, that it should make the promise of none effect."

Here's the argument: the promise was made to Abraham and subsequently confirmed by God. Once confirmed, the law certainly cannot nullify it, because the law didn't come along until 430 years later. (In a way, that's sort of a moot argument, since somehow at least parts of the law trickled out as early as Cain and Able. Remember they were doing sacrifices?)

But this referred to the Mosaic Law, making that a valid comment. The 430 years was the time the Israelites spent in bondage in Egypt. We learn that from Exodus 12:40. The law was given shortly after they escaped across the Red Sea. This suggests that God may have reiterated his promise just before, or as, the Jews went into Egypt. Let's suppose this promise was made to one of the original beneficiaries, like, for instance, Jacob.

THE PROMISE FOR JACOB

AS A MATTER OF FACT, THERE WAS ANOTHER PROMISE. AFTER Joseph had made himself known to his brothers, he asked them to bring his father, Jacob, to Egypt. Recall that God had renamed Jacob "Israel." The name was not original prior to God giving it to Jacob. So Jacob (Israel) brought all of his family into Egypt. In Genesis 45:28 we read, "And Israel said, it is enough; Joseph, my son is yet alive: I will go and see him before I die." (Notice Israel did not say, as the sitcom Jews do, "enough already.") And he went. And sometime about then, God spoke to him in a dream. This is recorded in Genesis chapter forty-six and is the confirmation to which the verse above refers: "Jacob, Jacob. And he said, Here am I. And he said, I am God, the God of thy father: fear not to go down into Egypt; for I will there make of thee a great nation: I will go down with thee into Egypt; and I will also surely bring thee up again" (Genesis 46: 2–4).

The New Testament book of Hebrews gives emphasis to the inability of the promise to be changed:

> Wherein God, willing more abundantly to shew unto the
> heirs of promise the immutability of his counsel, confirmed
> it by an oath: That by two immutable things, in which it was
> impossible for God to lie, we might have a strong consolation,
> who have fled for refuge to lay hold upon the hope set before
> us.
>
> Hebrews 6: 17–18

It seems likely that the reason God so often repeated his
message of the covenant, was to make it clear that the promised seed of Abraham was he who would bring salvation to all
nations. Moreover, that he would come through the bloodline
of Isaac and Jacob, not through that of Ishmael or Esau. This,
by the way, was shown in genealogies as far back as the book of
Ruth.

Paul now comes at the difference between the law and the
covenant yet another way. He is going to say, in effect, that if
someone received an inheritance as a result of having kept the
law, it would show that the inheritance had nothing whatever
to do with the covenant, or with a will. It therefore would not
be an inheritance based on a promise. Here is how Paul says it
in Galatians:

> For if the inheritance be of the law, it is no more of promise:
> but God gave it to Abraham by promise. Wherefore then
> serveth the law? It was added because of transgressions, till
> the seed should come to whom the promise was made; and it
> was ordained by angels in the hand of a mediator.
>
> Galatians 3: 18–19

Since God gave the inheritance (that is the whole focus of
the Bible) by a promise (verse eighteen), Paul assumes that some
might ask, "Okay, then what is the law for?" (verse nineteen).
Paul answers his own question in the Socratic style in which he
was educated at the feet of Gamaliel, the Greek scholar. What
purpose does it serve? That is not an extraneous question. Paul
says the exact opposite of what messianic and "regular" Jews
teach, as do the fundamentalist theologians, who evidently dis-

count the Bible. Paul declares in a statement somewhat cumbersome in English that the transgressions of Jews made the written law necessary but only until the promised seed (the singular seed) comes who will free his followers from that law. The law, he works in here, was in existence, as we mentioned earlier, from the beginning. Notice, he says it was "added," meaning the written law. The dispensationalists put it the other way around, saying the church era was the temporary expedient, operating only until the second coming. Obviously their doctrines do not depend at all on New Testament theology! They also then have to largely discount the teachings of Jesus, while continuing to think of themselves as Christians—at least according to their rhetoric.

Paul had the support of the entire history of his people to call upon in his teaching, And he had a lot of good common sense, no doubt bolstered by some fairly regular contact with Jesus after their meeting. He knew, for instance, and wrote about it in his letter to the Romans, that the law was given even to those who had no knowledge of, or contact with, God. This surprises some people, until they realize what it actually means. Here's how Paul says it in Romans 2:14–15: "For when the Gentiles which have not the law, do by nature the things contained in the law, these, having not the law, are a law unto themselves: which show the works of the law written in their hearts."

Must that not be how God was able to say of people before the flood, that they "were desperately wicked?" There were always at least a few standards by which men lived together. Again, we are reminded of the sacrifices given to God by the third and forth men ever created, eons before the written law came down off the mountain with Moses. Men were evidently all created with the law written in their hearts. If it was not, what could children rebel against?

But in order to officially and righteously, condemn mankind for sin, and have men understand what was going on, God was obliged to institute a written law. Once that had been done, God could say, and show, that all mankind are officially sinners! But the ceremonial aspects of the law given to the nation of Israel had a very different purpose. They were signs or representations in metaphorical language, usually pointing to the coming of the Messiah and his atonement for the sins of those God had decided, before the foundation of the world, to redeem from the curse of the second death, hell. These signs were intended to show to those who were believers back in Old Testament times, the nature of God's redemptive plan. Not many ever got the picture. But some did. That's where David got the idea, expressed in the fifty-first psalm, about the "tender mercies" and loving-kindness of the Lord who was his God.

There is one other point here to emphasize. That is the middle of verse nineteen, where Paul speaks of the seed to come. This is simply once more, from a different vantage point, delivering the message that the law was to be in effect only until Christ came to fulfill all of it. This makes it clear that Christ was meant to be the primary beneficiary of the promise. He is the seed! The law was to be in effect only until he came with the New Covenant. This emphasizes that there never was a single moment's deviation from God's original plan for his creation. It shows simply and clearly that the New Testament was in no way, an interim measure in God's playbook. Only the fundamentalists and dispensationalists could miss so evident a plan. That's why so many Reformed believers presume that their overlooking such biblical points must be intentional.

The ending of the verse we are examining has to do with angels and a mediator. There is similar language in Acts 7:53 and in Hebrews 2:2–3. So, what might angels have to do with the giving of the law? The word translated *angels* here is the Greek word *aggelos,* which often is also translated as *messengers.* John the Baptist, for instance, was definitely not an angel, yet Jesus called him an *aggelos* in Matthew 11:10. John was the messenger for the coming Messiah. In an effort to clarify what we are reading, it is sometimes instructive to substitute words in one place that carry a different translation in another. So, putting messenger in this passage, where the translators put angel, what do we get? Well it seems to make much better sense. Now we have a "messenger in the hands of a mediator." A messenger sent by a mediator maybe? Let's play a little with the word *mediator*. In 1 Timothy 2:5–6 we find some possible help. "For there is one God, and one mediator between God and men, the man Christ Jesus."

So, let's substitute Jesus into our verse, as the mediator and maybe the idea that the messengers were the prophets, because that was after all, their function, and see what we get. Let's keep Moses and maybe Jeremiah and Isaiah in mind, as we reconstruct the ending of Paul's sentence. So here's what it would sound like: "and it was ordained by the prophets of old, who were messengers who brought word of the coming of the Lord Jesus." They did after all, bring the message of redemption by grace. I believe this is approximately the intended message. Go back to the angels and the mediator if you prefer, no hard feelings. Actually, I talked you through this little exercise, to illustrate how it is nearly always possible, to bring the Bible more readily into view, but it takes a little extra work. The important objective of course, is always to try to understand the message our Lord wants us to get, out of his Word.

It may have been instructive to also have perused several other Bible versions to see how they presented this verse. But that is never a necessity, since the King James is always reliable, even if one has to "fiddle" it a little. You have doubtless recognized that we have sought no assistance, apart from the Bible itself, throughout this book. Our intent is to refer always, to the Bible alone in interpreting its content. In order to achieve that, the study effort must always be inductive, rather than deductive, if we are to come to the truth contained in the Bible.

There is just one remaining observation that should be made, concerning the mediator of verse nineteen, before we proceed to the next verse, where we will again encounter a mediator but from another aspect. The point we want to mention is this: it is significant to recognize that when the law was given, it was according to the will of Jesus Christ. This is so, because it illustrates and reinforces the idea that the grace of God is and always was, superior in every way to the law. God's original promise was to offer redemption by grace, not through the works of the law. It preceded the law, and has succeeded it. The written law has always been required to conform to the terms of the covenant! That explains why it cannot in any way change one jot or one tittle of the gospel, and that's exciting. Now, to verse twenty. Do you recall that we are studying Galatians chapter three? We left it a few pages back, so don't feel bad if you have forgotten where we were. "Now, a mediator is not a mediator of one, but God is one." I took the liberty of inserting a comma after the first word, feeling it lent to understanding, and that it might assist you as well. The first comma is not in the Bible.

Here Paul seems to be saying that a mediator does not appear where only one person is involved. A single person does his own mediating with himself. But where there are two opposing parties, a mediator can be a welcome addition. The Lord Jesus must still be in view as the mediator. That just seems correct.

If it is, then for whom is he the mediator? If God is one of the parties, it makes sense that man—sinful man—is the other. If man were not sinful, the parties would not be in opposition, ergo, no mediator would be required. But what is the requirement that can be assisted by the mediator? Well, we know Jesus died for the sins of those God sent him to save. So, God put Jesus between you and your redeemer! Why did Jesus die? He died to "activate" the promise. He is the testator of the will and is the main beneficiary of that will—the primary beneficiary, the first to receive the inheritance. He is all things necessary to the covenant. He is God! So, this is another way of illustrating that the entire salvation plan has come from the grace of God! He is the Alpha and the Omega—the originator and the finisher of our salvation. Nobody else, especially prideful man, can claim any of the credit. You can see from this, that if you were not in on the establishment of the covenant, then you were not involved in the plan! God does it all.

In the next verse, Paul's argument considers the possibility of tension between two of God's creative endeavors—the law and the covenant. Paul asks, "Is the law then against the promises of God? God forbid: for if there had been a law given which could have given life, verily righteousness should have been the law" (Galatians 3:21). Actually, the question is, are the law and the promise in competition? There are teachers in certain denominations who fail to understand the Bible, and so they suggest and teach that God has different salvation plans in different "dispensations." They have decided that keeping the law brought salvation for the Jews. Of course, they invented their own dispensational designations, then constrained themselves to inventing explanations for what went on separately (in their view) in each period. They teach that once the church age ends, God will institute yet another dispensation, during which Christ will reign for a literal thousand years on earth and will rule over national Israel, in which everyone living will have been saved. This requires, of course, that they totally ignore all of the end-times prophecy of the New Testament and much of that in the Old Testament. That cannot be a good trade off in the eyes of the Creator, because this is a plan they have themselves entirely invented.

But, the verse we are considering, answers the first query with, "God forbid." Meaning, "That's impossible!" The reason it has to be impossible, is that, had there been a law that could have given life eternal, then salvation itself would have come by the law, and we have already seen, in Paul's inspired reasoning, that this cannot happen. Those who want to believe in the law, or want to believe they can somehow influence their own salvation, forget, if in fact they ever paid attention to, what salvation requires. It is an incredibly complex process which to date we can say with authority, began sometime prior to fourteen thousand years ago. That's the approximate age of the earth, calculated from the genealogies presented in the Bible. We know from Ephesians 1:4–5 that God selected those he would save "before the foundation of the world!" Then we know that it was arranged about that same time for Christ to be the Lamb that would be sacrificed in order to justify all of those whom God decided to save. Then, God had to turn Jesus into a man and send him down to earth to be sacrificed. That took a lot of coordinating and selection of apostles and parents and a myriad of other details. Then we know from checking the dates of all the significant events that everything has to be planned and executed precisely and flawlessly to occur on the desired dates. No human could have done any of it in a thousand years, even with the most powerful computer ever invented. Then Christ had to die, experience hell (the wrath of God), and then be resurrected, right on schedule. It certainly takes a load of pride and self-aggrandizement to assume that God needs our help on top of all that, to get us saved! Yet, that's what the vast majority of churches hold to, in their doctrines. All such are works doctrines, which cannot get anyone saved. In fact, they may assure that many cannot be saved. Can you see how very silly they are?

I can give you an example of that reality. The preacher of a small congregation where I worshipped for a time, taught that baptism must precede, and be the point at which, salvation occurs. A family that came to that congregation from Catholicism, had all been previously baptized by sprinkling. Nevertheless, all of the family agreed to being re-baptized (for salvation) except for the wife's elderly mother, who saw no reason to be baptized more than once. Two years later, that wonderful Christian lady was called home to Christ. Her daughter asked the preacher if the mother was in heaven. He replied that she could not possibly be in heaven, since she had refused baptism by immersion. Crushed, that entire family left the congregation.

The preacher's insistence on an unbiblical requirement, cost his congregation eight of its most dedicated members! They had been nearly one quarter of his flock!

The next verse we want to consider is Galatians 3:22: "But the Scripture hath concluded all under sin, that the promise by faith of Jesus Christ might be given to them that believe."

The word *concluded* refers to a finishing or closing up together. The Scripture referred to has to be, or to represent, the law of God. In the New Testament times, that's where we find the law. You see, when we read "the law," it means the Bible, the entire Bible, and it is given not simply to Israel, but to all mankind. So, if one is a transgressor, a law breaker, he is locked up together in sin with all the other transgressors in the world. This passage does not indicate that we first must believe, and then we receive the promise. That's not how it works. We always have to remind ourselves that to believe means to have faith. The faith always comes from, or out of really, the faith of Christ. He has more than enough to supply everybody he came to save.

We have come to another of those places where two verses just can't seem to be separated, and provide the same meaning. That's how the next two verses seem to be, so we'll look at them as one entity or whole passage, just as they were originally written: "But before faith came, we were kept under the law, shut up unto the faith which should afterward be revealed. Wherefore the law was our schoolmaster to bring us unto Christ, that we might be justified by faith" (Galatians 3:23–24).

Paul is now employing more specifically, some of the varied functions of the law. We are not to be allowed to think that, since we are saved by grace, salvation bears no relationship to the law. We need to remember that the law is the same thing as the Word of God! After all, we know that "faith comes by hearing, and hearing by the Word of God" (Romans 10:17). God has used the written word—his written words—which are the law of God, in the process of saving us! Remember that we saw back in verse nineteen, that the law was added until Christ came?

Here we are seeing an amplification of the truth from the law of God. Until Jesus came, in other words, God brought in the written law, in order to keep every person he was then dealing with, under its demands and under its authority. That is what made the law like a schoolmaster. It gave instruction, it gave the authority to punish, and it allowed for the gaining of wisdom to guide people onto the correct path. So, until faith came in the person of Jesus Christ, who is faith, men were kept under the authority of the law. One of the functions of the law as school-master was to punish offenders with eternal damnation. But later it began to teach that punishment could be escaped simply by coming to the Lord Jesus Christ.

This was the "call" to those God had chosen to save. Then when faith came, the called could believe. There is a progression of the redemptive process seen in these two verses. Can you see that salvation is not an instantaneous thing, but a step-by-step process? That is not to imply that it has to be long and drawn out. But we all begin as sinners. Next we find out we are subject to eternal damnation. Now we cease to be quite as comfortable in our sin as we were previously. Then we learn that we might be able to have a savior, and we learn who that could be. If we are chosen for that privilege, we are given spiritual ears, and we begin to understand the message of redemption. Before long we recognize a certain portion of faith has found its way into our consciousness. Then, when Christ applies the gospel through the Holy Spirit, through our spiritual ears, into our heart, he *gives* us the faith necessary to believe in Christ. From that point on, our faith begins to grow. This is a representative example, which may not be precise in every case, but it's going to be similar. In the author's own case this took about fifteen years to come together. Some say their experience covered less than fifteen days. For some it could be fifteen hours I suppose. But it hardly seems possible that the process would be compacted into fifteen minutes as some, especially evangelicals, are taught to believe.

Then Paul says, in verse twenty-five, as we near the conclusion of our look into Galatians, "But after that faith is come, we are no longer under a schoolmaster." The authority is then taken away from the schoolmaster, and it rests entirely thereafter, with faith. In Romans 6:14 God tells us, "For sin shall not have dominion over you: for ye are not under the law, (once saved) but under grace." Then in Romans 7:6, we read, "but now we are delivered from the law, that being dead wherein we were held; that we should serve in newness of spirit, and not in the oldness of the letter." In short, once brought to Jesus by the schoolmaster, we no longer have to fear the penalty for sin! The law can no longer threaten us with eternal damnation. Summarizing that, Paul says simply, "For as many of you as have been baptized into Christ have put on Christ" (Galatians 3:27).

That should be fairly self-explanatory, with the probable exception of the meaning of *baptized*—that word that has been so divisive to the church. We could go through a litany of the various meanings of words used in the Bible to explain baptism, but the word used here in the Bible signifies "washing." But water is not in view here. To be baptized into Christ is the "one baptism" that matters, and that is the baptism of, the washing of—in and by—the Holy Spirit. Once that is settled, the next question becomes, "What does 'putting on Christ' mean?" This refers to the robe of Christ's righteousness in order to cover the spiritual nakedness in which we were accepted, with all our sins apparent, as happened to Adam and Eve. God also equated Judah's apostasy to nakedness in Ezekiel 23:28–29. This garment of salvation is mentioned in Isaiah 61:10 where we read, "he hath clothed me with the garments of salvation [...] with the robe of righteousness." We hope he did the same for you.

It is our earnest hope, that if you had not previously been led through this sort of inductive study, defining Bible words and ideas with other Bible definitions, using the Bible to explain and define the Bible, that you are beginning to appreciate the inerrancy and the satisfaction, to be found in this method of study. It always beats seeking answers from the catalogue of man's ideas. We pray, as we come nigh to the close of this look into Bible history, that this has been as enjoyable and interesting a time of searching the Scriptures for you, as it has been for me. Verses twenty-eight and twenty-nine of Galatians lie before us now. They are together, as rational and straightforward a wrap-up of Paul's sermon by mail, as could be hoped for. Here is verse twenty-eight—prelude to the bottom line—as Paul presents his list of opposites, which in Christ no longer exist spiritually: "There is neither Jew nor Greek, there is neither bond nor free, there is neither male nor female" (verse twenty-eight). And why does the apostle to the Gentiles believe this to be true? He gives us our answer in the last phrase of verse twenty-eight: "for ye are all one in Christ Jesus."

God is no respecter of persons. Everyone is the same in his sight, if they are among his elect. In Christ, all stand on the same holy ground. The miraculous change in each and all of these dirty, rotten, sinners was due to the grace of God.

Sadly, the simplicity and lovely truth of this miracle of which the Word of God himself speaks, has been distorted terribly by churchmen. Typically these are people who use the truth to further their own desires, through their distortions. An example of this, is someone who claims that, since there is "neither man nor woman," that women, like men, can preach, teach Sunday school, have authority over men as deacons in their congregation, etc. They deny the truth of God and will be judged by him. These people find what appear to be conflicting Bible statements, and rather than search out the truth, rather than find how they fit together, they build doctrine from one or two phrases. This has brought error and apostasy to virtually all of the corporate churches in our day. The equality of which Paul speaks, is totally referring, not to depleting God's rules of their authority, but to eligibility of the disparate types for salvation. All who are believers, who are among the elect of God, who were called by the Holy Spirit, justified in the blood of Christ, have been assured they will not perish, despite their differences. They share equal priority for eternal life. Paul's closing summation is all that remains. He reiterates the central theme for the Galatians and for you: "And if ye be Christ's, then are ye Abraham's seed, and heirs according to the promise" (Galatians 3:29).

Sadly, an overwhelming percentage of supposedly Christian denominations deny this last passage entirely. They choose to believe that, only the nation of Israel falls into this category, and they pursue that heresy, with revolutionary zeal. We will close by reminding ourselves that the inheritance of which Paul speaks, is a two-part deal. The first step is salvation of the soul, which we learned was the down payment or earnest of the inheritance. But the saved run around in the same old sinful body, until their reservation is called. Then comes the second step in the adoption process, the redemption of the body.

Absolute closing of the redemptive process comes only when Christ returns on the clouds at the last day. Then, the saints will all receive "resurrected" bodies and will move into the new heaven, as they inherit the new earth, and remain there forever. That's why true believers tend to long for his soon return. Selah!

INTRODUCTION TO PART II

W HAT MEN CALL "THE END TIMES" IS INCREASINGLY A LARGE part of today's church culture. Everybody associated with study of the Bible, or who attends a church today, is probably more concerned about the future, than anyone ever was, until about a decade ago.

The establishment of the secular State of Israel, a half century ago, and more recently news that the temple might be rebuilt and that "diggings" are going on under the presumed site of Solomon's Temple, have quickened the pulse of certain men. Some of these are men ready to believe almost anything associated with the legends and myths that have grown up around Israel and the revelation of Christ. But they also include some very distinguished scholars of the *Regime Ancien Religieus,* especially those who have a financial interest in delivering a little truth wrapped in a lot of assumption and some faulty prophesy.

It is certain that a lot of minute detail is absent from the biblical presentation of eschatology, the study of the "last days." But there seems to be a total lapse among many interested observers of any memory that "in the end times" and "in the last days" refers to what the Bible clearly presents as the end of time. The "end" signifies, without the vast majority of today's seminarians appearing to recognize it, the point beyond which there is no more world! There is no time beyond the "end" of the world! There will be no world, no creation, upon which time was established, after the "last day," since God tells us clearly in the Bible, that this will be the day he "melts" this planet with "fervent heat." That time is not far off, yet as we draw ever closer to it, men seem to be less inclined to believe that it can possibly occur. They are finding all sorts of diversionary "evidence" that some other scenario will play out. We are talking here about men with advanced degrees in things biblical!

They are mistaken. But that is not cause for despair, since God tells us in his recap of the end he has planned, that the day of salvation is *now!* He promises that, "A great multitude that no man can number," is being saved as you read this book (Revelations 7:9). That's part of why we know the "Great Tribulation," which precedes the last day, is going on right now and will continue until the last day. It also attests to the fact that that final day cannot be far off. You have finally come to proofs that make the pretenders wrong - the "meat" of my case- the proof of my thesis. Before you lies the real message from God, about the last day. Notice I did not choose to use a plural on the last word of that sentence. You will now experience God's plan, in six simple illustrations from the Bible. There are others. I challenge you to find them in the Bible, after you finish reading this book!

But we mustn't get ahead of ourselves. In the chapters ahead, I present six separate but intimately interrelated historical parables from the Bible. Think of them as scenarios. Or consider them trails-to truth. God gives these trails to us so we can learn right from the Bible, if we are willing to trust Him, what the last days of creation will look like. You see, when we study the writings we call the Bible, we find that God has a history of operating in a series of patterns, many (we might even be comfortable saying most) of which he repeats and repeats. For this reason it is not at all a stretch of the imagination to seek and discover patterns that fit what God instructs us that he intends yet to accomplish. But in order for that to occur, men must be willing to engage in such an inquiry. In these times, virtually none seem to have such a propensity!

What follows in this section is a series of such patterns or parables, or in God's lexicon, "shadows" of what is to come. Once you have observed and considered these patterns thoughtfully, these trails to truth, you too may begin to wonder about some of the things you have been taught. I hope you will be enlightened by what you are about to read. If you feel your knowledge of this area is somewhat sketchy, you will be broadened. If you feel comfortable with your knowledge about the end times, I hope you will be rewarded in confirming what you had believed. In either case, I expect that something in the pages ahead will surprise and I hope, delight each reader. As I wrote in the preamble to part one, no one who reads this book will be untouched by it.

Immediately following the final pattern from the Bible, explained in the next pages ahead, the author presents a point and counterpoint critique of these six discussions that exemplify what the Bible has to say about the last day. So, turn the page now, and look at the future, as God has planned it!

NOAH'S ARK, THE RAPTURE: IS THERE A CONNECTION?

We have heard with our ears, O God, our fathers have told us, what works thou did in their days, in the times of old.

Psalm 44:1

BEFORE READERS GET INTO THE TEXT, I ASK THEM TO PERFORM A short exercise. Please, before reading further, write, perhaps inside the back cover of this book, everything contained in your present understanding of the rapture. Write only what you have kept in your conscious mind about this subject and don't look anything up. Take some time to think about this, because it will be important, since what you can remember will be what you believe! After you complete your study in this part of this book, it will be a worthwhile exercise to compare your knowledge of the Bible,"before and after." It is only in the final analysis, after all, that anyone can know if he or she has spent time with this book wisely. If nothing is added to a person's understanding, the book will have been worth nothing. The writer sincerely hopes that this will not be your experience. So, begin this little exercise now, and when it is finished, set your notes aside until later. If that is finished, we will proceed.

There's one thing we ought to rehearse to begin with. What is contained here, will be covering things many readers may have formed varying opinions about. Then, there may be some readers relatively new to the Bible. So, we need to attempt to start on common ground. Therefore, I want to share what I have found to be the best way to get out of the Bible a fair measure for the personal effort one puts into it. There are dozens of books available on how to study the Bible. I choose to recommend absolutely none, despite how learned and scholarly they may seem to be.

What an earnest student needs is to clearly understand a few basic principles that have to do with proper, intelligently directed study of this book that is not at all easy to understand. The Bible is not an "easy read"! We need to be concerned with how to study this one of a kind book, because it is special. The learned theologians, most of them at least, have not a clue what is hidden from their view because they try to study it incorrectly. They have laid down rules for how the pastors are to direct study, and sadly, the less you know about their methods, the more you will learn from the Bible!

This really is not being flippant. It is a crying shame that the hermeneutic most "scholars" employ in studying God's Word will not allow them to gain the insights God intended for the diligent common man who wants to learn. It's alright if you choose to ignore the methodology you are about to read. Your pastor and ministers will not agree that it is the best. It may be that they do not want you to learn more than they know, because most of their church doctrines are likely as not built on faulty Bible interpretation. This is not intended to be unkind to anyone or to put down any denomination, but simply to tell you the honest truth. The reason is, that for at least a century, most of the seminaries have followed a hermeneutic which limits, rather than expands, what you're allowed to learn! A hermeneutic, if you've not heard that term, is simply a needlessly fancy and I think, arrogant way to say "method of Bible interpretation." Actually the men with their noses in the air call it a "science." And in their immaculate arrogance, they probably actually believe that is so. But it's simply a short set of rules for guiding concerted study of the Bible, nothing more.

So, without any two-dollar words to express what may appear to be two-bit suggestions, here is what this book recommends in studying God's Word. First of all, we must internalize the reality that the Bible alone, and in its entirety, is the Word of God.

Next, we need to recognize, before beginning study, that all of the Bible, every line, every word, is God's language—it is his revelation. Therefore, it is meant to be obeyed! All of it. Then keep in mind always that the Bible alone is where we can find God's Word. That makes the Bible alone the ultimate, the final, the only reliable, authority. Not creeds or confessions or church doctrines, all of which, when considered carefully, are the uninspired works of men. Last, remember this well: the Bible is its own dictionary and its own interpreter!

You will learn most, and learn it faster, if you set aside any and all reference materials you have typically used to "interpret" your Bible. Let the Bible teach you through attentive, *inductive* study of every line and word you want to actually learn about. You will need a good concordance, either Strong's or Young's, and an Interlinear Bible. Both are a bit spendy. You might try your local library until you can afford an Interlinear Bible. The man who wrote this book bought his at a yard sale for twenty-five cents! Don't overlook the Goodwill store.

You select a word you want to check the meaning of. So your first step is to look that English word up in the front part of your concordance. Then you check the meaning of it in the back section and the meaning of that word in every place it appears in the original language in which it was written. Check in the text of the Interlinear Bible every place that word (in Greek or Hebrew) appears and check the back of your concordance to learn what each occurrence of the word translates into. In this way you will begin to see that there are some poorly translated passages, in fact quite a few of them, and there are sometimes multiple meanings for words. Over time, you'll learn to interpret what the writer actually meant to teach you, and many meanings will surprise you. You'll quickly come to an appreciation also, of how inaccurate some of the things you have been taught really are. Be assured; you will find this sort of study an exciting experience.

Once you get comfortable working in languages you have never before seen in print, you will be delighted in the new experience of actually learning, through your own efforts, the truths that God personally put into his Bible. If you are like many whose eyes and hearts are opened to this experience for the first time, you may find yourself very seriously considering why you have not ever previously been similarly exposed to these truths by your church. God has been waiting for you to experience for yourself the truths of his Word. He has waited all your life to date. Enjoy the exhilaration of listening, possibly for your very first time, to the voice of *your* God speaking across the ages directly to *you!*

But now it's time for you to journey back through time, in an effort to ascertain just what it was that God has been waiting to show you from the Bible, concerning what the Bible characterizes as being "caught up" at the Lord's soon coming.

There are at least six identifiable areas, or perhaps more properly, "stories," in Scripture that seem to lead the reader down separate trails to a better understanding of just what the Bible is trying to tell us about the last days. If we are on the correct track to truth about our chosen area of interest, we should find ourselves coming to the same, or very similar, kinds of conclusions from reading each of these stories. That only makes good sense. If we are left wondering in any one area, or to the extent that any trail fails to illuminate our path to biblical truth, we should probably set aside that particular area of study for later analysis. If we find that happening in our progress through this book, it will be time to agree to close the gate on that particular trail. We will examine "at least" six areas, because competent Bible scholars have postulated at least seven. The author was led to this realization by reading the pamphlet *When Is the Rapture?* by Harold Camping of Family Radio, Inc. He lists seven "paths." I highly recommend that book for your reading.

All of what is contained herein has been written previously, since it's part of the Bible. However, it is not widely written of, or taught in many of the corporate churches. There are undoubtedly more than only six clear trails to correct understanding discernable, if we would but seek them. But seek with a true desire to learn, rather than with preconceived ideas gleaned from something other than the Bible itself, and in its entirety.

So, this book is in no sense meant to imply that after this inductive study you may not find other areas in the Bible that point to the rapture also. That could certainly include the verses typically used to define the end times. This book will primarily busy itself with, "pictures" of the end, not typically taught for that particular understanding. So, if the reader will keep an open mind to what the Bible actually contains, he may experience an exhilarating adventure resulting from reading this humble little book.

The first of the trails to truth we will explore here, will be the story of the flood and of Noah. This part of the Bible provides a striking image of the end of time—the last days of this world. The time of Noah was, after all, in every sense of the word, the end of the world for most of those living on it then. It also shows us a believable picture of the beginning of a "new" earth and reminds us that from the perspective of those few chosen to inhabit the new earth, it is entirely possible that "new" might simply refer to what could be "renewed."

In Noah's time, all but the elect of God, and the animals taken into the ark (and the fish), perished. But that was only after the elect, whom God had personally chosen, were "caught up" so to speak, into the ark. Also, by the way, if you had not recalled it, God told us in Genesis 7:16 that He Himself closed the door. Another way to say that might be, God chose who would be saved from the flood and who would not be saved. Before they were "caught up," the Noah family was predestined to be saved from the flood. It cannot have been coincidental, because God doesn't do things that way. Let's recall the words of Second Timothy 3:16, "All Scripture is given by inspiration of God, and is profitable for doctrine, for reproof, for correction, for instruction in righteousness." We should also be aware that in 2 Timothy 3:1–17, speaking of the coming of apostasy to the corporate churches (coming in Timothy's time and present in our day), the author says that church members will be, "Ever learning, and never able to come to the knowledge of the truth." Study this sentence again. That won't be entirely true of you with relation to our subject here, after you finish studying this book. Notice we did not say after you finish "reading" this book. By the time this trail has been illuminated and understood, you are likely to agree that the antediluvian (pre-flood) period in our biblical history was a very good representation of what is to come at the end of time.

What existed in those days was a situation where God was already grieved by man's sinfulness within a very short time after he invented man and woman. So, he drove them from his presence, out of his protection to some extent. Then, within another 1,500 years, he was so grieved by man that he vowed to destroy the entire batch, except for a tiny remnant; the single small family he chose to save from his flood. Notice again, how God selected them, and told them what he would do. He initiated it all! With that tiny remnant, God would begin to activate the "new world" he would create after the flood. In Genesis 6:14 God began his instructions for getting his chosen people, the

Noah family, to safety before he lowered the boom on the rest. You could say he takes, or "catches them up" out of harm's way into a haven of protection. Now notice that, as in salvation, God does all the work necessary to get the ones he chooses to safety. We can do nothing to ensure our own salvation from the result of God's wrath. God does it all! Noah has only to follow instructions of the master shipwright! It is true that Noah did the construction work on the ark, just as we have to "study to make ourselves approved," and bear the fruit God has in mind for his followers. You see, God had already saved Noah's soul, and Noah knew it! The important work, the gospel work, of Noah was done simultaneously with the building of the instrument of salvation. In other words, the construction was not why God delayed the flood. God could certainly have provided an ark himself in a moment, but he chose to have Noah do some of the work, possibly to give others the benefit of Noah's preaching while he glued and hammered. With the knowledge he possessed, Noah certainly would have been an adamant, animated preacher of the wrath of God. The important point to note is that Noah did not have a hand in the choosing of himself, or in the saving of his family, apart from building the ark. God told Noah to build, and Noah did what God directed. Nothing Noah did was of his own volition. God liked his attitude.

Have you heard that Noah worked on the ark for 120 years? That's what the author was taught years ago but later couldn't begin to find out where anyone got that idea. The solution is to be found by looking at what the Bible actually says. God tells us in Genesis 5:32 that Noah was 500 years old. The problem is, it does not say *when* he was that old. We can know from the genealogy given in Genesis five, however, that Lamech, Noah's father, was 182 years old when Noah was born. The Bible also says Lamech lived 777 years total but that he lived 595 years after Noah was born. This means that Noah had to be more than 595 years old when the door of the ark was closed, because Lamech did not die in the flood. Sure enough, in Genesis 7:6,

God teaches that when the flood came, Noah was 600 years old, so Lamech had been dead for five years. He tells the reader it rained forty days before the ark floated and 110 days afterward. Then the waters did not recede until another 150 days had passed. Next, the ark is found sitting on the mountain from the seventh month until the tenth month, as the waters receded. That's another two months, or about sixty days, possibly a little longer. So far, the information leads to a total from door closed to door open of something like a year plus a few days. We needn't attempt to find anything more with numbers from the story of Noah right now, unless someone is really bothered by those 120 years to build the boat! That's a really long time, but of course Noah had to build a really big boat. Finally, after the author had completely finished the first draft of this book, like walking into a wall that says "excuse me," he recognized again where that puzzler's solution lay previously buried to him. All the time it lay in Genesis chapter six. This may appear to be prior to God speaking to Noah about building the ark, but it is not. Chapter six begins with God being very unhappy with Adam and his family because of the conduct of "the sons of God." Now recall that this time period of God being fed up with man's sin is about 1,500 years after God placed man into Eden. Noah was born 1,054 years after Adam was born. Adam lived for 930 years of that time. There could not have been more than a few tens of thousands of people around yet. Some of them were obviously God's people (the elect), and some were not. The "sons of God" must have been from the few families of true believers around in those days, meaning that the "daughters of men" were not among God's people. God evidently began very early to desire marriages only between equally yoked families and individuals. God was not pleased with man's conduct. In verse three of chapter six, the Lord said, "for that he also is flesh." What are we to suppose that meant? The real question is why the "also" in that sentence. If you were to look at the original Hebrew rendering of that sentence, you would find there is no "also."

What it actually says is "in man's erring he is flesh." In other words his flesh, like the flesh of all who are among the elect of God, causes his sin. God is therefore describing elect sons who are sinning. They may have been given a new soul that does not want to sin; but until the last day they romp about in sinful, original, unsaved bodies, and God is sick of it!

Now wait a second; who is being addressed? The Bible really does not specifically say. It is certain that by verse thirteen God is talking to the world's first sea captain. So let's put Noah into the conversation way back in verse three and see how it reads. Not only that, let's replace the word *said,* the fourth word in that verse, with "told Noah" in order to find out if this makes the verse any more understandable. Now we have God telling Noah something about like this, "Noah, I'm sick and tired of these people, and I'm not going to take man's monkey business much longer. I'm going to cut his life span off 120 years from today. Jot that down and mark your calendar." Now everything from verse thirteen forward makes sense. For a long time it seemed God was here establishing man's normal future life span, but that cannot be since David says in Psalm 90:10 that God sets it at "three score and ten years." This writer now feels assured that this is where Noah learns that, 120 years later he's going to be adrift.

When you consider it (even if the Bible does not record it exactly), this also is the motivation for Noah to become a saw-horse preacher! It is not imaginable in God's plan that a man of God who, knowing what was coming, would not only do his ark work, but would not also be warning everyone around him of the judgment to come. The remarkable thing is that Noah followed God's instructions so well. One can only imagine the pandemonium had he not. But, have you ever asked yourself the question, "Why Noah?" What set Noah apart for saving? Moses answers this question in Genesis 6:8–9. It really is two separate things about Noah, which closely model what we are told about salvation in the New Testament. First, "Noah found grace in the eyes of the Lord." Found grace means he was saved by God's grace without any action on his part. We can know from this that he was among God's elect, because that is whom our Lord adorns with his grace. Next, we find that he was not just a man, but "was a just man" and "he walked with God." He showed the fruit that James talks about because he was a mature believer who kept God's commands. We can know he was saved because the Bible tells us that if we keep God's commandments it is because we love him! (1John 2 :5). God also calls Noah "perfect in his generations." What is that about?

Look at Genesis 6:9 again where the first phrase says, "These are the generations of Noah." It means the genealogy of Noah, but is there one here? No, it is not here! This actually refers back to chapter five, which is introduced as "the genera-tions of Adam." That's okay because that one genealogy actually is introduced for Noah's benefit, to prove something to us. We already know that all generations after Adam came from him and Eve. What we wouldn't know about in like manner, without God telling us, are the "generations of Noah."

God does not always make his Word easy to understand, but here clearly, are a couple of messages. First, that Adam was the first man in God's first design of the earth and Noah is the Adam of the second new earth! Adam, the reader may recall, simply means "mankind." For the second message let's look first at 2 Peter 2:4–6, 9. Here the message is that there are sure to be false teachers and that they will eventually be destroyed. Peter is saying, "God wouldn't save sinful angels, and he wouldn't save the entire old world, except for the Noah family; and he destroyed Sodom and Gomorrah but saved Lot. So, he certainly knows how to deliver his people—the true believers—and to select out the sinners for judgment!" God says it in this manner: "I will have compassion on whom I will have compassion, mercy upon whom I will have mercy" (Romans 9:15).

The message is "I choose you; you don't choose me!" (And he seems just a smidgin smug about it.) But we passed over the second message we promised (above) to share with you. Look back in 2 Peter 2, to verse five, where in the second phrase Peter calls Noah "the eighth person." Peter is not simply counting up the survivors on the ark. That would be too simplistic. Notice that in every reference to him in Genesis, Noah is the principal person, not the last. No, this is a completely separate topic buried in the message of that group of verses! This appears to be the way God hides his messages from all but the diligent searcher. Now turn back in your Bible again to Genesis, but this time to the *details* of the genealogy contained in chapter five.

There we find this list called "the book of the generations of Adam." Remember in the New Testament the genealogies serve a primary purpose? They are the trail of legitimacy, for a Savior who in his day, grew up being suspected by his neighbors, of not having a legitimate father. Each genealogy in the New Testament is a genealogy of Christ. The first in Matthew, traced forward from Abraham through Joseph. The second is found in Luke, traced backward from Mary to Adam, and it includes Noah. Here in Genesis chapter five, we trace the line (actually) from Seth, the first man whom we know was faithful to God (Adam was not). We can know this because of several pointers. First, we will see in this genealogy that Seth's line leads to Noah, and above we saw that Noah's line leads to Jesus through Mary. Jesus had no one in his ancestry who was not faithful—therein lay his legitimacy to be the king!

Next, we are told in chapter four, verse sixteen, that Cain, Seth's only brother at the time, "went out from the presence of the Lord." Cain became an outcast because of his sin and so (we are left to assume) did his parents. There is therefore, none but Seth to be seen by God as righteous! So now let's actually make our genealogical list. The list begins with Adam. Then comes Seth. (Seth, of course, was the third son, but the first *righteous* son to live and to produce heirs, hence the genealogy begins at Seth, not Adam.) Next is Enos, followed by Cainan, who gives us Mahalaleel. Then comes Jared, followed by Enoch, who was truly a good man because he was in a sense "raptured" leaving behind his son, Methusela, to give us Lamech, Noah's father. Then Noah has three sons. Notice that these genealogies are incomplete in that they are lists of only first sons. But a very accurate record of time can be established from them. Time is their true, if hidden, purpose.

So, if this list is examined from the context of it being a track from Seth (the first righteous first son) to Noah, the examiner will count seven between them. That makes Noah, as Peter said, the "eighth person," meaning the eighth *righteous* first son ever in the world! But why all this genealogy coverage in the Bible? We have to remember that the Bible is first a history, then several other things. Notice that the genealogy just examined contains a lifespan for each generation. With these, God accurately established for anyone willing to diligently study his Word, the true timeline of historical events! Adding backwards in the genealogy of Noah, for instance, we can know that if Noah was 600 years old when the flood came, the year was 1,656 years after God created Adam, and adding forward in other genealogies, we can know that the calendar year was 12,044 BC!

So you see, often there is a fountain of knowledge available in the Bible if we will diligently apply ourselves to finding it.

At this point, it is appropriate to examine Noah's preparation time, especially in light of the teaching already mentioned, assigning the four Noah men 120 years to build the ark. In Genesis chapter seven, God is speaking to Noah of his preparation for the survival of the passengers on the ark. In verse four God says, "After seven more days I will cause it to rain upon the earth forty days and forty nights." Noah has already built the ark, so we know he had but a week's notice of the departure, after that. Then in verse eleven we are told that Noah and all the animals entered the ark on the same day the rains began.

But Noah first learns in chapter six, what God wants him to do. Checking there again, we see that in neither chapter can be found any reference to the length of time Noah was given to build an ark. We do see, by comparing Genesis 7:11 with Genesis 8:13–14, that the Noah family and their animals were inside the ark exactly one year and ten days. Notice also in verse sixteen of chapter seven what the closing phrase reveals: "and the Lord shut him in." The focus of God's story of Noah is Noah! He does not say he shut "them" in. What the Lord wants us to learn from this entire book is what Noah said, what Noah experienced, and what Noah did. We are not even told the name of his wife! We need to learn to focus where God directs us, not on things we might be curious about. For instance, we learn that the people of Noah's time were detested by God because of their sinfulness, but what else does God take time to tell us about them during the rains? Absolutely nothing. That is not where God wants you to look. He wants our focus to be forward: to the new world he is creating for man. What one thing happened to all those other people that God does want us to know? They died in their sins! Said another way, "The wages of sin is death!" The message is unchanging from old world into new world, Old Testament to the beginning of the New Jerusalem!

Now, having said all that, turn in your Bible to where Christ looks back into history and read what Jesus has to say in Luke 17:26–27. "And as it was in the days of Noah, shall it be in the days of the Son of man (this ought to have exclamation marks all over it!). They did eat and drink, they married wives, they were given in marriage until the day that Noah entered into the ark, and the flood came, and destroyed them all." Here, Jesus is speaking of the end of that world. Notice he compares his own time, to what people were doing while Noah was building the family yacht. Now read verses thirty and thirty-one. This is the typical picture we have been taught about the day when what we call "the rapture" will occur. "Even thus shall it be in the day *when the Son of man is revealed.* In that day, if a man is on the housetop, and his treasured things are in the house, let him not come down for them. If he is in the field, likewise let him not turn back" (Luke 17:30–31). Home in on the words of Jesus: "when the Son of man is revealed." This is generally accepted to mean his second coming. The description of Noah's day in verse twenty-seven leads to the day "that Noah entered into the ark." That represents the "last day" for anybody who could not get into the ark. When the door was closed, Noah was not closed in as much as the world was shut out. This is a picture of what will happen to anyone who is not saved on the last day! So we are seeing two pictures: the last day and the day of the rapture "morphing," so to speak, into one. At that point, the reader knows those people were judged unworthy to enter the ark! So now, we see the curtain of judgment day creeping across our picture of the rapture and the last day. We might think that some could change right up to the last day, but we know that was not true, because God had already told Noah in chapter six, verse seventeen and on the first of the seven-day countdown, that Noah's family alone had tickets for the Cruise! They were the few previously chosen by God. They were his elect—the tiny remnant that would survive to be the seed in the new world. Likewise, only the elect in the end times can declare themselves (presumably) right up until the last day. When Christ reveals himself to nonbelievers on that day, the door will have been closed, just as in Noah's day. So, we can see a great, not to be ignored, similarity in the coming of Christ and the story of "the rapture of Noah." In fact, Jesus tells us that they are much alike in verse thirty. Then in verse thirty-one he begins his warnings concerning that day. Let's now read verse thirty-three: "Who- ever seeks to save his life shall lose it; and whoever shall lose his life shall preserve it."

Noah and his family turned their backs on their old life when they went willingly into the ark. Many others, who did not want to hear what Noah had to say, may have been given the opportunity to make the same choice as well, but did not. The decision of Noah's family opened up a whole new life that they would not have experienced, had they tried to stay and hold onto the old life. They were "born again," while all those people about them were perishing, as many are in our day. Those who ignored the prophets and clung to their old lives lost them when God closed the door and started the rain falling. On the last day that lies somewhere ahead of you and me, the same kind of activity will be acted out. Those who welcome "losing this life" and being gathered up "in the twinkling of an eye," "shall preserve it," as Jesus says. It's something to think about!

Before we continue, we need to digress for just a moment. Look back at the second paragraph on page 271, where it was written in the top line, that Christ "looks back into history." Now, in your mind's eye, add an extra *s* to the word *history*. Put it right after the existing **s**. Then separate the resulting word by creating a space between the pair of letters *s*. Do you see that "history" is "Christ's story"? Amen.

Now let's continue in Luke 17, where verses thirty-four through thirty-seven amplify a bit on that final day on this old earth for Christians. Now here is a little exercise for the diligent. In verse thirty-seven Jesus is speaking of dead bodies and eagles. What does Jesus mean by that? Theologians can't agree. Ponder that for a while, and we will come back later to see what the answer is.

In the meantime, the phrase "and knew not" in verse thirty-nine of Matthew 24 may be somewhat of a puzzle. There, of course, our Lord was speaking of the many who were nonbelievers. What is it that a nonbeliever does not believe, or does not know? He does not believe in, or expressed another way, does not know, Christ as the Savior. Obviously, those folks in Noah's time knew lots of things, but they did not know the redeemer until, as Matthew says, "the flood came." We think they instantly knew when the flood came, that they had missed the boat! They could see the salvation of a few taking place before their eyes, but it was too late for them to get into the ark of salvation—in a sense to be *"caught up"* to safety. "Likewise," Christ says, "will it be when he comes the second time." It has been well said that, there will be not one single nonbeliever in the entire world the moment they see Christ coming to claim his own people in the "rapture." Everyone everywhere will recognize in that moment, that like most of the people in Noah's time, they too missed the boat. They will then believe, but the Bible seems to suggest that it will be too late for that belief to register on the reservation list for the boat that will leave the dock that day.

After that, they will be here alone. The Bible doesn't say exactly what happens to them in the next instant. Are they killed? Are they transformed into a spiritual body and immediately transported to judgment, or do they have to die before joining the unsaved but resurrected nonbelievers before the judgment seat? This is not at all clear, but it may explain Luke 17:37, which this writer has never heard anyone translate. It is the same as Matthew 24:28, except Matthew uses "carcass" rather than "body," and I like it better. I say that because the usage in Matthew might have prevented theologians such as Matthew Henry, from making interpretive errors. Henry cut the "body" two ways, saying it could mean the eagles, as regal, beautiful birds, flock to the body of Christ, the believers, or that it could mean the eagles, being carrion eaters, go to pick at the dead nonbelievers. The Bible evidence appears to confirm that, Henry's latter interpretation would be the more correct. All the other commentaries skipped over that troublesome verse. Few theologians have any moxie! The author had already decided for himself that the eagles (or vultures in some translations) were after carrion and that could not be God's chosen people. That's what led to wondering where do the dead bodies come from? Although he does not feel competent to get much deeper into that search right now, we do know that the stars are going to fall on the earth (Revelations 6:13), and that cannot be healthy for anyone here. We also are told that unbelievers on that day will beg the mountains and rocks to fall on them to save them from God's wrath (Revelations 6:17). But then there is the battle of

Armageddon, in which many nonbelievers are projected to be slain. That seems to be the chief reason for the birds to gather.

So far, we have established that God wiped out all but one family because of the sin of the rest of the world. There is just one complication that makes that analysis too simplistic. Yes, there was just one family, but there were four wives. Each of them came from two families as did Noah, so really, there were ten families represented in the ark, if we look only one generation ahead of Noah's. So, we also know that God's hand had to be active in those families, ensuring the correct marriages were arranged, to produce a family line appropriate for the lineage of the Christ. But then there were grandparents too! You can see how complicated lineages could get. That's probably why God deals with only the line traced through each firstborn son. What we have read but have not mentioned is, that the story of Noah is the story of the gospel of Christ that threads its way through the entire Bible, tracing the generations of Jesus all the way from Adam. There has always been, and will be finally, an escape for whom God has chosen that escape. This is the message that will play itself out on judgment day.

Once again, as he demonstrates over and over again in the pages of his book, God will destroy the entire creature while saving a small remnant, which he will lift up to safety. In this chapter of God's story, Noah took his family into a heaven—or into the haven—that God provided for his own when destruction came. The last point that it would be good to tuck away for later examination is to reiterate that the rapture of Noah, and the symbolic "last day" of the world along with the symbolic "judgment day" of nonbelievers, all came on the very same day. We can say in closing that there are a lot of similarities intentionally pointed out to us in the Bible between Noah's time and the coming end of the world. Sadly, just as the resurrection was spoken of for thousands of years before it occurred, the rapture is laid out for us many times in the Word. Yet, many churches and denominations, many pastors and teachers have chosen, just as did many synagogues, to believe something else. "We have also a more sure word of prophecy, whereunto ye do well that ye take heed, as unto a light that shineth in a dark place" (2 Peter 1:19).

NIGHT TIME, WHEN THIEVES LURK

THERE ARE SEVERAL PLACES IN THE BIBLE WHERE GOD CONFIRMS that the return of our Lord may be likened to the appearance of a thief in the night. That is not a pretty allusion, but we cannot argue with the Word of truth. One thing is evident, God never asks us to "like" the story line of his Word. But he does say, it is the truth; and we had better accept it, or perish! So, we can puzzle over why God uses that kind of reference, and then we have to come to terms with it as best we can. After all, it is given to teach even the simplest minds how our God works. He has repeated it often enough to get the attention of even a sleepy-headed researcher, who has now finally settled for accepting that the two distinct happenings are in fact, related. Speaking of his sometime return, immediately after speaking of how the rapture works, Jesus gives the following definite guidance for all to see.

Watch therefore: for you do not know in what hour your Lord comes. But know this, that if the master of the house had known in what hour the thief would come, he would have watched, and would not have suffered his house to be broken into. Therefore also be ready: for at an hour you will not expect him, the Son of man will come.

Matthew 24: 42–44

So, what exactly are we supposed to be watching for? Are we watching because if he comes like a thief in the night, he will come silently and we might miss him? Some churches teach that, and there is a superficial appearance of validity to it, but there is a bit of a deeper meaning to be sought. One might look at First Thessalonians, chapter five to see if he could find agreement. There, Paul is speaking specifically about his personal description of the, "day of the Lord," the second coming of Christ. This, and 2 Peter 3:10, are where we get the "thief in the night" business. Both agree, "the day of the Lord comes as a thief in the night." But notice, it does not say there, as many believe, that the Lord will come as a thief in the night. It says the day he will arrive comes that way. Peter tells us that the day comes like a thief all right, but when it gets here, "the heavens shall pass away with a great noise"! Not only that, Matthew 24 assures everybody that when he comes, Jesus will come with "a great sound of a trumpet," courtesy of his angels. Luke records that "there will be signs in the sun, and in the moon, and in the stars, and upon the earth distress of nations." This last agrees with Mark, who writes:

But in those days, after the tribulation, the sun shall be darkened, and the moon shall not give her light. And the stars of heaven shall fall, and the powers that are in heaven shall be shaken. And then shall they see the Son of man coming in the clouds with great power and glory.

Mark13:24

So, we see that our Lord in no way resembles a thief in the night when he comes, or at any other time for that matter. He will come triumphantly, and on the clouds, heralded noisily by trumpets and preceded by some pretty nasty signs in the heavens, that nobody is going to miss if he is watching. Here, watching seems to mean be vigilant, to be awake to what is going on. It also carries the sense of being prepared to act. The watching then, may be for signs that will precede the day of his coming. That day will sneak up on anybody who is not paying attention, or is unfamiliar with what is contained in God's Word. Let's look at one other description of Christ's coming, this from the Apostle Paul, in his first letter to the church at Thessalonica. Turn in your Bible, to First Thessalonians 4:16. There we find the Apostle Paul saying, "For the Lord himself shall descend from heaven with a shout, with the voice of the archangel, and with the trump of God."

That's a bit different from Peter's version, but what's a shout by an angel between friends? It's consistent, in that it agrees that our Lord will not be sneaking up on anybody he comes to save! Like the other verses, this characterizes anything but a silent approach. One other point needs to be made. The very fact that all of this is in print and available to everyone, makes it impossible for anyone to be surprised that he will be coming. That begins to remove excuses. It's wonderful how the Bible satisfies our need for truth, and even for interpretation. There is one other reference that bears on the situation of the second coming. Recall that Jesus, speaking to unbelievers in Mark 8:12, said, "there shall be no sign given unto this generation." But to the astute—and this means true believers—the only sign he said, "will be that of the prophet Jonas." Jesus meant, understand the gospel, and that means study the Bible! So, it must be time to find out just what it means to come like a thief in the night. To begin, let's turn to 2 Peter 3:10 again. Here we find some clear confirmation that only the unsuspecting could possibly miss an event accompanied by "great noise and the melting of the earth!" Great noise and burning of the elements hardly constitute a surreptitious coming. But they could make quite a diversion! But that's not what you need to look in Second Peter for. There is another great truth here that the Lord does not want true believers to overlook. It was mentioned in other verses, but Peter makes it impossible to ignore. It was mentioned above. Peter tells us clearly that the day the Lord comes again, is the same day that the earth is destroyed! It is the day of "fervent heat!" This adds a dimension to our study, namely that the day of the Lord is also the last day—the end of the world. Now, ask yourself this: if true believers are watching for this day, as we just learned from the Bible, is it possible they were previously "raptured"? You can answer that for yourself. There is another clue that all "premillennialists" miss, even though it just hangs out in space, begging to be noticed by anyone reading even lightly through Scripture. Their "missing" is intentional! Turn back again in your Bible to Mark 13:24. Read that as a favor to yourself. When does it say the sky will be darkened? When will the stars fall out of heaven? When will Jesus be seen coming in the clouds? Then, very importantly, when will the "rapture" occur? This is Jesus talking, so we should be able to expect that what he says is likely to be the way it will play out. After all, the Bible does consider him to be God. Why do you suppose the authors of the *Left Behind* books and the vast majority of so-called "evangelical" Christian pastors, cannot read this and believe it? Your Bible says all this comes *after* "the tribulation!" Well, saints preserve us! How did that get in there?

But let's continue in order to see if that contention is in any way modified or reinforced elsewhere in the Bible. Our study technique is to allow the Bible to define, to prove, to possibly modify, the Bible. In order for a text to be understood as it is written (the goal of hermeneutics) it must agree with all other areas of text in the Bible. Look into Revelation 3:3. Here is found no less a personage than Jesus Christ himself, declaring that believers must watch if they want to know when he is coming! That alone, if one considers it, tells how we will make ourselves ready for his coming. Why be ready? That's where the warning not to go downstairs if you are on the housetop comes in. Don't look back! It is all going to happen quickly, and if someone is not ready, physically and mentally, it may be possible that he too may miss the boat. Remember that Noah had only a short time to be ready? This next time is going to be something like that, possibly shorter. If a believer is vigilant, having thought through what will happen to him in that time, it won't matter when the Lord comes for him. He'll be ready. He does not, after all, have to pack a bag! It's evidently not knowing the day that will catch unawares all of the unbelievers, who, as in the time of Noah, we learned in the first chapter, will be busy doing their everyday ignoring of God and his salvation program. That day will sneak up on them like a thief, but we hope not on God's chosen people. There is an interesting warning by Jesus in Revelation 16:15 that fits into what we are talking about here. Take a look at it now, if you will. "Behold, I come as a thief. Blessed is he who watches, and keeps his garments, lest he walk naked and they see his shame." This adds something of a wrinkle to the idea of watching for the coming of the Lord. Does our Lord mean it may be embarrassing to be in the shower the moment he comes? Does he mean the elect will be clothed in heaven with whatever they were wearing when Christ takes them up in the rapture of the last day? That's certainly possible, but it seems that "garments" here refers to keeping our garments "white" in purity. That's Bible language for being righteous or blessed (redeemed)—covered when others around you are showing their nakedness (sin). They are not blessed, and our Lord will have no trouble spotting his sheep when he comes. A sense of appropriate dress does seem to fit in here. Notice also that there is a change in how Jesus says he will come. He says he, not the day, will come as a thief! Personally, the writer tends to think that this is only a variation in the way the chosen scribe expressed an idea. We are probably not intended to see it as having any physical import different from what is contained elsewhere in Scripture. It could however, be our Lord's way of highlighting our need to be ready. The main message remains that he will surprise the unbelievers whenever he comes. On this score, however, the author is certainly open to hearing ideas he may not have considered as long as some biblical support can be shown.

Now, if we look into First Thessalonians, we can see some more reflections of Noah's day, and along with those reflections, maybe somebody who does not believe anyone will sneak up on him.

> But of the times and the seasons, brethren, ye have no need that I write unto you. For you yourselves know perfectly that the day of the Lord so cometh as a thief in the night. For when they shall say, peace and safety; then sudden destruction cometh upon them, as travail upon a woman with child; and they shall not escape.
>
> 1 Thessalonians 5:1–9

This is consistent with what we have read up to now. "They," of course, are the same sort of "they" who were present in Noah's day—the unbelievers who again, will not be ready. The meaning of "ready" we can begin to recognize, has nothing to do with their actions. It is a readiness instilled in believers by their Savior. Those who do not have the truth, can never be ready. Notice we are back to the day being like a thief, but let's not make too much of that. Of more import, is the opening sentence. The times and the seasons, we are being told, are in fact discernable to believers, if they are paying any attention at all to the Word of God. We will come back to that though, because it is inextricably connected to, so it goes along with, that thing after which the rapture occurs, according to Christ. But let's return to our unfinished Scripture:

> But ye brethren, are not in darkness, that that day should overtake you as a thief. Ye are all the children of light, and the children of the day: we are not of the night, nor of darkness. Therefore let us not sleep, as do others; but let us watch and be sober. For they that sleep in the night; and they that be

drunken, are drunken in the night. But let us, who are of the day, be sober, putting on the breastplate of faith and love; and for an helmet, the hope of salvation. For God has not appointed us to wrath, but to obtain salvation by our Lord Jesus Christ."

1 Thessalonians 5:4–9

For many readers, this has always been a very difficult passage of verses to comprehend at all. But it is certainly possible, if not easy, to understand at least some of what God is telling us here. It all boils down to this: the unsaved have no hope of being caught up by Christ at the second coming, in the manner that God's children will be caught up, if they are paying attention. Consequently, his children are to be sober of mind, expectant of heart, and thankful to be chosen to be with Christ for eternity. Everyone else will be surprised again, as they were in Noah's day. They dwell in darkness and will not see the light as the elect have seen it. Those who walk with Christ are in the light of his gospel and are saved by that wonderful light. That light forms the "day" of which the Lord speaks.

What this is talking about, and it is mentioned in verse two, is the "day of the Lord." This is the day everybody worries so, about coming surreptitiously. We learned in Mark 13:24 that the day when Christ appears will coincide with the last day. There must be other Scriptures to confirm that. Second Peter 3:10 said that this is the day when "the earth and the works therein shall be burned up." Revelation 19:20 is clear that on the same day that Christ comes "the beast and the false prophet will both be thrown into the lake of fire." That certainly sounds a lot like judgment day. That is especially so, when coupled with the words of Jesus in Revelation 22:12, where, speaking of his second coming, Jesus says, "His reward is with him, to give every man according as his work shall be." That carries a very strong suggestion—in fact, a threat of judgment coming on the same day. So what the Bible seems surely to be teaching, is the "day of the Lord" being the day he returns in the clouds, in "great power and glory" as King of Kings. The faithful will be expecting him, because they have read the times and seasons to be ripe for his coming. Everyone else will be surprised and in fact horrified! "Peace and safety, then sudden destruction" (1 Thessalonians 5: 3). There is your thief in the night!

Sad to say, this true gospel is unacceptable to the vast majority of people who claim to be true believers. That surely must be because although the true gospel teaches the love of God through the Lord Jesus, and almost anybody can buy into that, it also insists that mankind is under the wrath of God. Many churches today will not teach the latter message, possibly because it might affect their bottom line! Of course, they would phrase it differently! That has to mean those pastors and those they lead, will likely be among the surprised when Christ comes, because they are not being true to his commands. He is very tough on teachers who fail to do the job he asks to have done. The reality is, that on the Lord's day, there will be an abundance of people surprised not to be among those God knows as his own. They may be surprised all the way to hell. What an awful moment that will be.

Now, we have seen this whole thing set up in Scripture, suggesting that there will be true believers here for Christ to take up on that day. That must mean there are believers here on the last day—on judgment day. That suggests that the rapture has not yet occurred. Since the judgment day occurs on the last day of time, that's when the rapture has to occur also, if there are still believers remaining on earth. That also has to mean that the believers have already been judged. It happened when Jesus endured the wrath of God for them beginning at Gethsemane and ending at Calvary, when our Lord announced, "it is finished." This is confirmed by First Thessalonians 5:9. We all ought to write that verse down and memorize it.

There are some who will say that the wrath spoken of in the Bible, is the "Great Tribulation." That's unstudied hooey, but it is a common misinterpretation in today's churches. But it is also an unstudied one, to be sure. You just finished satisfying your-self with Scripture that the rapture occurs on judgment day. So, we can know with certainty that the church will endure the final tribulation. We can, therefore, deduce that since the unsaved get their punishment in the lake of fire, the tribulation is designed specifically for the church. That means the "tribulation" is not the "wrath" spoken of in First Thessalonians 5:9. The wrath of God is what is going to make the unsaved very uncomfortable for all of eternity. It is the wages of sin! The true believers, who are likewise sinners, have already had their sins covered by the blood of Christ. There is a nice, succinct, explanation of God's wrath in Revelation 6:15–17. Take a good look at that now and know exactly whereof God speaks.

The only way we can make sense of all the Scriptures we covered in this lesson, and the only way First Thessalonians chapter five makes any sense at all, is if the rapture and judg-ment day occur on the same day. The "they" who are surprised, are those who have not trusted in Christ. Those who have trusted, are in the light as Christ is in the light, so there is no way they can be surprised by a thief in the night. Turn finally, to Revelation chapter eleven. Here, speaking of the two proph-ets, who represent the corporate congregations sending out the gospel, we read:

> And they of the peoples and kindreds and tongues and nations shall see their dead bodies three and one half days and shall not suffer their dead bodies to be put in graves. And they that dwell upon the earth shall rejoice over them, and make merry, and shall send gifts one to another; because these two prophets tormented them that dwell on the earth.
>
> Revelation 11:9–10

What in the world would it be that these prophets tor-mented the "kindreds and tongues and nations" with? It would have been the same thing that torments the world today, the gospel of Christ. The two dead men represent the churches that no longer send out the true and complete gospel of Christ. Absolutely nobody is sad to see them perish. So here's a clue to the seasons and times. What is the clue? It is that the gospel must be silenced before Christ returns!

Looking now at verse twelve of Revelation eleven, the reader virtually sees the eternal, true church, made up exclusively of true believers, and here these two prophets are, being, "caught up" to heaven in a cloud. What's more, "their enemies beheld them." It is also clear in verse thirteen that in the "same hour" the destruction of the earth begins, according to God. We just now read the official heavenly version of the "last day." Of course, God probably had not read the *Left Behind* books yet!

Now, to complete the picture being reflected from what is painted in the Bible, just imagine the reaction. The great gnashing of teeth and wringing of hands when that great many who think they are true believers, discover that the gospel they have been following is not at all the one taught by Christ! "Depart from me" they will hear, "I never knew you." His coming will be surreptitious to them, just as it will be to all unbelievers, including those who claim to be saved, but sadly, are in fact not known to God at all. First Thessalonians 5:3 says, "sudden destruction shall come upon them." This could account for the gathering of eagles. So, all believers should join in praying for the unsaved, some of whom may be sitting next to you in church on Sunday. This is the language of judgment day and is why true believers fear the Lord just as he has commanded!

Now, it's time for the reader to direct himself back to First Thessalonians five, but this time to verse ten. This is a good verse to emphasize, since even though it is not required for this study, it does contain an interesting and wonderful, if slightly camouflaged, thought. Verse ten is God's way of assuring us that whether we are alive when he comes, or in the grave when he comes, if he has chosen us and saved us, we will live together with God for eternity. This is simply God's way to handle the promise contained back a few verses in chapter four, beginning with verse fifteen, of First Thessalonians, chapter four. There he assures us, that he has planned an orderly and complete "rapture" for all who have ever believed. This is an oft-quoted explanation of the rapture, which many say will come before the tribulation. This little group of verses assures us that even the dead in Christ will be taken care of. They will, in fact, come with Christ when he returns (verse fourteen). Those who are living at the time of the rapture will in no way cut the dead out of the picture. There is room in the ark for everyone God has saved. His haven (heaven) is open for business to all comers on that day. He has assured all generations that the dead in Christ "will rise first" (verse sixteen). Then, after the dead in Christ are taken up, those who are alive will join them in the clouds, and all of the saved will "ever be with the Lord" (verse seventeen). That should make you wonder when the so-called "millennial" reign will be. But we'll come to that in good time.

Before we get to that, let's investigate another place in the Bible where we will find a picture of the end times and the second coming of Jesus. We have to go way back, into the Old Testament for this next excursion into the rapture.

FEASTS OF LEVITICUS
WHISPER, "RAPTURE"

IN THE LAST CHAPTER, WE COMPARED SCRIPTURE WITH SCRIPTURE, proving some very definite conclusions about the "last days." For one thing, we learned that every believer who ever lived will be either resurrected if he is dead, or taken up if he is alive, when our Lord returns.

We haven't yet nailed down the case of the nonbeliever precisely, but we will. Now it's time to offer you two verses that you very likely have never read in association with the return of Christ, but that's what they deal with. First, is John 7:37; "In the last day, that great day of the feast, Jesus stood and cried, saying, if any man thirst, let him come unto me, and drink"

Second is Nehemiah 8:18; "Also day by day, from the first day unto the last day, he read in the book of the law of God. And they kept the feast seven days; and on the eighth day was a solemn assembly, according unto the manner."

Both of these passages mention "the last day," but both are relating to the Feast of Tabernacles! This feast was instituted by God himself to commemorate two events in the very checkered history of the nation of Israel. The first event was the sojourn of the Israelites in the wilderness for forty years, when they constantly whined and complained about God and about Moses. The second reason for the feast was to mark the time when the annual harvest was completed. The "last day," the day Jesus comes, is related to the Feast of Tabernacles because the feast refers to judgment, the sorting of wheat and tares which comes at the end of the harvest, or the end of the year. Join us in reading from the book of Leviticus, chapter twenty-three, where we read, "Ye shall dwell in booths seven days, all that are Israelites born shall dwell in booths; that your generation may know that I made the children of Israel to dwell in booths, when I brought them out of the land of Egypt: I am the Lord your God" (Leviticus 23: 42–43).

The Feast of Tabernacles is also called the Feast of Booths by Israelites, for obvious reasons. It looks back on a not-so-pleasant time in the wilderness. Believers today are living in a wilderness also, but when Christ comes, they will be led out of the wilderness into the promised land, just as the children of Israel were led, long ago. That leading was a picture of the leading to come. For our meaning here, we will ignore the biblical fact, that none of the adult Red Sea pedestrians lived to cross Jordan. When they receive their resurrected bodies, the elect will dwell forever with Christ. "Then we which are alive and remain shall be caught up together with them in the clouds, to meet the Lord in the air: and so shall we ever be with the Lord" (1 Thessalonians 4:17).

So, you can see that this ancient Jewish feast actually identifies with the return of our Lord Jesus, and therefore with the last days. Like the ancient Israelites, those who are true believers are looking forward to ending their time in the wilderness. But the feast has another meaning as well. It marks the end of harvest. "And the Feast of Harvest, the first fruits of thy labors, which thou hast sown in the field: and the Feast of Ingathering, which is in the end of the year, when thou hast gathered in thy labors out of the field" (Exodus 23:16). So, this is also referred to as the "Feast of the Ingathering," which comes at the end of the Jewish year. Not the end of the sacred year, which runs from our April to March, but in God's reckoning, whenever the harvest is complete for all practical purposes, the year has ended. Then, in Leviticus 23:34, we read, "Speak unto the children of Israel, saying, the fifteenth day of this seventh month shall be the Feast of Tabernacles for seven days unto the Lord." This was God, setting up the Jewish "ceremonial" laws with Moses. We see that the fifteenth day of Tishri, the seventh month of the Jewish year, which falls around the middle of our October, begins the seven-day Feast of Tabernacles, or "Booths," or "Ingathering." Consider again this seventh month, which God considered the end of the year. What do we find in the book of Matthew that might bear on this? How about Matthew 13:30, 39? Speaking in a parable, Jesus said of tares and grain, "Let both grow together until the harvest: and in the time of harvest I will say to the reapers, gather together first the tares, and bind them in bundles to burn them: but gather the wheat into my barn." The tares are a biblical representation of the people who go to church but never become true believers. Tares are weeds that come up with the wheat and grow up looking so much like wheat that it is very hard to tell them apart. This results in allowing them to grow alongside the wheat until time to harvest them, when the seed is finally separated. The weeds are burned to prevent their reseeding into the field. Actually, it is believed that the designation "tare" referred to a grain known as "Bearded Darnell." This was a type of rye grass common to wheat fields, but that could be dangerous to livestock, because of a fungus that readily attached itself to that variety of grain.[15] In Matthew 13:39, Jesus continues his discussion of tares, with an explanation of the meaning of the parable, "The enemy that sowed them is the devil; the harvest is the end of the world; and the reapers are angels." So, we can appreciate the connection God has made between the Feast of Tabernacles, which was instituted by God as a picture of things to come (as were all of the ceremonial observances and feasts), and the plan for the return of Jesus at the end of the world. That will be the harvest of souls, the last day, the day of judgment and damnation for the unbelievers, all rolled into one. It's the end of the season of earth!

We have just experienced the total connection of the two testaments, illustrated in only one of the Jewish feast days. Imagine what lies hidden in the others! You can get an inkling in the emphasis God put upon the observance of those feasts (see Exodus 23: 14–17). Let's briefly review the three required feasts, recognizing there were several others.

The first was the Feast of Unleavened Bread, which was buried in the Passover Feast that ran from the fourteenth through the twenty-first of Nisan. That's the first month of the Jewish holy year, which approximates our April. The Feast of Unleavened Bread falls on the fifteenth day of Nisan. If you want to track these feast days, you have to remember that all Jewish days run from sundown to sundown. The Passover was a week-long celebration that anticipated the future shedding of the blood of the Messiah—the Passover Lamb—the sacrifice for God's chosen people. That's what was going on in Jerusalem the week the Jews crucified their Passover Lamb in a.d. 33!

The second celebration was the Feast of Harvest, or "firstfruits." It was also called the "Feast of Weeks." It seems like the Jews couldn't all agree on what to call their holidays! This one came on the sixth of the month of Sivan, roughly equivalent to our month of June. It was fifty days after the Passover Sabbath. We Christians know it best as "Pentecost," so named for the Latin *penta,* which had to do with groups of five. This day anticipated the spiritual harvest expected to result from the Messiah being sacrificed. We know from the book of Acts that this is precisely what happened.

Third, and the last we will discuss, involved all males of Israel. It was known as the Feast of Tabernacles, which we talked about earlier, as an entry to our discussion of Jewish Feasts. This was immediately preceded by the Day of Atonement (tenth day of the seventh month). Effectively, if not admittedly, this feast celebrated the "last day."

Now, how do these things we have been discussing all come together? You are now going to read something you likely have never heard before. If you look for it in the Bible, however, you will find it is there! At some point in history, on the very days of the year when Israel was celebrating these feasts, God brought about the exact spiritual event or phenomena, represented by the particular feast being celebrated! To illustrate: AD 33—the Jews hung the Passover lamb on a cross, while they celebrated Passover without him.

A few weeks after the cross, the church of Jesus began the harvest of souls during the Feast of Weeks. First fruits included approximately 3,000 people from sixteen nations on the day of Pentecost.

Will Christ complete the pattern by returning during the Feast of Tabernacles, or Ingathering, to complete the feasts of Israel on the last day? Could this knowledge give a "leg up" on being ready? It certainly seems that two of the three most significant Jewish Feasts, actually became their own literal conclusions—the exact times of God's plan of redemption being carried out in the sight of the people who killed the Passover Lamb! We also saw in this chapter that the rapture comes simultaneously with the resurrection of believers spoken of in Thessalonians, chapter four. In John six we saw that the resurrection of believers will happen on the last day. John chapter twelve led us to the truth that was buried in the Feast of Tabernacles—that the last day is the day of judgment. So far, all three trails of study appear to agree completely. So let's go on to a fourth area of examination. It will be left to the reader to examine the remaining Jewish feasts to determine how or if, they are connected to the end times.

TIMES OF SODOM
AND GOMORRAH

THE READER MAY WELL BE WONDERING HOW THE DESTRUCTION of places so sinful as these two cities and as relatively unimportant seeming, could possibly be a representation of the judgment day that will accompany the end of the whole world.

Even more puzzling might be the question, "What has this event way back in early history to do with shedding light on the rapture of God's church during the last days?" If you are wondering, that's good news, because that means you are thinking, and it also means you just may be open to allowing this book to help you find an answer—the biblical answer. People seldom come to recognition of God's truth, unless they are actively seeking an answer. God did not make understanding the true meanings of the Bible, like a stroll through the park. It often takes some serious digging to unearth some of the bones God has buried in the Word. Then too we know, because Scripture tells us, that some things we were not intended to know, until God figured we were ready. Some, in fact, were hidden until the end times, which we are in today, when much is being revealed that has laid unfathomed for centuries. It is exciting to suddenly come to an awareness of what our Lord now wants us to hear and understand. Some of it is not what we might wish for.

But, before we go back in time to the pages of Genesis—back from the end times, to near the beginning, to read of Sodom and Gomorrah, let's see what we can find in the New Testament. We'll be looking for what might bear on our search for truth concerning what picture, the story of these evil cities may hold for New Testament believers. We should begin with an examination of First Corinthians, chapter fifteen. This is a letter from the Apostle Paul to the church at Corinth, thousands of years after Sodom and Gomorrah disappeared. Let's listen in, as Paul speaks to the Corinthian Christians concerning believers and the last day of the world, in verses fifty-one through fifty-three: "Behold, I show you a mystery. We shall not sleep, but we shall all be changed. In a moment, in the twinkling of an eye, at the last trump: for the trumpet shall sound, and the dead shall be raised incorruptible, and we shall be changed."

Paul is speaking of the last day demonstration of the victory of Christ over death. He is speaking of the scenario painted so vividly in Matthew 24:31, by our Lord Jesus, as he describes to his followers, what will happen on the day of his return. Jesus tells them an angel will blow a trumpet, which will herald the gathering together of all his elect scattered "from one end of heaven to the other." We know from these last words that he was there speaking of the elect who already died, and whose souls were in heaven, which we might think of as a "haven" that protects them from judgment. But Paul is focused here, not on the dead, but on the living. All the apostles seem to have been certain that the second coming of Jesus would occur in their lifetimes. They had been told that those of the elect who are alive when Jesus returns, will not die. But they certainly will be changed by Christ, into new 'glorified bodies,' along with the dead whose bodies will also be made new (Philippians 3:21). Then, in those new bodies, they'll be "caught up" into heaven with, or shortly after, the glorified bodies of all those believers who had previously died.

The important message was, that neither the dead nor those still alive, had any significant advantage on getting into heaven. Theologians, pastors, and teachers speak of this as "the Rapture of the saints." The church, meaning all true believers from all history, will be called by trumpet to report and receive a new body to accompany the cleansed soul of salvation on the trip to heaven. This is the seventh and last trumpet spoken of in Revelation 11:15–19. It is also spoken of as the "last trumpet" in First Corinthians, chapter fifteen. This event is also heralded in First Thessalonians 4:15–17, where we are told that those who are alive and "remain unto the coming of the Lord" shall be caught up together with the risen dead, to meet Jesus in the "air." But what are we to suppose Paul meant by the word *remain?* It certainly is possible that Paul's words were meant to refer to "those who are still alive" at the coming of the Lord. Being ever Paul, however, Paul the evangelist, it is likely he was more concerned with ensuring that none "fall away" from their reliance on the Lord Jesus and become ineligible to receive a "glorified" body on the day Jesus returns. That sense of Paul's meaning just feels better. In Philippians 3:20–21, Paul confirms that it is Jesus who takes care of getting the saints fitted into new bodies:

> For our citizenship is in heaven; from whence also we look for the Savior, the Lord Jesus Christ: Who shall change our vile body, that it may be fashioned like unto his glorious body, according to the working whereby he is able even to subdue all things even unto himself.
>
> Philippians 3:20–21

So, we see that it is Christ who not only has justified us, but also will convert us into a form of bodily acceptability to enter the Father's heaven, joined to the soul he originally made new, when we were saved. Hallelujah!

The prophet Isaiah said of this day we are examining, "he will swallow up death in victory [...] And it shall be said in that day, Lo, this is our God; we have waited for him, and he will save us" (Isaiah 25: 8,9).

Now, please turn in your Bible to Revelation chapter eleven. We looked at verses fifteen through nineteen earlier, in relation to the seventh trumpet. Lets focus now on something else. We have just learned that the Rapture occurs virtually simultaneously with the second coming of Christ. We also read in the Bible, that the dead shall rise on that day and the believers will go to heaven on that day, in new, heavenly bodies, united with their souls that had been reigning in heaven with Christ. So let's look at verse eighteen of Revelation eleven. The Bible is a bit wordy in this explanation, but only because God does not want us to mistake what he is telling us. This verse clearly says that the day when the seventh trumpet is blown, some other things also occur: the wrath of God has come upon the nations. What is the "wrath of God"? It is *judgment!* It is the time when the dead will be judged—both believers and unbelievers.

So, we also know that the rapture and judgment day occur on the same day. Now we have arrived at the point where the vast majority of evangelical Christians choose to stop reading, or at least to stop perceiving. Many will say (we know because we have heard them), "The book of Revelation is just too hard to understand!" That statement is hooey if one is a true believer. If a true believer will attempt to understand, God will reward his effort. The author knows that's true because that was what happened to him, once he stopped running away from God's truth! Can anybody reading this page today, honestly say this has been too hard to understand?

Take a second to look again, at Revelation eleven, verse fifteen. But this time, we want to sort of just get a sense of what the main message of this verse is. Ok, we read it through, then we ponder, asking ourselves, "What is the purpose of this verse?" Let's phrase it another way to ourselves: "What is this verse announcing?" Announcing? Why of course—it's announcing that "The end has begun." It is heralding judgment day—the last day—the end of the world—the end of time. It's all the same day! Now, read through verse eighteen again, and be ready for a little quiz.

Q. Why are the nations angry in verse eighteen?

A. They were warned but were still surprised (like a thief in the night). Add your own ideas.

Q. What does it mean to "destroy them which destroy the earth?"

A. Here's one approach to answering this question: simply ask yourself, "What caused God to want to destroy the earth? The answer is, it was sin. So in God's view, it is sinners, not himself, not messy campers, who are destroying the earth on the last day. That's justice, and is probably why he is so full of wrath at sinners, and why the wages of sin is death. They are spoilers!

Now one last time, at the risk of being redundant, we know Christ comes on the day the last trumpet sounds. Also, verse eighteen says it's a time for the dead to be judged. What does that make this day we are looking at? It makes it judgment day. We also know that we call the day when Christ comes the "rapture." So, using that old mathematical axiom that says, "Things equal to the same thing are equal to each other," we can say we have several equal signs working here on this one day!

But, we are past due on our arrival in Sodom and Gomorrah, and we are heading there right now. But, on the way (isn't *but* an important word?) you need to be introduced to a fellow called Luke, because he has some information that is going to bear on the situation in the two nasty cities. So, you are invited to find Luke 17:28–37, and to read the whole thing.

This is a good introduction to what happened in Genesis, and notice that it ties in with the day that Luke terms, "the day when the Son of man is revealed." He characterizes that time for us as one in which, "they did eat, they drank, they bought, they sold, they planted, they builded." In other words, life as usual was going on right up to the time when God took action against them. Notice, Luke is not describing cities; he is describing the people who lived in them. The cities were not the sinners, the inhabitants were, and the same day that Lot left, "God rained fire and brimstone from heaven, and destroyed them all." God destroyed "them," and additionally the cities were torn apart.

But how did it happen that Lot was spared? Well, Lot was the son of Abram's brother. Abram's father, Terah, had left the land of Ur (Iraq) and took his son, daughter-in-law, and nephew Lot, along with him to settle in Canaan. We do not know how old Lot was, but he was probably somewhat younger than Abram, who had been born 2861 years after Noah's son Shem was born. This information is given simply to establish that Lot, despite choosing to live in Sodom and to marry a woman from there, who was probably not a believer, as Lot evidently was, came from good stock. We have to assume that Lot was a believer, since God did select him from all the people of the city to be saved from destruction. We know from Genesis 19:1 that Lot met two messengers (possibly angels) at the gate of the city, then invited them to stay the night at his house. They accepted after an initial declination, and Lot made a big dinner for them (verse three). Men of the city came to the house and wanted Lot to turn the two over to them for vile conduct. The messengers told Lot to gather up his family and, "bring them out of this place." In other words, "get out of town," because they intended to destroy all the people there. Lot was in no hurry to leave, but finally he was told to take his wife and two daughters and leave immediately, or they would perish! After much hand-wringing, Lot finally agreed to leave, but would not go to where the Lord wanted him. Instead, he went to a small city named Zoar (verse twenty-two). So, Lot and his two daughters were saved from the wrath of God, which brought utter destruction to Sodom and to Gomorrah. Lot's wife couldn't turn her back on evil, so she was turned into a pillar of salt. Lot's own conduct is worth study, but we leave that to another day. That was judgment day—the end of the world—for the people who lived in those cities. They were utterly destroyed, but messengers from God took Lot out of the devastation. Lot was watching at the gate and was present, when the time of destruction was at hand. Lot's wife just couldn't put worldly things behind her, although they were warned in a manner very similar to the warning Jesus gives in Luke 17. There he warns, "he that is in the field, let him [...] not return back." Jesus says clearly "remember Lot's wife. Whoever shall seek to save his life shall lose it, and whosoever shall lose his life shall preserve it."

Jesus is clear that, as it was in the days of Abram and Lot, "even thus shall it be when the son of man is revealed" (verse thirty). So, we can say with assurance, that another picture of the last day is found in Lot's departure and the fate of Sodom and Gomorrah. Everything associated with that event, happened in a single day: judgment, removal of God's chosen, and the last day (end of the world).

It is time now, with Sodom and Gomorrah fresh in our minds, to open the book of Revelation again. Find chapter seven, verse nine. Here the Bible is talking about the great multitude, which no man could number, who are standing before the Lamb. They are all saved Gentiles, and in verse fourteen, we learn that they "came out of great tribulation." They were saved, evidently during the tribulation, or were already Christians who went through the tribulation. This means that the Christians could not have all been raptured before the tribulation. If they had been, who was around to bring the gospel to all these who were saved during the tribulation? In any case, we know that the tribulation has just ended, and that believers were involved in it. We know it just ended for two reasons. First, this multitude is standing before the throne, so this is judgment day. Second, we were told in Matthew 24:29 that, "Immediately *after* the tribulation of those days, shall the sun be darkened." It is speaking here of the end of the world!

So, we see that the Lord himself actually links the last day of the earth with the destruction of Sodom and Gomorrah! He is talking about the last day—the day Christ comes—the day the angels come—the eagles come—the day Judgment comes—the day the dead are raised and the day the church of God is changed into a transportable form and "beamed up" to join Christ in the clouds. That's a big day, in case you hadn't noticed! Since there is so little difference between then and now, why would we not expect the Lord to apply a tried and true stratagem? The message we ought to focus on, is, *be committed* and *be ready*, so we do not look back, or pause to reconsider. Committed, if you consider it, will be extremely important.

RESURRECTION DAY AND THE RAPTURE

W E HAVE NOW STUFFED OURSELVES WITH FOUR-CHAPTERS WORTH of information that cannot have failed to cause us to at least begin seeing some connections the Bible has made for our edification. Certainly, anyone who has been to church more than a few times, already recognizes that there is a link between the resurrection of the dead and what we call the rapture. The rapture in fact, is a resurrection from death, if you think about it! To the living, it is every bit as important as resurrection is to the dead.

But there are quite a few biblical truths that many who are, or think they are, Christians, have never been exposed to, for one reason or another. If that is actually true, then there is conjecture and opinion, fancy and misinterpretation, which can stand some brushing aside.

This chapter deals with another one of the scriptural areas or "trails" spoken about at the beginning of this part of the book. The particular Scriptures are some of the same you have already followed to trace one or more of the other separate trails in the preceding chapters. You may be getting a feeling of redundancy, but don't think that means you are not covering new ground, because you are. That's the nature of inductive study. This chapter traces an entirely separate trail from those we have previously followed.

Once again, we will allow the Bible, and the Bible alone, to lead us to uncovering the truth that God is leading us to. The Lord is trying to tell us, but some simply will not listen! By the end of this book, you will be able to see that any one of these scriptural trails is sufficient to show the utter inability of the premillennialist position to be considered biblical, in any stretch of the human imagination. Linked together, they highlight the truth of what God wants us to know and to teach.

Let's begin this section of our study, by looking again into First Thessalonians chapter four. This area of the Bible contains a wealth of often quoted Scriptures, which are some of the most used when discussing or teaching the rapture. We referenced these verses in an earlier chapter, but let's read them again to begin afresh this particular view of God's Word.

> For if we believe that Jesus died and rose again, even so them also which are dead in Jesus will God bring with him. For this we say to you by the word of the Lord, that we which are alive and remain unto the coming of the Lord shall not precede them which are dead. For the Lord himself shall descend from heaven with a shout, with the voice of the archangel, and with the trump of God: and the dead in Christ shall rise first: Then we which are alive and remain shall be caught up together with them in the clouds, to meet the Lord in the air: and so shall we ever be with the Lord.
>
> 1 Thessalonians 4:14–17

Notice that this particular passage does not in fact say clearly, that both groups of believers, the dead and the alive, will be accompanying our Lord in the same hour, or even on the same day! We can get very used to assuming things that we "just know," without actually including the proofs of them in a particular discussion.

So, allow the Bible to remind you what John 6:40 has to say: "And this is the will of him that sent me, that every one which seeth the Son, and believes on him, may have everlasting life: and I will raise him up on the last day." This then, is how we know that true believers will be raised in one day, and that the day will be the last day. Now hear what Jesus has to say in John 12:48 about those who do not believe: "He that rejects me, and receives not my words, has one who judges him: the word that I have spoken, the same shall judge him in the last day."

So, if we can believe that our Lord means that a day is truly a day, he will not only be raising the believers on the last day, but also judging the nonbelievers on the same day. In order to do that, he will have to also raise them, and we know that the Bible refers often to "the day of the Lord." So we feel safe, when we couple being told that the last day is also judgment day, with an educated assumption that the unsaved dead are raised the same day also. We can confirm this decision with the words of the Apostle John: "the hour is coming in which all that are in the graves shall hear his voice, and shall come forth, they that have done good, unto the resurrection of life; they that have done evil, unto the resurrection of damnation" (John 5:28–29). With this, we certainly appear to be on firm ground in our contentions concerning the last day. We have established the order of events on the last day, including the timing of the rapture, in relation to the resurrection, in the words of 1 Thessalonians 4 above. Let's reiterate them for you, verse by verse:

First: verse fourteen–Christ comes, bringing with him the souls of the saved dead. Then,

Second: verse fifteen–we learn that the living believers will not hinder the connection of the dead saints with God, because:

Third: verse sixteen—the bodies of the dead souls who are with Christ, rise at Christ's command. Then, verse seventeen—the living saints are "caught up together with the newly risen dead, in the clouds!" How could anything be clearer?

Isn't it interesting how one single group of verses can lay out the entire catalogue of events at the end of time? Yet, many refuse to accept what the Bible has to say and may even refuse any attempt to understand it, relying instead on something someone who never studied the Bible carefully, told them years ago! What other explanation can there be for so many Christian denominations teaching that the church will be "raptured" out of the tribulation, and not have to endure it? We have just seen that they will be caught up on the last day of the Great Tribulation, which is the day of the Lord! It will be a day of business as usual, not tribulation at all, for the unbelievers-until they see what's going on!

The reader is correct, if he has gotten the idea that the end of time will be a rather busy day. How in the dickens is Christ going to be able to judge all those sinners in one day? Of course the Scriptures speak of "judgment day," and perhaps that is only the beginning of God's workweek! That may be fuel for another study. Has it been obvious, as we have worked through these chapters, that they have gotten progressively shorter? Yes, that was intentional. It just so happens, as each reader is no doubt recognizing, that there are not all that many separate Scriptures necessary to prove our points about this subject. The important and informative ones keep turning up in our proofs, regardless of the trail we are following to the truth of the rapture, as it is told in the Bible. But that fact does not invalidate the separateness of the trails to truth, which God has woven throughout his Word. Only one trail remains in our particular, chosen proof of God's plan.

So, come on along with me now, as we finish off our search for God's truth about the "last day," The Great Tribulation, and finally, the "catching up" of the saints, as our God says repeatedly in the Bible, on the "last day."

TIMES OF THE PROPHET DANIEL

WELCOME TO THE FINAL CHAPTER OF THIS PORTION OF THE book. This is the last of my attempts to show you that the Bible is quite clear about the events of the final days. Although you noticed the trend of successively shorter chapters, this one breaks that trend, and gets longer. We have thus far traced our way along five distinct trails, each leading in its own way, to the truth of the great miracle that somewhere, at sometime, somebody dubbed, "the Rapture." The author does not claim to know where the term finds its origins, nor does he particularly care, since it has been the root of so much mistaken scholarship. He also doesn't think much of it!

That, by the way, is the typical hallmark of the errant gospels of men that so abound among the denominations in our day. In their *Illustrated Bible Dictionary,* Zondervan takes a rather enjoyable position on the term. They don't mention it at all!

Of course, that's because the term is not contained in the written Word, but was coined by someone as a shorthand reference to a major event. It's almost an insulting term. God certainly did not name "it." "It" is not even a single, isolated event, but rather consists in several separate and distinct special, supernatural occurrences. The several occurrences just happen to seem sufficiently simultaneous to merit having been labeled by lazy theologians, with an actually non-descriptive term. Then, it also has the disadvantage, that in order to be understood, it has to be explained. That alone should tend to discourage its use in theological discussion, but it does not. Oh well, it's another sign our time, that we so often settle for less than truly meaningful discussions of the gospel.

Tribulation, on the other hand, is a biblical term. It is a phenomenon actually described in the Bible, yet experience has been, that churchgoers know a lot more about the made-up term than they do about the biblically described event. I'm not exaggerating. God inextricably entwines that event with the made-up term. The word *tribulation* can be found in Scripture, but alas, that has not meant that it could be widely understood by teachers, pastors, or even authors who write books like this one. This author was flippant enough recently, to offhandedly ask a friend, who happens to be a pastor in a major denomination, if he knew how to determine when the "Great Tribulation" might begin. As was suspected, the longtime pastor was not at all conversant with that particular reference in Scripture. He also happens to be a premillennialist. It's widespread, ignorance is!

Only this past week, a relative who is firmly convinced that if the tribulation begins, he will already have been "raptured," was asked to show the author where it says that in the Bible. Needless to say, he had something about a fingernail far more pressing, that required immediate attention, and his presence elsewhere. Evangelicals don't even know what the Bible says about that subject and evidently do not want to know! They just want to be left alone to believe whatever they choose to believe. That is a tragic truth. At any rate, here we are—just the two of us—and the author of this book will take the liberty to presume that you, its reader, desire to learn something, and that's why you have this book in your hand. This is your last chapter about the last day, so treat it kindly, and it will be good to you as well. In chapters past, we have concluded by Scripture search alone, that the last day of the existence of this earth, at least as we know it, whenever it comes, will be coincident with the resurrection of all the dead everywhere. We have also concluded that such time will essentially be simultaneous for saved and unsaved alike, but we could be argued out of that position by a sufficiently passionate argument. It will also be coincident with the "catching up," as the Bible puts it, of the saved people living at that time, and it will begin the time when the unsaved of all generations come before the judgment seat of almighty God. All this is according to clear passages, found by ourselves, in the Bible. We have used no other reference book, no well-known seminarian authority on the Bible, no commentaries by famous but long-dead theologians or preachers, as they do in the seminaries, in preference to reading the Bible. And, we've done reasonably well.

But the Bible has more to say on this subject. Might it be, therefore, that in further study, we could find evidence to contradict what we think we know as a result of our studies in one or more of the previous chapters? Indeed it could, but there is only one way to know the answer to that question, so let's continue by examining this subject from yet another aspect. But before we go on, know with certainty, that the Bible assures us, that the concept of progressive revelation is quite seriously among the major premises of Scripture. That means it is always possible that tomorrow may bring enlightenment one had not achieved today. But that's only going to happen to someone who is regularly and diligently, studying the Bible. Most of what is contained between the covers of the book you are holding had not been revealed to the author five years ago.

Christ Jesus has provided us an outline of things we should look for—the signs and events that will occur shortly before we hear his shout and the trumpet heralding his coming. Let's begin in Matthew 24, verses four through thirty-one, where Jesus answers two questions from his disciples, as he sits on the Mount of Olives. Immediately, many of us get a picture of somebody standing on the very top of a mountain, almost up in the clouds, and everyone listening is down below, because there is not room at the top for the entire crowd. That's the image this writer always used to get reading this chapter in Matthew. But then he did something clever. He checked his geographical atlas and was disappointed. The Mount of Olives, the top of which is approximately one half mile east of the east wall of Jerusalem, is not much of a mountain. The city is at an elevation of approximately 2,600 feet above sea level, and the wide, flattish top of the mount is only 250 feet above the city! It's a sort of flattened, roundish ridge about a mile long where olive trees grew in ancient times. So, our Savior could have been sitting anywhere on that big, rounded mound they call a "mount." Sorry!

The disciples asked Jesus, just after He told them the temple would be totally destroyed, "Tell us, when will these things be?" And they asked Him, "What will be the sign of your coming, and of the end of the world?" So, here is our first question:

Q. "Do we highlight what is not popular with the church?" Or asked another way, "What does this teach us that the disciples already knew, but that most evangelical Christians don't want to know today?"

A. It's obvious from their second question that the disciples already knew, because their Lord taught them, that the end of the world was simultaneous with the second coming of the Christ! Look again if you didn't catch it. Check it out! Now here is an even tougher question that is not actually part of our lesson, but that really cannot be separated from it.

Q. If what is obvious in the Bible is true, can there be a "millennial reign" of the believers with Christ on earth after Jesus returns?

A. Definitely not, if God has anything to say about it! (This one requires some serious digging, with an application of common sense. Perhaps that's a subject for another book.)

Q. Why did they ask Jesus, in this discussion, about the end of the world?

A. Obviously, Jesus had connected the events, as in the first answer above, and they wondered if there would be separate signs.

Beginning in verse four, Jesus answers the disciples, speaking about what is in store for them. Then in verse fifteen, he warns everyone who will ever read the Bible, what to do when they see a certain thing happen. He calls the thing they will see, "The abomination of desolation," which Daniel the prophet spoke of, in the Old Testament. Notice that Jesus is positive about this happening. He does not say "if" we see it. He says "when" we see it. In order to begin to find out what this means, we had better go read what Daniel had to say, because we are given a parenthetical admonishment to be certain we understand this passage.

The Scriptures to which Jesus was referring are in Daniel chapters nine, eleven, and twelve. Shall we start with the smallest number? Good, that would be Daniel 9:23. Actually, this smallest number refers to the parenthetical information that comes last in the verse. Here's what it says, and remember this admonition is coming from God, through Gabriel, through Daniel, to you! It's something God definitely wants you to know: "The commandment came forth, and I am come to show you; for you are greatly beloved: therefore understand the matter, and consider the vision." Isn't it nice to hear something like that from Jesus? Especially so, after being basically told, "Now pay attention to this!" What comes next is the instruction concerning the revelation of what we know as "the seventy weeks of Daniel." Do you recall what instruction wrapped up this part of Daniel? In Daniel 12:4, the prophet was told to close and seal the book until the time of the end. Daniel did that, and only now, because we are legitimately in the end times (in fact, in the tribulation), have a very few had their eyes opened by God. As a result, some have been able to see what was in the book that has been sealed for all these years. Much that was previously hidden to Christians for almost 2,000 years, is being revealed now to serious Bible scholars. They are few! Let's go on, so that you are presented with the opportunity to "understand the matter," to "consider the vision." The one who wrote this book you are holding is confident that if you are studying this book, you too, are "greatly beloved."

Having briefly visited Daniel, let's now return to the verse we were reading in Matthew, and we will revisit Daniel as we go along. Remember, we are told that we will see, "The abomination of desolation [...] stand in the holy place." When we see that, Jesus instructs us, beginning in the next verse,

> Then let them which be in Judaea flee into the mountains. Let him which is on the housetop not come down to take anything out of his house: Neither let him which is in the field return back to take his clothes. [...] For then shall be great tribulation, such as was not since the beginning of the world to this time, no, nor ever shall be.
>
> Matthew 24: 16–18, 21

So, despite the inescapable fact that most pastors cannot tell you when the tribulation begins, here in the words of Jesus that beginning is clearly defined! The tribulation is kicked off by somebody—anyone—not necessarily everyone—seeing the abomination of desolation standing in the holy place! Our task now of course, is to define two things for ourselves:

1. The "abomination of desolation" and

2. The "holy place"

The author can personally remember struggling over the meaning of the quote when he first attempted to apply it to our time. We are about to see how, "fleeing to the mountains" and "being in Judea," fit in for Christians today. But right now, it's time to quietly return to Daniel chapter nine to see if there might be some definitional assistance lurking there. Find Daniel 9:4, and let's see if we can find a parallel to the time of Daniel and the time we are living in today. We find the prophet praying, "And I prayed to the Lord my God, and made my confession, and said, Oh Lord [...] We have sinned, and have committed iniquity, and have rebelled, even departing from thy precepts and thy judgments."

Then jumping down to verse ten, Daniel tells us, "Neither have we obeyed the voice of the Lord our God, to walk in his laws, which he set before us by his servants the prophets."

Of course, though he was living in Babylon during the time of the "captivity," Daniel was speaking for all the nation of Israel. His concerns were for the apostasy of his people and their spiritual leaders. It would hardly be farfetched to suppose that we today face a similar problem. The world has more of a stranglehold on "Christians" today than it ever had before. The Christian world permits the murder of the unborn, we allow our children to watch smutty TV programs and our girls to wear clothing that only a decade ago would have branded them as sexually promiscuous. If we can believe the reports of numerous studies of teenagers, sexually promiscuous is exactly what children today are. In the Western democracies, teen pregnancy rates among churchgoing families, along with rates of sexually transmitted diseases (STDs) mirrors the secular world. Forty years ago our country had about four STDs. Today the number is twenty-three and climbing! "Christians" think nothing of enjoying R-rated movies, and the divorce rate in Western countries is the highest it has ever been, and equally high within the congregations! The entire fabric of our families has been rent asunder as our morality and humanity are being eroded away by current attitudes. Most corporate churches today sanction divorce and remarriage in the church, where sixty years ago divorce was virtually unknown. "Christian" music of today is often taken right out of the "rap" of mid-city gangs and dope rings, as is the dress and behavior of many young churchgoers. There is an "anything-goes" attitude that pervades many corporate churches today and which is often supported by the denominational leaders. There is a widespread interest in "miracles," signs and wonders, including "faith healing," falling over backwards, barking like dogs, "holy laughter," and especially speaking in tongues, all of which pass for worship! The tongues phenomena has spread rapidly through many mainstream churches, where it is always closely followed by signs and wonders, falling backward, and so-called "faith healings." The corporate churches today are in a sad state of spiritual disrepair, and are going more downhill every day. That means that in biblical terms we, who call ourselves God's church, are in a state of constant fornication! The bottom line is that it sounds like we are no better off as believers, than were the Hebrews of Daniel's time, maybe even worse.

Now, let's go back and see what else Daniel has to say about his time and ours. There may be an interesting parallel in the words of verse sixteen with our own time. "O Lord, according to all thy righteousness, I beseech thee, let thine anger and thy fury be turned away from thy city Jerusalem, thy holy mountain; because of our sins, and for the iniquities of our fathers." Daniel is showing us here that Jerusalem, especially because of the temple, was a "holy place" in his day (but it was an evil place too). One might say that, despite God not dwelling there, it was "*the* holy place," the center of worship, the location of the holy articles of the Jews, the place they went to sacrifice and worship. It was their "sanctuary." We see that amplified in the next verse, "Now therefore O our God, hear the prayer of thy servant, and his supplications, and cause thy face to shine upon thy sanctuary that is desolate, for the Lord's sake" (Daniel 9:17). Well, this seems to be saying that the sanctuary is desolate because of the sins of the people. It appears that Daniel was rather concerned for the safety of that desolate sanctuary, from the wrath of God! He cries out to the Lord in verse nineteen, of chapter nine, "O Lord, hear; O Lord, forgive; O Lord, hearken and do: defer not." We can be sure, because of Daniel's words, that the holy place, the desolate place, was the temple—the sanctuary—in Jerusalem, the holy city, so that the "holy place" included the city of Jerusalem!

So, where is our sanctuary, our holy place? It's not Jerusalem! The fundamentalist will say that it is, because he values the Old Testament over the teaching of Christ. But in our culture, our religion, there really is no one place we could call a "holy city" unless it was an agglomeration of our sanctuaries, our church meeting places. There is no single spot that Christians make pilgrimages to, or go to worship. Taken together, our places of worship in our neighborhood church buildings may be said to represent our "holy city." So, if we were to designate a holy place, we would have to say it was inside our meeting places, or what we commonly refer to as our "churches." This is not to suggest that the true holy of holies is not within each true believer, since we, both individually and collectively are the dwelling place of the Holy Spirit. Christ lives within us, praise the Lord! But when we go to the meeting place—to church—that is where the Spirit is (or is not!), where the candlestick is, or is not! The Bible says the Spirit there, is the candlestick of that church. The book of Revelation speaks of God removing the candlesticks of churches that are not true to the gospel. That means the Holy Spirit leaves those churches! If you are not familiar with that, you should read chapters one through three of the book of Revelations.

Now let's go back to Daniel, and when we get there, please read verses twenty-four through twenty-seven of chapter nine, where the messenger (angel) Gabriel is talking confidentially to Daniel. Here is that conversation:

> Seventy weeks are determined upon thy people and upon thy holy city, to finish the transgression, and to make an end of sins, and to make reconciliation for iniquity, and to bring in everlasting righteousness, and to seal up the vision and prophesy, and to anoint the most holy. Know therefore and understand, that from the going forth of the Commandment to restore and to build Jerusalem, unto the Messiah the Prince shall be seven weeks, and threescore and two weeks: the street shall be built again and the wall, even in troublous times. And after threescore and two weeks shall Messiah be cut off, but not for himself: and the people of the prince that shall come shall destroy the city and the sanctuary; and the end thereof shall be with a flood, and unto the end of the war desolations are determined. And he shall confirm the covenant with many for one week: and in the midst of the week he shall cause the sacrifice and the oblation to cease, and for the overspreading of abominations he shall make it desolate, even until the consummation, and that determined shall be poured upon the desolate.
>
> Daniel 9:24–27

We have not really found the most facile of language samples have we? This is tough stuff to make out. That may be why nobody had much success in understanding it for the past 2,000 years or so. But that does not mean we should not make every effort to understand what God is here saying for our edification. After all, God told Daniel to seal the book until the end times, and that's exactly where we are today! That is precisely why some of us are just now coming to understandings that have eluded scholars for nearly two millennia. We are actually not going to "lift" a lot out of this part of Daniel, for this particular study. Mainly, just a sense of what is going on. What may be important to think about here, is a simple question that may not have such a simple answer. The question is:

Q. What is meant by "desolate?" (desolation)

A. It's likely we each have a tip-of-the-tongue definition, but is it accurate with regard to the Bible usage? Let's go back to the Bible again for a definition.

Reading slowly and carefully through verses twenty-four through twenty-seven of Daniel 9, we see that the Messiah (who speaks for God through Scripture) will be "cut off" (verse twenty-six). The time periods here are important but not for this particular study. This is reminiscent of the two witnesses of God in Revelation 11, who are a representation of the church, which carries the word. They are cut off (killed) and lie dead in the street for three days, before coming back to life. And we see that another prince (not capitalized, so not holy) shall come and destroy the city and the sanctuary, and "desolations are determined." Daniel does not say this other prince is "standing in the sanctuary" (who, let's assume, is Satan, just for now, because he is Christ's chief adversary throughout the Bible). Daniel says only that this other prince destroys it. It is his presence then, that causes the destruction of the sanctuary or "holy place" or city (Jerusalem) that represents God's holy mountain to the Jews.

So, we can say that the very presence of Satan (or his emissaries and activists) is enough to destroy what the Holy City represents. Notice in verse twenty-seven that he has stopped the worship practices. And there will be an "overspreading of," or we might correctly say "a substitution with," abominations of some sort. He has spread his abominations over the holy things of the sanctuary, making it desolate because God the Holy Spirit is no longer operating there. Whatever these abominations are, they effectively ruin the sanctuary, making it of no account to God.

But, do you see the hope expressed in verse twenty-seven? Look again. He promises that when the "consummation" comes - the ending that has already been determined, that whatever that end is (he does not disclose what it is here), it will be "poured upon the desolator!" If we really think about it, this has to be the wrath of God. Could this be a hint that in the end, God will triumph? We do know that in Revelation, when those two witnesses come back to life, God once again reigns in victory over death and evil. That's about as exhaustive as we want to get in Daniel right now. So, let's flee back to Matthew, but before we do, consider this question. Are you beginning to get a feeling for this back and forth interplay of Scriptures and times (always returning to find truth for our time), which makes inductive study, with its word-by-word, thought-by-thought analysis of meaning, so rewarding? Okay, now back to Matthew and chapter twenty-four, with the new knowledge of the definitions we went looking for in Daniel.

We learned that the "abomination of desolation" is the same as the "abomination that makes desolate," or Satan, who ruins the sanctuary for God's purpose, so that the Holy Spirit is no longer operating there. So, we can insert this into verse fifteen and know that it is telling us, that when Satan was ruling in the sanctuary of Daniel's time, God left, and it became desolate. Likewise, cranking that meaning forward a couple of thousand years (God is the same yesterday, today, and forever), we read, parenthetically; "when you see Satan standing in the church congregations or denominations, you Christians are commanded to do the stuff in the next few verses!" Why? Because, as Jesus tells us in verse twenty-one, that's when we will experience the Great Tribulation! Has the rapture already happened? It cannot have happened, because Jesus is not telling the unsaved to run for the hills, he's telling Christians! Then too, who was it that we learned, in Daniel's time, caused the abomination to take over? It was the people who were supposed to be the chosen of God! In our day we are talking about the corporate churches and the people in them. Satan cannot come in to take over, so long as the Holy Spirit is functioning in the congregations. Notice please, that there is no suggestion here anywhere, that every single church has to be recognized as belonging to Satan, before Christians are to take action. It says, in essence, as soon as you see it happening, run for cover *out* of the corporate church! But that is an entirely different study also, and one that is not fun, so let's just leave the churches being in the midst of the Great Tribulation, with all their membership still waiting to be raptured. We did agree, however, to cover the "flee to the mountains" of Mathew 24:15, when you see Satan taking over the corporate churches.

There are numerous references in both Testaments of the Bible, where mountains or certain mountains (Zion and others) represent the sanctuary, or special place, of God, or represent God Himself. We saw this, as a matter of fact, when we looked at Daniel 9, where we saw: "thy city Jerusalem, thy holy mountain." It is not necessary to belabor the point, but a bit of study will show that the reference would mean in essence, "flee to where God is." The Judea part seems to refer to the temple (a sign of the corporate churches as the place of worship) in Jerusalem, which is in Judea. This carries the connotation that we cannot serve two masters. There is a symbolic treatment of this truth in the Book of Ezra. In chapter ten, Ezra informs the people that the men who married wives who were not Hebrew, must separate from those wives and their children. The men agreed that they would do so. They could not go into the temple while in opposition to God's law, and the simile is that we cannot serve God and worship Satan at the same time. That's probably enough of that to let our reader see how we prove the Bible with the Bible.

But yes, before any accusation of short cutting, there certainly are some warning signs of the coming tribulation and the end of the world. These preconditions are often mistakenly taught as being part of the tribulation. Let's look at why they are not part of it. We are given a list, beginning in verse five and running through verse twelve, of Matthew 24. The list seems not to be necessarily meant to be arranged in a chronological order, nor is it necessarily exhaustive. Its purpose is simply to alert believers to the things that Jesus knows are going to happen. As you read through the list, number those things you believe have already occurred in your lifetime. Here's the list:

False Christs	Strife among nations
Famines	Persecution of believers
Pestilence	Church goers betraying one another
Earthquakes in many places	Hatred among church members
Wars and rumors of wars	False prophets
Love of God wearing away	

According to Jesus, the first five are simply "the beginning of sorrows" (Matthew 24:8). The rest are evidently full-blown sorrows. But we should recognize that only three of the above are unique to churchgoers, and none may apply to true believers. None of this is the tribulation Jesus speaks of. Nothing men can do, is the cause of the Great Tribulation, with the exception of not keeping God's commandments, if one is of the church. The Great Tribulation is strictly the result of the corporate churches (but not the true, eternal church) being taken over by Satan. That is just about the worst thing true believers can imagine happening! The one thing from these passages that does affect true Christians, is not listed because it did not belong with the others. Matthew 24:9 says, "Then shall they deliver you up to be afflicted, and shall kill you: And ye shall be hated of all Nations for my name's sake." This is already going on in parts of the world today, even here in America, and it applies only to true believers. True believers are certainly hated today by much of the secular world. The reason it is already going on, is because it is a part of the Great Tribulation. That's just one way we can know that we are already in the first part of that tribulation. The chief indicator is in verse fifteen, and in the conduct of the various congregations. We have already discussed those two indicators, but recall what verses fifteen and sixteen tell us, because it is so key to our analysis: "When ye shall therefore see the abomination of desolation, spoken of by Daniel the prophet, stand in the holy place, (whoso readeth, let him understand) Then let them which be in Judaea flee into the mountains."

It is time then, for those who care, to conclude that the rapture cannot precede the tribulation because tribulation is here—it has begun! The author cannot say with authority exactly when it began, but according to the indicators, it is here. But the rapture is not (At least we who think we're Christians better hope it's not!). But we can narrow down to a rather precise conclusion, when the rapture will occur in relation to the other end-time events described in the Bible. Now here's another exercise:

Speaking of the "Great Tribulation," Jesus, whom we can rely on as an expert in these matters, says in verse twenty-two of Matthew 24, that God will shorten the tribulation for the sake of the elect.

Q. Why would God have to shorten the Tribulation, if the believers (the elect) had already been "taken up" in a "pre-trib" rapture?

A. ?

God has given us a fairly precise outline of the end times—a chronology really, leading up to the judgment day. This is found in Matthew 24:29–30. There, God declares that not some time after, not even soon after, but "*Immediately* after the tribulation of those days," some definite things are going to occur. In other words these things will end the tribulation, instantly if not sooner! That's why the Bible warns us to watch-to be ready-to figure out in advance, just exactly what we will do, when God makes that instant transition, happen.

1. The sun will be darkened

2. The moon will not give light

3. The stars will fall from heaven

4. The powers of the heaven shall be shaken (gravity, tides, rotation, etc.)

God does not divulge the means of these results, but presumably these things could be caused by more than one means, making it dark, and in other ways, scary! Will the planets fly out of our solar system, or will they crash into one another, or blow up? We don't know, and if you think about it, who cares? It's the end of everything, so precisely how it ends kind of falls into the "why worry?" category. The point is, what ends the tribulation, is destruction of everything except the elect! There is one thing that might merit some consideration. Remember that the sun and the moon are what our entire calendar and planetary system of time are based upon? If they are suddenly gone, or moved, is that not the end of time as we know it? The last day is the last of time. Now, as to the real significance of our stars falling, let's take a look at Revelation 6:12–17.

There we find God describing, in a detailed way, some things that are going to happen at the opening of the sixth seal:

1. A great earthquake (the ground splits open; rocks and buildings tumble down)

2. The sun turns black (it's totally dark)

3. The moon becomes red as blood (it's no longer a reflector)

4. The stars fall to earth (this alone could be fatal!)

5. Heaven is rolled together like a scroll (ouch!)

6. Every mountain and island is moved (tidal wave time!)

Does this sound like anything but the last day? How many stars do you figure any one neighborhood can absorb? How long can man last without sunlight and heat? This is definitely the end of our world! We find similar language in 2 Peter 3:10–13. The message is, this is the wrath of God, of which the Bible says the judgment is a part. This is the utter end-similar to Noah's day. Considering this pile of rubble God just created, can you see Christ returning here to set up an earthly throne right after the tribulation? Yet some denominations insist this will happen. Again, let's recall that what makes this time period the Great Tribulation, is not all this destruction of the world, but that Satan has taken over in the corporate churches. Non-believers are ecstatic until day zero, not sharing in the misery that believers are experiencing. Then destruction ends it. The misery comes later for the nonbelievers and lasts a whole lot longer. It starts on the last day, then goes on for eternity, while true believers have only the tribulation period to endure before the end. Jesus takes them out, just moments before that end. The only activity that separates the Great Tribulation and the end of the world is the last day, when the true believers will be caught up to be with Jesus. After that, they are in paradise, as the universe is rearranged into whatever God wants it to be. If believers were raptured before the tribulation, why would it be called tribulation? Who would it be tribulation for? Certainly, the followers of Satan would not get too upset to wake up and find their hero in the churches that everybody else has left. Just look around at today's churches. It may be that God has given us another foreshadowing, in the national elections of 2008.

Let's also recall that, immediately *following* the tribulation, God's timetable calls for the Rapture to occur, so we can know that the timing of the Rapture is completely dependent on the occurrence of the Great Tribulation. Once Christ returns in the clouds, there is one day filled with last-minute tasks for Jesus, just before the world falls in on the unbelievers. Did you follow this? This is the nutshell, if you've been looking for one.

It should now be safe to observe that we have been diligent in our application of the Bible to the solutions of our questions. We have patiently examined no fewer than six separate and distinct relational situations that form trails to understanding what the Scriptures can teach us about the end times and the events associated with those times. It is this researcher's earnest desire that you can agree that the truth is very clearly stated, once we decide to use the Bible and the Bible alone, to lead us. God has documented everything that he feels is important for us to know. It is our task to dig and sift until the truth comes shining through the obscurity that is, in every case, intentional in God's divine Word. He does not intend for all to know, and certainly not one of us knows even the beginning of what there is yet lying unknown in the Scriptures. We should always leave some room for misinterpretation also. The author recognizes and readily admits, that the reader or someone else may, after diligent study, very well find him wanting in interpretation. That's why he is completely open to correction so long as that correction comes entirely from the Bible, not from denominational doctrines or confessions, Rabbinical traditions, folk tales, manuscripts of wandering gnomes, or the indignation of some pop singer. Some readers will totally ignore this admonition, especially die-hard pew warmers who take exception to something they find here, on the basis of something they read in a magazine.

Each of us owes it to himself, to take time to ask himself, if he is prepared for the last day, whether it comes after the tribulation, or tomorrow. This chapter is being finished late in the evening, with full knowledge that perhaps more than 100,000 people, just in this country alone, will not rise from their beds in the morning. Many of them will not be in heaven tomorrow night.

It is the duty of God's elect to carry the gospel to the

unsaved. I hope that in some way, something of what has been written here, will reach someone who might otherwise have heard nothing of Jesus Christ, nor of the wrath of God against the unrighteous. God is good. He is a God of love, to be sure, but he is also an awesome, fearsome God to those who do not acknowledge him, or who slight him. Praise God for his Word, for it will carry his people who trust in his mercy, to glory.

AUTHOR'S NOTES
CONCERNING PART TWO

ONCE I HAD FINISHED THE FIRST DRAFT OF MY ORIGINAL MANU-script for this book, which has now become Part Two, I sent it to my friend Chuck Grove, a friend in Reedsport, Oregon who is a gifted author. Chuck is also a practicing and self-proclaimed, critic of other people's writing and the only person I ever met who left a Protestant church background to become a Roman Catholic! That was immediately of interest to me, because I'm a very conservative Reformed Protestant who was raised in a Catholic family! We make quite a pair.

For many years before I met him, Chuck had written under the nom de plume, "Howard Bond." He agreed to act as reader for this book, proofing and critiquing my manuscript. Most of my other friends thought I had slipped my trolley, having a Catholic writer critique a Protestant-oriented Christian book. Yes, Howard Bond was cut from entirely different spiritual cloth, but I was comfortable with the challenge, and anticipated some interesting counterpoint to my own views. That was precisely what I received. Now, Bond is a poet, and a newspaper columnist like myself, and is very quick witted with a great, expressive, comedic personality. He has the best command of the English language of anyone in my immediate acquaintance.

Because his comments were not only right to the point, but also clever and sometimes a giggle, while being well researched from a typical, everyday Christian point of view, I decided immediately to wrap them, somehow, into my manuscript. So, the critique you are about to read, became part and parcel of the proofs of what I believe is a truly biblical position on these spiritual issues. So, what lies before you at this point, are the perspectives of my Catholic friend and the responses those comments elicited from me. Our exchange went back and forth by snail mail for some months, but don't worry, it won't take more than seven or eight weeks for you to read this part of the book. (only kidding, honest). His comments refer to the several chapters of Part II, which originally was intended to be the complete book, and what you already read in the final version.

What follows are Howard Bond's actual notes and comments, almost exactly as I received them, but organized a little here and there for ease of reading, and somewhat shortened. You will also see the exact responses I sent back to him on "issues" he introduced, with very little excised. We had a lot of fun writing this, so I hope you will enjoy reading it. Charles is the kind of writer who will call me, as he did last night, when he likes something particularly inspiring in my weekly newspaper column. Last night, the phone rang. When I answered, a hushed voice said briefly, "You wrote it masterfully. I loved it." And he hung up! That's the sort of reader response, that writers thrive on, especially when it comes from someone critical, like a good friend.

So in this part of the book, I have edited out little of substance, preferring that my readers share the criticism I was honored to have my friend and fellow writer, offer - coupled to my own immediate reactions. So now, the arrow having been shot, I cannot call back a single line. It is therefore my earnest hope that you will find my responses as biblical as I intended for them to be. May our God bless your reading.

Note: On the following pages, passages of critique commentary are indented while my own responses remain at normal line width.

A CRITIQUE OF PART TWO

BY HOWARD BOND

Querido Miguel,

At long last, after reading and rereading your MS, I think I can make an effort to assess it both objectively and subjectively. I will indicate parts where I think you might want to make corrections, as well as parts where I think you may not want to make corrections, but I think you should.

First, as regards style and technique overall, your style is catchy and should hold your reader's attention. Perhaps your most glaring error is your repeated misspelling of Noah's boat as the *arc*. It was *not* an *arc*—it was an "*ark*." So called because he used an ark welder to put the thing together.

He had me. That was embarrassing, but it was also nec-essary-and clever! I replied; Thanks C.L., I was using an old family spelling of that word, but I don't mind humoring you by changing it.

"Nissan" Nissan? Oh that's right, you're a theologian, and can't be expected to know the difference between a Jewish month and a Japanese car. By the way, I am wait-ing for a response from the NISSAN motor company for a suggestion I submitted to upper management. I suggested they change the spelling of their product to "NISSIN." That way, it would read the same whether it was right side up or upside down. (Oh yeah—try "Nisan" for the Jewish month.)

I wrote: "I admit to sins of omission. Also, I was sure the Max-ima was named for a Jewish month. I cannot believe I mis-spelled *ark!* Perhaps if Noah had painted a name on the prow? Or Moses? Okay, I have corrected this category of irritant, so you were in fact, worth something.

"Believers and unbelievers." At that point in time, I don't think there will be any unbelievers.

(He is speaking of the Second Coming of Jesus on the clouds.) On that line I now have "saved and unsaved."

"Lot and his daughters." "Ah yes, Lot and his daughters! Let's not forget that they got him drunk on wine, incested him, and got pregnant with Moab and Benammi. I must say, Lot was a "lot" more capable when he was drunk than I ever was! By the way, when did incest become "incest"?

The cave where "it" originally happened, as you are doubtless aware, was commonly known as "cest" by the ancients. The name happened the first time somebody asked "where?" The rabbis, later changed it to "incense," which they thought was a snappier name. By the time the Bible was written, the word *incest* was no longer in popular use, apart from the temple ceremonies. We do know, however, that "incense" was practiced for centuries in populating the earth. Twelve of those "incensed" families became a "people." One time when God got mad at them, he admitted he never had liked the smell of their burning "incest."

> *Phenomenon* is singular. *Phenomena* are plural.
> Speaking of Noah and his boat, have you ever wondered how Noah fed all those critters over such a long time? Especially the herbivores. The carnivores no doubt extincted some species at dinner time.

My response: Clever use of *are*—single word with a plural meaning! I don't know how Noah fed all those critters. I do know, however, that the ark influenced nautical terminology. One example is the deck on which Noah walked the animals. That area, that had to be shoveled, still carries an unusual name.

> Well, now on to some more "contentious" considerations. First, let's consider the "Bible only" theory, which you frequently employ. You ask: "Is the Bible (the Word of God) the final authority, or is your denomination, or your pastor, the final authority?" (P.III of Introduction) "It cannot make sense at all to suggest that the final authority for truth lies in the church, and not God, yet this is precisely what is taught in some denominational creed and confessions! That of course would affect dramatically the way the authority of Scripture is viewed." (Hey, that's great! Only problem: Greek is all Greek to me.)

Okay, I know that my "Bible only" philosophy irks the pope. I hasten to point out that this is a fundamental premise of all the great Bible scholars. Reformers Luther, Calvin, Zwingli, and Huss, had been "priesting" long before they ever laid eyes on a Bible. Each completely changed his theology upon reading the truth contained in that book! Anyone who wants to, by the way, can get hold of a concordance and an Interlinear Bible and convert all that Greek to English!

You say, "Once again we will allow the Bible, and the Bible alone, to lead us to uncovering the truth that God is leading us to." It might gall you to learn that you adhere to some defined Catholic doctrines. For example, the Council of Trent defined infallibility that: "If anyone does not accept (all the books of the Bible) as sacred and canonical, in their entirety, together with all their parts [...] let him be anathema." And the Vatican Council made the unqualified statement that "the books of the Old and New Testament [...] have God for their author. This is the ancient and continuous belief of the church." And there is more, but that should suffice.

Au contraire, I'm not galled, since I am quite aware of the confessions and creeds that abound, chiefly, but not exclusively, in the world of the liturgical sects. We also had them in the Presbyterian Reformed church I formerly attended. The problem with all of these, is that their proponents believe them, but don't practice them! They are works of men, not at all infallible! They began because the church didn't always allow its people to see the Bible! Then, when that changed, they were so comfortable chanting their memorized creeds and confessions, that these documents continued to have more authority in their minds than did the Bible! Such documents are necessary only for men to establish their own authority. In the final analysis, they weaken God's authority. (His instructions are already in the Bible).

I characterize such activities as products of men not content to be just part of the body of Christ's church. Every so often they try to shinny up the neck and be part of the head. I don't find anywhere in the Bible that God asks for that kind of help.

Then you say, "that should suffice." But you know, the documents—whatever they had—never sufficed! Such prescriptions have never caused men to abide by the supreme law of God!

Howard next expands his previous argument ;

> But let's not rely on defined Catholic doctrine for the truth of this matter. Let's go right to the Good Book itself, which tells us: "all Scripture is inspired by God, and useful for teaching, for reproving, for correcting, for instruction in Justice" (2 Timothy 3:16). But that doesn't translate to a "Bible Only" theory. Indeed, the Bible itself scuttles that idea. Christ founded the Church, sometimes called his "mystical Body," to teach his religion to all mankind. He didn't print and distribute Bibles. Some few, of course, had access to the Scriptures, as implied above. But not even those who did have access to the Scriptures were necessarily capable of reading them properly. "This then, you must understand first of all, that no prophecy of Scripture is made of private interpretation" (2 Peter 1:20). "In these epistles there are certain things difficult to understand, which the learned and the unstable distort, just as they do the rest of the Scriptures also, to their own destruction" (2 Peter 3:16).

"Wow," I responded, There are at least three major ideas contained here. I do appreciate that you choose 'not to rely on defined Catholic doctrine for the truth of the matter.' I believe that if we are to serve our God appropriately, we need to serve him, not the men who call themselves "the church," and write those things.

To begin, the King James translation uses the words *teach-*

ing and *doctrine* interchangeably, Then where you have quoted "Justice" (a new one on me), my curiosity is piqued by the capital letter, knowing you make few errors of grammar. I searched the word *justice* in both Young's and Strong's Concordances and found no evidence of the Greek word for *Justice* being used anywhere in the New Testament. Then I looked up the word *righteousness* that I was familiar with as appearing in this passage in 2 Timothy. I found that word to be *dikaiosune* (it's Greek to me too), which is equivalent, according to Strong, to *righteousness*, but according to Young is actually *rightness*. Happily, Young throws in a second meaning—*justice*, but doesn't capitalize it. I wonder if you use a mainly Catholic-friendly version of the Bible, because I have always heard the word "righteousness" used there. This is a passage intended for those who are God's elect, his chosen who make up Christ's universal, invisible body of believers, which he calls "his church." *Justice* and *Righteousness* may have been "morphed" here by the translators, since they are interchangeable in Old Testament Hebrew, on occasion, such as in Psalm 89:14, where David says "Justice [righteousness] and judgment are the habitation [foundation] of thy throne." Judgment, Justice, and equity are linked by Solomon in his description of the wisdom of godly instruction in Proverbs 1: 3, and the twin *J*s are inseparable in numerous Old Testament renditions. Did you notice how lightly I passed over the business of that capital letter?

By the way, 2 Timothy 3:16 was an excellent opener here. But allow me to dive into the Interlinear Bible to get what was actually written. The beauty of this book is that every individual word is translated separately, then the whole is put together to arrive at a slightly more accurate description. I'm fond of this reference, and have comfort concerning its validity. Ready for this? I believe that the Scripture in reference, does indeed present a very comfortable "Bible only" message, and it is not a theory, because I believe in the inerrancy of Scripture! I'm quoting, not inventing, as is so often the wont of "theologians." What this passage does not do, is limit the need for teaching, which God has described adequately in other passages. It nowhere refers to the teaching of the doctrines of men.

Okay, it says in a word-by-word translation "every Scripture," (says a little more than "all,") but I can't explain that technically. Like other "articles," the word *is* does not appear in the Hebrew, but is assumed. Now here's the part I home in on: "God breathed [to me that's significantly beyond 'inspired'] and profitable [the Greek word *ophelimos*, which has a sense of being extra worthwhile to learning] for teaching, for reproof, for correction, for instruction in righteousness [there's my word], that fitted may be the of God man for every work good having been furnished." So you see, God himself is here saying, that man will be "perfectly" fitted to do God's work by studying *only* God's Word! Of course he really means, "diligently study it." In effect, man needs nothing else. Now, this does indicate that all things necessary to fulfill the assignment of Jesus called the "Great Commission" are found in his Word. I'll allow you to eat my hat! Man needs to add *nothing* to the written words of the Bible. In fact, God warns in Revelation 22:18–19 that anyone who does add or subtract, is in for a dose of the thunder of God's wrath!

So, if we will admit to what God is clearly saying, we can hardly escape the conclusion that there is a God-defined sufficiency in the Bible alone, and in its entirety. This is what electrified the reformers back in the 1500s! We need nothing more to get saved or to carry the message of salvation to others. So, in my humble opinion, doctrinal things, oft quoted in the pulpits regularly fail the test of conformity with God's authority.

Continuing, you say, "the Bible itself scuttles that idea" (the idea of sole authority resting in the Word). To the contrary, all of the early disciples of Jesus were, with the possible exceptions of Matthew and Luke, well tutored in the synagogue! Then they all got precisely what is now contained in the Gospels, directly from the greatest preacher who ever lived. The Mosaic

Law was read in the synagogues every Sabbath, for every Jewish boy while he grew up. On top of that, God spoke to men through his creation, as well as with signs and wonders. You're right about one thing. God was not in the Bible printing or distributing business, but he made sure the Word got out through those he chose for the express purpose of sending it out. In fundamental Christianity as taught in the Bible, there is little of the ceremonial aspect which characterizes "religion"—the overdone, outward "show and blow" of belief.

We must remember that it certainly can be no coincidence, that this document has survived the attempts of the Jews, the heathens, kings, Popes, Satan, and others, to destroy it, down through the ages! God himself has guaranteed that we have it, because he made it necessary to his chosen process of salvation, for those he sovereignly has chosen to reign in heaven as heirs with Christ.

Recall with me, that he tells us, "Faith comes by hearing, and hearing by the Word of God" (Romans 10:17). It is God's imperative that we have the Scriptures, and that those whom he chooses, rely on them for truth. I think that's why Bibles have survived centuries of man's attempts to destroy and to suppress them. This truth is what Jesus specifically said he would build his church on. That has been widely misinterpreted, probably because man wants to have authority not given to him in the Bible.

It is so clear, that men of every stripe will attempt to interject themselves into God's affairs, and between you and God, and me and God, whenever they have an opportunity. Their motivation, I can only guess, is to get between God and those who want to serve him. That can only mean that, whether such men know it or not, they are not working for God, and there is only one competing alternative. The only way to be sure where we are going, is to make God and God alone, our focus and reference for everything we do.

Let's simply take literally, what the Pooh-Bahs at the Grand

Council of Trent passed down and which you quoted saying, essentially, "there can be no complete authority apart from God." That means not the corporate churches, not me, not you. Only God, and he says he speaks only through the Bible.

May I disagree with your studious concept that, "God designed his church to teach his religion to all mankind? Jesus sent individuals out who had never been to a seminary, to just spread the good word. "To teach them to observe all things whatsoever I have commanded you," is the way our Lord put it. There really wasn't a church yet, and those sent out, were few. If what you say was the motivation for Jesus to establish his church, he certainly did not choose a cadre of the best teachers around! Mostly they were totally uneducated men.

But let me get on with addressing your concerns with my lovely manuscript! Your "not even those who did have access to the Scriptures were capable of reading them properly" actually does not fit. Peter is not speaking of the reader when he says "no prophecy of Scripture is of private interpretation" (2 Peter 1:20). He is saying that, what we find in Scripture was, "God breathed" as I properly translated 2 Timothy 3:16 for you above. Peter is speaking of the veracity, the reliability, and truth of what is written. I'm sure you'll agree if you reread it. But don't believe me. I'm not the authority, the Bible is, so let's read it in Greek, converted word by word into English. It says: "every prophecy of Scripture, of (its) unloosing, did not come into being not for by will of man was borne at any time, prophesy, but by Spirit Holy" (2 Timothy 3:16).

See it? He's talking about the origin of the words, not the dispensing of them. In 2 Peter 3:16, ol' Pete is taking a shot specifically at Paul's epistles. But let's examine carefully what is being said. What and who, are these folks who have trouble reading Paul's letters? (we don't know if the ones Pete speaks of are even included in the Bible.) Peter says in verse seventeen that he is speaking of "the wicked." He also calls them "unlearned and unstable," but he himself is also unlearned and demonstratedly unstable at times, So, he has to *not* be talking about men of limited education who can't read the epistles, but the same kind of people for whom Jesus spoke in parables. He's talking about nonbelievers! But even if some cannot understand the epistles, there's still a lot of Bible to lead them who seek it, to truth.

I have to say, I find it difficult to agree that "the church was necessary for a proper, uniform understanding of Holy Writ." If that was true, how can we understand the incontrovertible truth, that no two sects of the corporate representation of the body of Christ believe the same doctrine? Now, as touching upon your prior contention, look at second Thessalonians 2:15. If I understand your point correctly, it would be that letters of the apostles are equally valid with Scripture. The passage you quoted is, "Therefore brethren, stand fast, and hold the traditions which ye have been taught, whether by word, or an epistle" (2 Thessalonians 2:15).

You used the more common "teachings" and the common usage "our letters," suggesting Paul's since he often used a collective, instead of taking full credit upon himself. In the Greek, however, we find it referring not to teachings, but to "traditions." That may include some of the older Jewish traditions taught in the synagogues, since quite a few members of the early church, were Messianic Jews. The epistles, obviously, might have been from any writer. But the most important word in this whole sentence is *word*. This had to refer to a *verbal* teaching by someone approved by Paul, because this was prior to the writing of the New Testament, and New Testament teachers did not refer to the Old Testament as the "Word." The sayings of Jesus, yes, or it could have been Paul's preaching. Either way, this conversation does not support a contention that there ever was, "uniform understanding." The teaching was fairly, but not precisely uniform, but we have many examples of spurious practices and understandings among the earliest churches, all through the New Testament.

Then, there is our black friend, the Ethiopian eunuch,

who "was struggling with reading Scriptures." The man who instructed the Ethiopian was not a cleric, not a scholar, but a simple disciple of Jesus, who told the story of his redeemer, and it touched the listener. This was an example of how to spread the gospel, not a treatise on the need for an organized church, or a uniform understanding of Scripture. Philip simply shared what he knew; the eunuch heard what was said, and believed. Nobody wrote Philip a pamphlet approved by the church hierarchy, or a script that guaranteed he said just the correct stuff. That's not what gets people saved. It is hearing about Jesus from somebody who obviously loves him. That's all that has ever been desired by Jesus, according to the Bible. Jesus didn't bother with any lessons, classes, catechisms, or confessions, apart from what he personally explained to them. There were no Bibles, but the example of the Ethiopian is one of reading the Holy Scriptures. The Old Testament was plenty to get all the people saved, who got that way during and immediately after the ministry and the misery, of Jesus on earth. The church is, in no way, *ever* mentioned as an agent of salvation, in the only instruction book the Christ left for us.

You are quite correct about Mark 16:15–16 being "our Lord's final command to his disciples." This is Mark's recollection. I prefer the reality expressed by the tax collector. Matthew remembered his Lord's words to be, "Go and teach." That's a doable assignment, yet in the last one hundred years at least, his church has not really done a bang up job of being involved on a personal basis in doing that.

His early disciples probably did a pretty fair job of going forth as you suggest, and naturally they carried no Bibles. There were none to carry. That came later when the men who had toasted marshmallows over a hot fire with Jesus, were gone and the goer-outers had no personal experience with our Lord. Being able to read was never included in the requirement for salvation. It was to *hear* the gospel preached. That's what one does every time he hears the Lord speak through the only source of his voice available today, the Bible.

Yes, the Bible tells us that salvation is entirely the work of God alone, and says we can do nothing to ensure our own salvation. The Mormons, Jehovah Witnesses, Baptists to some degree, Nazarenes, Christian Church, and certainly the Church of Christ, all hold works doctrines, some of the latter being interwoven with a smattering of faith teaching. But, if we read the Bible, we find out none of them get saved, in the way they teach that salvation comes! I'm not implying none of them are saved; that's God's business. But if some are saved, it was not though any works of theirs.

> Well, I hate to seem picky, but what about the fact that our Lord Himself became man precisely to teach us what we must *do* to be saved?

What Christ came expressly for, was to be the Passover Lamb—the propitiation for the sins of all those God had sent him to justify forming the external church with. He suffered the wrath of God to pay for the sins of those he came to save. Not the sins of the whole world as the Bible appears superficially to say, but only for the sins of his elect, chosen from before the foundation of the world (Matthew 25:34, Ephesians 1:4). He taught many things in parables we must remember, and his purpose was to intentionally prevent the multitudes from understanding his message!

> You know, even as he instructed Noah as to what he must *do* to be saved.

God, in fact, did tell Noah what to do to be saved from getting his jammies wet, but I'm sorry to tell you after all your work, that Noah's soul was already saved! Look at the last verse of Genesis chapter five. Right at the end of listing the "generations of Adam," God shows us that he has his eye on Noah, since he stops his list with Noah and his sons. We will find out later that Noah is entirely the reason for this list. God tells us, after complaining vociferously about how sinful man was, that he was going to put an end to man. But he also said, "But Noah found grace in the eyes of the Lord" (Genesis 6:8). The grace is God's, because Noah, like everyone else Christ will later go to the cross to save, has already had his sins paid for. God has already saved him by God's grace. So when he is introduced to us, Noah has already been saved.

The last thing you mentioned was the following:

> You fail to distinguish the most important difference between man and beast. God made us "in his image and likeness." He gave us "free will." He gave us the power to choose to believe or not to believe, to obey or not to obey. Remember Adam and Eve? They had to believe because they were in intimate contact with their Creator. But even so, they *chose* to disobey.

To begin with, I am attempting to teach the Bible. That book does not, to the best of my recollection, bother itself with the difference between man and the beasts, other than to say man has dominion over them. I am presuming that you are arguing from the perspective of man, not of the beasts ?

I would say, despite no direct commentary on this subject that I can recall, the Bible somehow does not make "free will" the discriminator, contrary to what some sects teach. It seems to me that the fact that one has a soul, while a soul is not mentioned for the other, is the most significant factor, but I don't want to seem argumentative. Actually, I spent this morning with a beautiful, white German Shepherd. I can guarantee you, that dog has a free will. Oh, his master has a modicum of control over him, but only when the dog relinquishes his will to the man's! Contrariwise, I think that if you will review the Scriptures, then consider what happened to Paul on the Damascus road, and the experience of Lazarus coming out of the tomb at the call of his Creator, you may begin to correct your perception concerning "free will." Certainly we have freedom to choose which socks to wear and what to have for breakfast, but when it comes to thumbs up or thumbs down on our direction of spiritual travel, we do not see any hint of a vote being allowed us, in properly interpreted Scriptures.

As a matter of biblical fact, even Jesus had no will of his own. That's clear from John 4:34. "My food is to do the will of him that sent me." In a similar vein, our Lord defers to the will of his heavenly Father at least half a dozen times in the book of Matthew alone! He taught us to pray, and part of that prayer in Matthew 6: 9–13, is to affirm that it is God's own sovereign will that we are to do! In verse ten of that prayer Jesus again calls for God's will, not our own, to be done. If that is a new concept to anyone, he should read again, where Jesus says that anyone who wants to go to heaven must "do the will of my father which is in heaven" (Matthew 7:21). A fellow ought to refresh himself on what Jesus says in Matthew 12:48, 50, in Matthew 26:39, John 5:30, and John 6:38, just to name a few places where the Christ tells us that the saved have to shed free will. It is a luxury for only the unsaved.

Ah, yes, the Adam and Eve caper. No, I do not remember Adam, and barely knew Eve. I knew they left Eden under some sort of cloud, but I didn't have the real story on that pair for a long time. They never write, they never call!

It is true, Adam and Eve knew who God was, but they rebelled, nonetheless. But we must remember that they were not as we are. They were created with "free will." They were, according to God's own appraisal, part of what was "very good." You see, they were created perfect. You were not, because you were hatched after "the fall." God evidently learned his lesson about making perfect humans and made the rest of us devoid of free will about certain things. Yes, they chose to disobey. But to Eve, the decision concerned what to eat, not how to get saved. There also was no pattern of behavior they could emulate for how to conduct themselves. Also, they may have suffered because there was not much of God's law handed down yet in their day. That lack might make someone a good study.

I liked your final wrap-up of the critique. It was simple and tasteful, with a dash of hopelessness. You said,

> Well, so much for my critique. It is probably not exactly what you had hoped for, but at least it is candid. And I'm sorry, but I cannot affix my imprimature to it. Although I love you as a brother and cherish you as a friend, I reject you as my pope.
>
> God bless, amigo!
> Ceil

This is one of this man's trademark closures. His initials are C.L., so he signs himself in a very inventive way! At this point this writer responded with:

It is actually more than I had hoped for, Charles. Knowing our differences regarding the subject matter, I expected even less agreement than I encountered. Perhaps a slightly stronger statement of appreciation was anticipated, but then you did manage, "the style was catchy." Seriously, brother, what you have given me is a cherished gift. My surprise for you is that it will have life as an entire additional section of the book, with your byline, added onto what you previously read. I have made up a catchy name for it -"Part Two." What do you think?

I thank you for that opportunity, my brother, and appreciate your substantial contribution to the book. It started out as "my book," but has become "our book" since you succeeded in dragging me entirely away from the primary topic! Personally, I thought "masterful" might have just covered it appropriately!

> As usual, su amigo,
> Miguel

A CHRISTIAN ZIONIST
AUTHOR

NOW IT'S TIME TO RETURN TO, AND COMPLETE, MY LOOK AT dispensationalist inspired fundamentalism in America. In this chapter, I will highlight one of the "Giant's" of fundamentalism, and attempt to show how such folks have been mistaken for so very long. The next chapter after this, will provide insight into the beliefs of a large segment of what is considered the "Christian Right." Let's begin.

In his bestselling book *The Late Great Planet Earth*, first printed in 1970, and which made him famous for its "amazing biblical prophesies about this generation," Hal Lindsey, in typical "Christian" fashion, took credit for the work of C.C. Carlson, the real author, and made most of the money. If you doubt that to be typical of many of the top-selling books by the big names in the fundamentalist and evangelical ranks, simply look about you. That's just the way it works. Believe it!

D. James Kennedy, Tim LaHaye, even Vestal Goodman, the "Queen of Gospel," and many of the other big names in "religious" books of the past seventy-five years, sailed out of mediocrity on the backs of real writers, whose names appear as a "with" in small letters after the banner headline of the "star" who actually did little, if any, of the actual manuscript, in most cases. Some don't even mention the "ghost writer."

Lindsey laid the responsibility for the end of the world at the feet of war. God, of course, considers war not to be the real causative factor at all. In fact, it isn't even considered. Rather, God sees *himself* as the ultimate terror. Evidently, Lindsey hadn't read that part of the Bible yet. A careful reading and thoughtful analysis of the Bible, will always disclose that God himself will finish the world he created. He will do that for the same reason he has always "whacked" man, in one way or another, through-out the Bible! It's not "the economy, stupid," it's sin! Being a confirmed dispensationalist, as are virtually all fundamentalist Christians, Lindsey never answers the question of why God, who throughout the Bible, has never really had an interlude of real happiness about the Hebrew people, would immediately, after a one thousand year period of peace, prosperity, gaiety and brotherhood, suddenly destroy the whole thing! Could it be simply because that was what he planned all the time to do? That would make no sense whatever. Lindsey must think you're stupid, if he expects you to believe that. All through the (then) perhaps fifteen thousand years of the world's existence, there is this one and only "millennium" of great happiness and peace. So, then he wipes that out with the wave of his hand? Do you really think that fits the God of the Bible?

No, that makes no sense when we consider the divine econ-omy of God in his world, particularly if we carefully study the clues to the end times, he gave us within the Bible. The dispen-sationalists worry about war, for a particular reason that they cannot speak of openly. We will deal with that shortly. Lindsey spends several pages on the horrors of war. Then he tries to convince the reader that when there is nobody living on earth apart from the Jews and those they have brought into their confidence and have suitably "trimmed" in their nether regions—only after that wonderful period, will God burn up the planet on schedule. Two pages later, Lindsey says the solution to war is for everybody to accept Christ. Christ, however, has a different "take" on things. He tells us in the Bible, that nobody will ever accept him, unless God has intervened on behalf of that person. He also assures us, that such intervention is reserved for just a very few! So much for Lindsey's gospel on war!

But, we really ought to attempt to understand that peculiar fundamentalist scenario, because that's what the dispensationalists have been teaching their members for at least seven or eight decades now. You see, they are convinced, that in this increasingly sinful world, at the very zenith of world need for more people who are believers in Christ, according to Lindsey (one of their chiefest spokesmen), just before the "Great Tribulation" spoken of in the Bible, God is going to snatch away all of the believers! Then, despite the adverse effect that must have on the prospects of increased wars in the world, Christ will found a peaceful, no-wars kingdom in Jerusalem—the one in Palestine—for one thousand years. That would, they believe, act as some sort of palliative before God destroys the entire world. Lindsey also finesses Israel into being the patsy for the tribulation. We will examine that a bit later also.

Then Lindsey writes, "There will be people who will become believers at that time" (during the Great Tribulation). He does not explain how, in an environment where there is nobody who is a believer, nobody to tell anyone about the gospel, believers will magically be manufactured. Certainly God could do that, if he chooses to. We are left to wonder, why? Why what? Oh! Why did God not include any of that stuff in the plan he laid out in his Bible? Are we to suppose God has whispered that design only to Lindsey, while he left the rest of us in the dark? Or, did Lindsey read all of this in the Schofield Bible? At any rate, these new believers-presumably believers in Christ- are somehow manufactured during the Great Tribulation, the very thing that all existing Christians had escaped. Then, according to the dispensationalists, they will be taken by their Savior, to live with Israel, in Israel, and under the law of Israel!

Yes, under this salvation plan for the state of Israel, the old law is to be reinstituted with a few exceptions. We're talking here (Lindsey's book) about the very Savior who himself refused to live under Jewish tradition or law, requiring Christians to suddenly do that! I for one, am wondering how these new Christians are going to get saved without any Holy Spirit, no working church, no preachers, none of the apparatus God set up for evangelizing the world originally! You'll have to ask a premillennialist if you want to know about that! If, as they believe, God will reverse himself, wiping out entirely, the work of and necessity for, his Son Christ, are we to presume the Jews will be finally convinced by God that they ought to accept their Messiah? Then they will tell these pagans, who never were religious Jews, about Jesus, and everybody will live happily and in harmony for a thousand years. Somebody surely deserves to be wondering why God did not put all of that into the Bible. Again, there has been no rebuttal of this presentation from any living theologian I am aware of!

In order to recognize how the fundamentalists must enter into manmade reconstructions of what the Bible says, an interested reader might look at what Lindsey has built on page 127 of his sales pitch for Zionism. At the top of that page, he confesses (against other Christians) that "Christians have a tendency sometimes to toss out words which have no meaning to the non-Christian." By "toss out" we might deduce from what follows, that he means "not use." That seems, however, not to be his intent, but rather he appears to mean something like "use to disadvantage" or "invent," because that is precisely what he is about to do. You have to follow these fundamentalists carefully sometimes to recognize that they are about to pass a handful of wool at you, at just about eye level! Watch what Lindsey does. He next says *rapture* may be the sort of word that turns "an unbeliever [...] from the simple truth of God's Word." It seems just a bit arrogant for him to "toss out" the word *rapture,* which was invented by precisely the people whom he represents, the dispensationalists, only to make up another new term. This new word of Lindsey's also is not found in the Bible to describe what is generally known among the corporate churches as "the rapture." Lindsey decides that it should instead be called *translation.* He gives as a reason, that "some Christians" (presumably his denomination, since that term is not commonly known among the other denominations, if books, newsletters, preaching, and media-evangelist preaching are any indication) don't understand the Bible version. The truth is that *rapture* is not such a hot descriptor, but is commonly used by doctors, lawyers, liars, friars, banana-boat first mates and every preacher you are likely to encounter. It certainly is not disagreeable to cashier the term *rapture* out of the evangelical lexicon. But, if one is decided that such a change is necessary, why not replace the offending word, with terminology actually used in the Bible to describe this miracle? Lindsey writes that, "The word *rapture* means to 'snatch away or take out.'" The gullible no doubt have believed this misdirection. But Lindsey did not do his homework (why is anyone surprised?). He apparently preferred to simply concoct something else that suited his purpose.

In the interest of honesty and clarity, this area of study should be more closely examined, because there is usually at least some naked truth masked by denominational vocabulary if we're willing to look for it. First of all, it should be only appropriate and God glorifying, to recognize that our Lord, through the apostles John and Paul, used the phrase "caught up to God" to describe what will happen when Christ returns. Do you personally have a problem with "caught up"? Neither does anyone else who is willing to go on record. One may be permitted therefore to ask why the term *rapture?* Why *translation?* Why not "caught up" as it is presented in our Bible by Jehovah God? Why is it only the evangelicals seem to have a problem closely following the Bible? But, in fairness to the author we are discussing, let's see what else he says on page 126. In his second paragraph he gives us only choices he personally recognizes. "But whether we call this event 'the rapture' or the 'translation' makes no difference—the important thing is that it will happen." Makes no difference? Isn't it interesting that this man cannot allow the actual words of the Bible to creep into his reasoning? In fairness, it is possible that he is able to think only in verbs he himself chooses. He is, after all, who he is, and evidently, he greatly admires that person.

There is a large brown book that some writers often employ at times such as we are here facing. It's non-fiction, written by a fellow named Noah Webster. He called it his "study in lexicography," but it is generally known today as his "dictionary." Anyone can share the wisdom of the lexicographer on this matter, simply by finding, for instance, the word *rapture*, which happens to be found listed *and* defined in our language, within the *Merriam Webster Collegiate Dictionary* on page 957. Isn't it sad that Lindsey had not (evidently) the aid of such a volume, but chose instead to conjure up his own definitions? It must be admitted that dictionaries may contain errors on occasion. But in general, they are found trustworthy. Even, it might be reasonable to suppose, for such advanced biblical scholars as Hal Lindsey. Here is what is contained on page 957:

rapture \'rap-cher\ n [L raptus] 1.a: a state or experience of being carried away by overwhelming emotion. b. A mystical experience in which the spirit is exalted to a knowledge of divine things. 2: an expression or manifestation of ecstasy or passion.

Ah, perhaps we have ourselves a clue here. Did you happen to notice that this is, by definition, expressly an emotional, not a physical, experience? 1 b. might be bent to fit the occasion, but it is not a word made naturally for what is described in the Bible. The most noticeable mismatch is between what Lindsey says and what the dictionary says. Lindsey, remember, says that "The word, *rapture* means to "snatch away or take out." He is too kind to mention the purely spiritual aspect of the word's application.

But to continue the examination of this veritable "gospel" of evangelicalism, let's wallow out here in fundamentalist left field, as we examine Lindsey's first choice, "*translate.*" This verb is found once in the King James Bible, according to *Strong's Exhaustive Concordance* and also according to *Young's Analytical Concordance.* Both admit also, the use of the past tense, three times and to its extension into a transitive noun on one occasion. Both volumes agree that the only use of the word in the KJV (2 Samuel 3:10) is the Hebrew word *abar* meaning "to cross over." The Modern Language Bible (MLB) uses *transfer* while the Living Bible has "give it to." The RSV and NIV both copy the King James (no matter what their many champions say), and the New American Standard sets the pace for the MLB. Most damaging to the choice of words to replace what is contained in the Bible however, may be the inescapable fact of Strong's list of meanings. In the twenty-three lines of potential meanings of the Hebrew word *abar*—word number 5674 in *Strong's Concordance,* the synonym *translate* appears next to last! One has to reach almost to the bottom of the synonym barrel of potential meanings, to come out with *translate!*

The most important piece of work we should concern ourselves with, however, is what the Interlinear Bible says of the "translate" idea. This Bible presents a word-by-word translation from the Hebrew (or Greek) into English words and then also presents a less accurate, but more English-like, paragraph to place the Hebrew into a more English-friendly framework. This is our only true look at how the Hebrew phrase would have been originally constructed and written by its author, writing in the Hebrew language, or in the Greek. Beginning in English, as presented identically by the King James, New American Standard and the New International Version Bibles (suggesting there is no better original translation than the KJV), we read in 1 Thessalonians 4:17, about the departure for heaven, of living true believers at Christ's soon return. There we read: "Then we which are alive and remain shall be *caught up* together with them in the clouds, to meet the Lord in the air: and so shall we ever be with the Lord" (emphasis added). Here is what the Interlinear Bible says in the word-by-word translation, arranged into a more English-friendly reading style. It is identical to the King James Version, once again testifying to the overall accuracy of that particular Bible. So, if it is the best selection for the translators of the Interlinear Bible, the King James, New American Standard, and the New International, why is that wording not good enough for the dispensationalist, Christian Zionist, Hal Lindsey?

It's clear that Lindsey did not get the idea about *translate* from any version of the Bible, as it is written in 1 Thessalonians 4:17. It is quite possible that such departures from God's version make it easier for the evangelicals to teach their version of the "end times." That version is truly somewhat different from the construction to be derived from a more careful rendering of the texts-any of the texts- mentioned above. Of course, there may indeed be other, less sinister motives, hidden among the twists and turns of logic employed by those whose banner Lindsey carries. But why would they go to such extremes to obscure the original meanings of the Bible, if not to concoct their own desired outcomes, which are distinctly different from the teachings of the Reformers who dragged Christianity out of the clutches of the Popes?

If we were to examine the Greek words of Revelation 12:5, where John is telling the parable of the woman clothed with the sun, whose son is taken alive to be with God, we would not find that child being "translated." No, there we find a Greek word that is number 726 of Strong's list of Greek meanings. That word is *harpazo,* a derivative of a Greek verb that means "to take for one's self," in this case by God, for himself. It is an act of God, not just some strange kind of "happening" that comes upon the child. Word 726 means to seize, to catch up, to pluck up, or pull! That's what God is doing in Revelation 12:5. The same Greek word appears in 2 Corinthians 12, where, in verse two, Paul explains about the man he used to know, who was "caught up" to the third heaven. Then, God uses the same word as Paul recounts how the man was "caught up" into paradise. Philip was "caught away" in Acts 8:39. It seems clear that our Lord intended to have us accept his rendition of this miraculous "snatching" by himself of those he has so chosen. The translators of the KJV, NIV, MLB, Living Bible, NAS, and RSV have all agreed that "caught up" is the appropriate expression. Only Mr. Lindsey seems intent to insist that there is a better expression for the evangelicals to use, and to the best of our knowledge, no Christian author has ever taken him to task over that. But, "As for me and my house, we will trust in the Lord."

So, we ought perhaps to ask ourselves, "Can dispensationalism possibly be scriptural?" Can a dispensationalist be a Christian? Let's begin by asking something more difficult. "What exactly is dispensationalism?" Writing for the publication *Chapel Library,* I.C. Herendeen defined this phenomenon as "a system of prophetic interpretation." Not an entirely forthcoming sort of definition! Fortunately, this definition is widely accepted today among evangelicals who identify with "fundamentalism" as their system of Bible exegesis, despite some difficulty in actually pinning down a definition. They identify dispensationalism as a "new light" from God concerning the interpretation of his Word. So, let me ask you. Does it seem consistent that something "new" can, at the same time, also be fundamental? Doesn't newness destroy the ability for something to be the fundamental example? As recently as fifty years ago, anyone who called himself a fundamentalist would have understood that the limits imposed by our Lord in Revelation 22:18–19 would absolutely preclude there being any sort of "new light" outside the Bible, subsequent to the completion of the Scriptures.

In his third sentence, Herendeen changes his mind. He decides to call dispensationalism a "system of teaching." This comes closer to the mark, since it is entirely a manmade approach to rewriting parts of the Bible that do not reflect pre-tribulation rapture thinking. Such thinking is presumed to flow out of the dispensational teaching of the people who call themselves "fundamentalists," i.e., those evangelicals, who teach a version of radical Zionism. At any rate, after this retrenchment, Herendeen proceeds to uncover his own spiritual nakedness as a somewhat arrogant, prideful, anti-fundamentalist, academic. "Anti" since fundamentalists do not accept all of the Bible as fundamental to their teaching.

He first condemns the dispensational "system" because it was "unknown to the spiritual giants of the past, and was never incorporated into the creeds of any of the evangelical denominations." In other words, "It's new. "One would be hard pressed to imagine a weaker argument about anything having to do with the teachings of God! How many denominations existing today have ever updated their creeds to reflect what they are currently teaching or allowing to occur on their premises? We can be assured that "virtually none" would be comfortably close to the mark. This is surely the case, since so many of the corporations have drastically amended what they teach today, as compared to sixty years ago. They would, however, hardly admit their present apostasy in their creeds.

Herendeen also failed to mention just who was included under the banner of his personal "giants" of the gospel. Then, almost immediately, he admits to the great lack of direction evangelicals currently enjoy, by saying, "Its adherents seem, nevertheless as convinced that it (dispensationalism) is as much the teaching of Scripture, as they are of the divine inspiration of the Bible." He is correct that they have strayed far from biblical teaching, but without direction? It would seem that the specific direction lacking in evangelical teaching today, is that of the Bible.

There seems to be plenty of unison when it comes to the peculiar beliefs they share among themselves. This attests to some direction, but it is not from the Lord or from his Word. From this, many have concluded that the abomination of desolation spoken of by Daniel, is indeed installed in the holy place. This means, of course, that Satan has come as that angel of light, into their denominations, precisely as the Bible plainly prophecies! It is he who leads there. If that is true of course, we can know that we are indeed living in the Great Tribulation spoken of by the Apostle Matthew.

Mr. Herendeen eventually gets around to accusing the evangelicals of "modernism for the orthodox" or what is commonly known as "false doctrines" not inspired by the Holy Ghost. I spoke of this in an earlier chapter. I reiterate it here, as support for my contentions concerning the times we are living in. Such doctrines are sponsored by the man of sin and are utterly devoid of scriptural support. Each of us must judge for himself, whether Mr. Herendeen is correct. That can be done, but only by applying diligent personal study of Scripture, to what is coming out of the evangelical camps. Some who are reading this may be relieved to realize that there were indeed some accusers during the past decade, as the *Left Behind* books swept away all records for popularity among professing "Christians." Not many. But there were some. Some folks-not many-recognized those books as being a mockery of the Bible. We must remember that those books, like Lindsey's more than two decades earlier, are nothing more than attempts to keep alive the spark of fundamentalist Zionism. They do not rely on biblical truth for their popularity, since their readers are mostly ignorant of the contents of the Bible. Such readers are, therefore, generally unable to recognize their divergence. Even the seminaries did not speak out against such obviously misconstrued tales, because they are mostly "Pre-trib" rapturists also. Since the seminaries and universities employ mostly atheists to teach today's pastors their trade, we ought to give no credence whatever to any approbation they might offer for supposedly "religious"-oriented writings. Let them scribble their creeds and doctrinal statements behind the curtain of respectability they find in academia.

There is only one true test of whether or not some teaching warrants the attention of a true believer. That test may be found in 1 Thessalonians 5:21, where the Apostle Paul wrote, "prove all things; hold fast that which is good." The proof is the Word of God. Writing to his beloved Timothy, Paul said, "Study to show thyself approved unto God, a workman that needeth not to be ashamed, [but] rightly dividing the word of truth" (2 Timothy 2:15). The problem with such an approach, however, is that it appears that no test of "scripturalness" is ever desired by the evangelicals! That is a rather harsh indictment, but it does appear to be true. For validation, one need merely look at the immediate aftermath of the publication of the very first of LaHaye's *Left Behind* fantasy series. At that time, the author's understanding of fundamentalism was very under-developed, but he did ask some fundamentalists where in the Bible they got their belief in a pre-tribulation "catching up" of the saints. None could recall where such teaching might appear in that book. The author had personally never even heard the term *rapture* mentioned until the early 1990s, when it seemed to suddenly be the standard preoccupation of the evangelical churches. Now, how in the world can respectable pastors believe, and teach, a concept for which they cannot recall any biblical support whatever?

It appears to be entirely possible, that many presumed believers are finding many large segments of the Bible entirely unprofitable for their attention. Since they can't find what they are being taught, in Scripture, they get used to not referring to the Bible at all! This is quite likely, given the propensity these days toward premillennial teaching, which is the inclination of all dispensationalists. It seems they may not believe all Scripture to be either valuable or necessary as we are told it is, in 2 Timothy 3:16. There certainly cannot be a great effort to "rightly divide the word of truth, in those who believe what they read in the *Left Behind* books. This is not meant to necessarily imply that premillennialists are necessarily emissaries of Satan—at least not knowingly. But the result turns out to be the same, and in Satan's favor! Here's another thought: Consider for a moment the Alfred E. Newman approach to Bible study. Just how much of Scripture can be said to be unnecessary to one's learning if a person has the blessing of complete reliance on being "caught up" before all the heartache and aggravation that will accompany the Great Tribulation? What, me worry?

The evangelicals have been taught that the tribulation is for only the pagans and the Jews—that true believers will be removed from all the nastiness before it begins. So there is a growing sense among the evangelical churches that ought not to be there. It would not be there if they were taught what the Bible actually says, including its warnings. Briefly, the Scriptures make clear that the tribulation ahead is *only* for (my emphasis) the true believers (the elect). Anyone interested in the truth of God's Word on this subject need spend only a bit of effort understanding what the definition of "Great Tribulation" in the Bible amounts to. That definition certainly does not include wars and famines we need to worry about!

THE IMMORTALS
THE FINAL CURTAIN

I T IS UNKNOWN PRECISELY HOW MANY PEOPLE THERE ARE LIVING IN this country today. Estimates vary, and are typically rounded off to what the observer figures is the nearest ten million. Two hundred seventy million seems a popular number. But we do know that between twenty and thirty million of them in the United States and, presumably some large number elsewhere, believe they will never die-that they will achieve immortality!

This is the earnest belief of a group of men and women who call themselves "Fundamentalist Christians." Most employ the Schofield Reference Bible in arriving at their beliefs concerning "things eschatological." That is, about the last days of mankind on the earth. They also lean heavily on the Hal Lindsey novel of 1971, a best seller, because every Fundamentalist and Dispensationist must have bought at least one copy of *The Late Great Planet Earth* since that book sold approximately 30 million copies! If Lindsey's royalty was only thirty - five cents per copy, he would have pocketed about ten million dollars. Lindsey was the second generation from Schofield, to profit handsomely from making up prophecy as he went along. That meager sum convinced another generation of like-minded Fundamentalist profit (not prophet) seekers, that indeed, a tidy "killing" could be made in Dispensationism! In fact, in the intervening years, numerous "prophets" have been using television "ministries" to prove what a great business venture C.I. Schofield invented back in 1909.

Not only that, a comparatively smaller number of them, when compared to twenty million, are actively engaged in attempting to manipulate events and governments in a mis-guided effort to make God's program conform to their personal gospels. These are concerted and very likely desperate, attempts to ensure that God is not only following their plan, but will be coerced into being prompt about it! This may sound a bit pre-posterous to some, but it will not sound that way at all to any confirmed Fundamentalist.

In the journalistic community, typically referred to these days as the "major media" or as the "liberal media", there is a general, but vague, awareness of support for the hawkish ele-ments within the Israeli Government, being continuously and openly advocated, by what they term the "Religious Right" in America, or the "radical Right." There is a strong, if inappropri-ate prophetic rationale for Fundamentalist support of National, secular, Israel. Unknown to the Fundamentalists, however, it is a pipe dream, since it is based on totally inadequate interpreta-tion of the word of God contained in the Bible! It is entirely unconnected to God's plan for His church.

The fundamentalist view is that Christ will return to earth, in order to establish a worldwide temporal kingdom, which they have christened the "millennial kingdom." They extracted the rudiments of that idea from the Bible, as a result of erroneous conclusions based loosely on passages taken out of context. But before God does that, they believe He will return to "Rapture" all the members with paid up tithes, of the various corporate churches. That means they expect God to take them bodily up to heaven, without them ever having to die first! That's a strong motivator! Then, after one thousand years of reigning here on earth, God will judge all the sinners. But the timing and apparatus of all this, is open to discussion depending upon which of several "schools" is doing the telling! The common factor for all Christians, not only fundamentalist ones, is that sometime in the course of human events, what they call the "Rapture" will definitely occur. There is widespread disagreement on when, fed by the inescapable and obvious conclusion that Christians prefer to be told what to believe, rather than to study it for themselves.

The true goal of Fundamentalist leaders, who believe they can nudge things along, rather than waiting for God to finish His plan, is to ensure their survivability. Can you see that, this makes it a work against God, not for Him? If anything should occur in world events, to remove Israel from the Near East, they believe that the expected Great Tribulation, which they are convinced postdates the Rapture of the saints, but predates the end of the world, will have to be postponed, possibly for centuries. That would mean, that even the lavishly wealthy Fundamentalists who control that movement, would have to experience death in order to get into heaven. That's unacceptable to the fundamentalist barons. That would be beneath their perceived station in life (and death). That's simply not to be tolerated! So, they actively attempt to manipulate world events connected to the State of Israel, evidently in the belief that they really have the power to decide for God, how things will go. The last "big shot" who believed that was his destiny, wound up getting his name changed and being booted out of heaven.

This rarely stated, well-guarded agenda, intended to assure them death-free living, is the psychological motivation behind American Fundamentalism's unwavering support for Israel and all things Israeli. But timing is everything. Let me emphasize that again. Timing is everything. They must make it alive, to a time exactly three and a half years before all the Jews in the world return to Palestine. That's Fundamentalism's date. That's why they send money to Jewish organizations, and sponsor Christian Ministries that help Jews get to Palestine. At the top, it has nothing to do with benevolence, or with caring a whit about Jews or about Jesus! Their purpose is actually to get lots of Jews there to die! That's part of the agenda they believe is set by the Bible, in Zechariah 13:8,9, where according to that prophet, as they choose to read him, two thirds of the Jews will die in the battle of Armageddon, and the remainder will then go to a special heaven for Jews. In reality, Since all the Christians have been already "taken up" into heaven when the slaughter of the Jews and other non-Christians begins, according to the Fundamentalist view of the New Testament, there will be no benevolent Christians here to help Israel!

So, the bottom line is that, Fundamentalists pray for the day when two thirds of all Jews must die, in order that the last act of the play will be the Fundamentalists being transported to heaven! That's the tradeoff of their Gospel, and the central motivation for their political support of Israel. They believe, as do most thinking Christians, that the end is right around the corner. Therefore, they are more than ready to have the Great Tribulation begin, which they believe is for Jews and pagans only.

So one can see exactly why it is that the Fundamentalists and their spin-off Evangelical movement, thrive on the doctrine of "imminent Rapture." That's followed closely by imminent and unavoidable holocaust among their Jewish friends. They support political "hawks" in Israel, in the hope that such men will hasten the coming holocaust, which in fact, Fundamentalist doctrine knows as the "Great Tribulation."

The specific motivation for Dispensationism's support of Israel is never mentioned from the pulpit. Down in their pews, the faithful hear many sermons about the Pretribulation Rapture. They also hear sermons on the Great Tribulation, regularly. They do not however, hear the two themes preached in a connected way. Do Fundamentalist ministers expect their congregations to add things up for themselves? Perhaps, but we know for certain they consider the two events to be a politically incorrect topic for treatment in public. No one wants to be asked, "So we can avoid death, but only because two thirds of the Jews in Israel will die shortly after we are taken out of there? Their political intent then, although unannounced, amounts to the political 'scapegoating' of the Israeli state- men, women, and children. The temporary national survival of Israel in Palestine is of course, mandatory if it is to be the national sacrifice for Christianity, as Fundamentalists perceive it. Certainly, they will include in their rationales for U.S. support of Israel, the importance of maintaining democracy in that region, and a strong geopolitical ally as a cornerstone in the Near East. But the real motivation needs none of that, so long as Christians believe they may avoid death, by spending U.S. treasure on Israel.

Will this situation change? To imagine that people deluded by such doctrines will choose to abandon their beliefs and symbolically sign their own death certificates, and therefore choose to abandon their support for the government of Israel, is to imagine a five year old abandoning his Santa Claus vigil on the 24th of December! Pretribulation Rapture teaching has been the foundation of Fundamentalist and most Evangelical teaching for more than 175 years. Certainly, these people could abandon their beliefs in Dispensational doctrines. But sadly, they are probably more apt to abandon God. This is so, because they are already quite comfortable ignoring the Biblical fact that their ministry is the tool of the "Evil One" spoken of in the Bible. It has to be so, since it is not consistent with Bible teaching! There is an extremely high psychological price involved in turning away from Dispensationism and back to the teaching of the Bible. Not many, if any, complacent fundamentalist, is likely to take that death defying step. That's the trouble with being immortal.

NOTES

1. In his 2002 book, *Who Is This Jesus: Is He Risen?* The late Dr. D. James Kennedy, Presbyterian Church in America, with Jerry Newcombe, wrote some rather revealing anecdotes.

2. Charles Ryrie, *Dispensationalism Today.* Originally published in 1965, the book has been updated at least twice, most recently in 2007. Note that the Publisher is one of the two largest and most "prestigious" Bible Colleges in this country. Both support the "D" word.

3. Ibid., pg.312

4. See, "Kingdom of God," in Zondervan Pictorial Bible Dictionary, Grand Rapids, 1967.

5. Albertus Pieters, in *The Schofield Bible,* insists, "The entire "dispensational" scheme ... when subjected to examination in light of Holy Scripture, breaks down completely ... "

6. See Shields in "Gospel Witness" magazine.

7. Mauro, in his pamphlet, *I was robbed,* Chapel library, undated.

8. In his book, *The Hope of Israel,* Philip Mauro cited what he termed, "dispensationalist dementia". See also Google, *www.preteristarchive.com,* Dec.3, 2005.

9. Lewis Berkhof, *The History of Christian Doctrines,* Banner of Truth Trust, London,1969, p.262. Berkhof had relatively little to report in support of dispensationalist history, presumably since it had existed only a little more than a century. He found "no trace" of such a concept in writings of, Clement of Rome, Ignatius, Polycarp, Tatian, Athenagoras, Theophilus, Clement of Alexandria, Origen, Dionysius, or any other "important" church father.

10. One of them was Charles D. Alexander, in his book, *MOSES or CHRIST?-Paul's Reply to Dispensational Error.* The other, if one reads him carefully in Galatians 6:16, was the Apostle, Paul of Tarsus.

11. J. S. Brown, in his book review, *The Three Rs- Rapture, Revision, Robbery,* cited in "Dispensational Dementia", P.4.

12. "Some Fundamentalists Ache for Armageddon" in *Christianity Today,* Quoted in "Dispensational Dementia."

13. *"How Evangelicals Became Israel's Best friend,"* www.Preteristarchive.com,p.5.

14. Gary Bauer, Ibid.

15. Today's Dictionary of the Bible, See "Tares", pg.606, Also Webster's Collegiate Dictionary. under "Tares" pg., 1192. The Pictorial Bible Dictionary, Zondervan, Grand Rapids, MI, 1967, Listed under "Plants," An annual, "Lolium Temulentum" (Latin) or Zizanion (Greek), which flourished in the wheat fields of the Holy land. Its seeds were smaller than the kernels of wheat, so they fell through a special sieve used in the threshing process, because the Darnell was a serious poison for man and beasts if it carried (as it often did) the Ergot-like fungus.

BIBLIOGRAPHY

Alexander, Charles D. *"Moses or Christ? Paul's Reply to dispensational Error."* Heartland, as presented in geocities.com. December 12, 2006. 1–14.

Allis, Oswald T. *Prophesy and the Church*. Phillipsburg, New Jersey: Presbyterian and Reformed Publishing, 1945.

Barth, Karl. *Evangelical Theory*. Wm. B. Eerdman's Publishing Co., 1963.

Brown, David. *Christ's Second Coming*. Edinburgh: T. & T. Clark, 1882.

Brown, J.S. *"The Three Rs–Rapture, Revision, Robbery."* Book Review.

Bray, Gerald. *"Still an Evangelical."* Modern Reformation Magazine. November / December 2001.

Campbell, Donald. *"Essays in Honor of J.D. Pentecost."* 1985.

Canfield, Joseph M. *"Some Fundamentalists Ache for Armageddon."* Christianity Today. Wikipedia. Org. 2008.

Chafer, Lewis S. *Systematic Theology*. Dallas: Seminary Press, 1936.

Chilton, David. *The Days of Vengeance: An Exposition of the Book of Revelation*. Ft. Worth: Dominion Publishing, 1987.

Clouse, Robert G., Ed., *The Meaning of the Millennium*, InterVarsity Press, Downers Grove, IL 1977.

Cox, W.E. *"The Scriptures–Without Note or Comment."* Alden, New York: Bible Tracts, 1970.

De Mar, Gary. *Last Days Madness*. American Vision Inc., Powder Springs, GA, 4th Ed., 1999.

Green, John C. "*Comments on 2004 American Religious Landscape Report.*" *Evangelicalism.* wikipedia.org. December12, 2006.

Green Jay P. Sr., Ed., *The Interlinear Bible,* Sovereign Grace Publishers, Lafayette, IN, 2nd Ed., 1986

Gunn, Grover. "*Dispensationalism: Christian Zionism.*" www.grovergunn.net. December 22, 2006. 14.

Harvey, V.A. *A Handbook of Theological Terms.* New York: McMillan,1964.

Herendeen, I. C. "*Is Modern Dispensationalism Scriptural?*" Chapel Library. Venice, Florida. Undated.

"*History of Christian Doctrine.*" The Banner of Truth Trust. 1937 and 1969.

Jackson, Wayne. "*Examining Premillennialism.*" Christian Courier. February 2001.

Jeffrey, Grant. *Apocalypse.* New York: Random House, 1997.

Kant, Immanuel, Transl., *The Critique of Judgment,* Prometheus Books, Amherst, NY 2000.

Kevan, Ernest F., in *Wycliffe Dictionary of Theology.* Harrison, E.F., et als, Eds. New York: Hendrickson Publishing, 1999.

Kuizera, John E. "*Conversation with Albertus Pieters.*" Hope College, 1923.

Lindsey, Hal. *The Late, Great Planet Earth.* Grand Rapids: Zondervan, 1970

MacPherson, Dave. *The Incredible Cover-up.* Plainfield, New Jersey: Logos Int'l, 1975.

Mathison, Keith A. *Dispensationalism: Rightly Dividing the People of God?* P&R Publishing Co., Phillipsburg, NJ, 1995.

Mauro, Philip quoted in Allis. "*The Church in Prophecy.*" 67.

Murray, George. *Millennial Studies.* Grand Rapids: Baker Books,1948.

Netanyahu, Benjamin. Conference address to Voices United for Israel. Washington, DC. April, 1998.

North, Gary. *Fundamentalism's Bloody Homeland for Jews.* Lew Rockwell.com. December 21, 2005.

North, Gary. "*The Foreign Policy of 20 Million Would-be Immortals.*" Lew Rockwell.com. December 21, 2005.

Pentecost, Dwight J. *Things to Come: A Study in Biblical Eschatology.* Grand Rapids: Zondervan,1958.

Pieters, Albertus. *The Schofield Bible.* Booklet, Venice, Florida: Chapel Library, 1919.

Ryrie, Charles C. *Dispensationalism Today.* Chicago: Moody Press,1965.

Ryrie, Charles C. *Dispensationalism-Revised and Expanded,* Moody Press, Chicago, 2007.

Salmon, T.H. "*Have We a Correct Understanding of the Times?*" Alden, New York,1971.

Schwerley, Brian M. Excerpt from *Is The Pretribulation Rapture Biblical?* in reformed.com/pub. 2007.

Shields, T.T. "*Gospel Witness.*" Pamphlet. April 7,1932.

Sizer, Stephen, "*An Alternative Theology of the Holy Land.*" Comments on Dispensationalism, DVD, *On the Road to Armageddon.*

Snowden, James. "*The Coming of the Lord, Will it be Premillennial?* American Journal of Theology. Vol. 23, No. 4, Oct 1919.

Stoney, J. Butler. Quote from 1875, in Miles J. Stanford's *Israel's Messianic Kingdom.* West Sussex, U.K., 1973.

Strong, James. *Strong's Exhaustive Concordance of the Bible.* Nashville: Thomas Nelson, 1997.

Tenney, Merrill C. Ed. *Zondervan Pictorial Bible Dictionary.* Grand Rapids: Zondervan, 1967.

Trumbull, Charles D. Ed. *"The Life Story of C.I. Schofield."* in Sunday School Times, 1945.

Vos, Geerhardus. *International Standard Bible Encyclopedia,* 2nd ed. James Orr, ed. Grand Rapids, 1939.

Walvoord, John F. *Israel in Prophesy.* Grand Rapids: Zondervan, 1959.

Walvoord, John F. *The Millennial Kingdom.* Grand Rapids: Zondervan, 1959.

Woolf, Henry B. Ed. *Webster's New Collegiate Dictionary.* Springfield, Massachusetts: G.C. Merriam &Co., 1976.

Young, Robert. *Analytical Concordance to the Bible.* 22nd ed. Grand Rapids: Wm B. Eerdman's Publishing Co., 1970.